WAR IN A STRINGBAG

WAR IN A STRINGBAG

CHARLES LAMB
DSO DSC

Foreword by
VICE-ADMIRAL SIR CHARLES EVANS
KCB CBE DSO DSC

CASSELL&CO

Cassell Military Paperbacks

Cassell
Wellington House, 125 Strand,
London WC2R 0BB

First published by Cassell 1977
This Cassell Military Paperbacks edition 2001
Reprinted 2002

British Library Cataloguing-in-Publication Data
A catalogue record for this book is available from the British Library

ISBN 0-304-35841-X

Printed and bound in Great Britain by
Cox & Wyman Ltd., Reading, Berks.

To my sons and yours, and to
every Burns and Brown
in the Royal Navy:
then, now and in the future

Contents

Foreword

Vice-Admiral Sir Charles Evans, KCB, CBE, DSO, DSC

When the Royal Navy took over the Fleet Air Arm from the Royal Air Force in 1938, it inherited obsolete aircraft. It was apparent, moreover, to the naval aircrew which remained that they could expect no replacements from the British aircraft industry because its resources were, quite rightly, concentrated on producing Hurricanes and Spitfires to enable the RAF to ensure that, in the event of war, Great Britain could remain secure as an arsenal and a base for offensive operations.

When a year later in 1939 war was declared on Germany, the Fleet Air Arm was required not only to fight a war at sea but also, in their obsolete aircraft, to support the RAF in the face of the very modern aircraft of the Luftwaffe.

If some Fleet Air Arm aircrew did not rate their chances of survival as high, they were proved right, for some of the very best men were lost before the United States entered the war and was able gradually to re-equip the Fleet Air Arm with modern aircraft under Lease-Lend.

What enabled those few aircrew of the Fleet Air Arm to play such a vital part in the critical years of peril between 1939 and 1943?

Whenever I think about this, my thoughts invariably return to Charles Lamb, for he epitomized all the qualities which enabled his contemporaries to achieve so much with so little; professionalism, courage obviously, ingenuity, infectious optimism and, above all, superior power of leadership.

For many of the survivors the Second World War is a dim memory, others have a sharper reminder. As I write this Foreword Charles Lamb is entering hospital for the twenty-seventh operation resulting from the experiences described in this book.

I hope that in reading this book you will gather a small part of the inspiration which is mine through associating over the years with this remarkable man.

C.L.G.E.

Acknowledgements

I would like to express my thanks to all those listed below for the many ways in which their patience and generosity have helped me to write this book:

Dr Guy Beauchamp and Dr James Drummond – for keeping me alive.

Mr E. M. Boyle, Reference Librarian, Salisbury Division Library, Wiltshire Library and Museum Service.

Mr Maurice Buxton.

Mr J.B. Cannell, The Commodore, and all the members of the Association of Dunkirk Little Ships.

Cartographic Enterprises, Tregony, Cornwall.

The Drafting and Records office, Royal Marines, HMS *Centurion*, Gosport, Hants.

The Fleet Air Arm Officers' Association, and the staff of the Fleet Air Arm Museum, RN Air Station, Yeovilton, Somerset.

Mrs Wendy Garcin.

Messrs. Gieves & Hawkes, Savile Row, W.1.

Sir Donald Gosling.

Miss Mary Griffith.

Mr Robert Hardy, who bullied me into writing this book.

Miss Susanna Lamb, my granddaughter, without whose help I would have finished in half the time.

Mr Mike Legat.

Mr and Mrs Jeremy Peyton-Jones.

Mr Chris Nicholls (Cameras), Salisbury.

Miss Christine Sawicki, of Toronto, Canada.

Mr James Scrimgeour, CMG, OBE

Captain Colin Shand, DSC, Royal Navy.

Mr Ken Sims, and all the members of the Telegraphist Air Gunners' Association.

Miss Jane Whigham, Public Relations Officer, Union Castle Line.

The London *Sunday Express*, for permission to reproduce extracts from the article by C. G. Grey published in 1940.

The Council of Management, and Staff, of The White Ensign Association HMS *Belfast*.

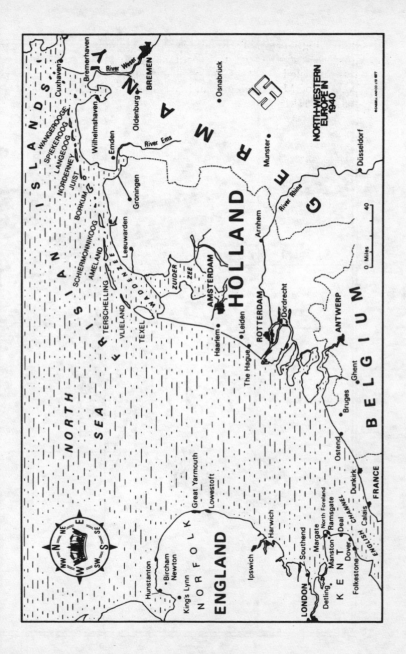

NORTH-WESTERN
EUROPE IN
1940

© CASSELL AND CO. LTD 1957

0 Miles 40

NORTH SEA

FRISIAN ISLANDS

Hunstanton
King's Lynn
Bircham Newton
NORFOLK
Great Yarmouth
Lowestoft
ENGLAND
Ipswich
Harwich
LONDON
Southend
Margate
North Foreland
Ramsgate
Manston
Deal
KENT
Detling
Dover
Folkestone
ENGLISH CHANNEL
Calais
Dunkirk
Ostend
FRANCE
Bruges
Ghent
BELGIUM
ANTWERP
Dordrecht
ROTTERDAM
The Hague
Haarlem
Leiden
HOLLAND
AMSTERDAM
ZUIDER ZEE
WADDEN ZEE
Texel
Vlieland
Terschelling
Ameland
Schiermonnikoog
Borkum
Just
Norderney
Langeoog
Spiekeroog
Wangerooge
Cuxhaven
Bremerhaven
River Weser
BREMEN
Oldenburg
Wilhelmshaven
Emden
Groningen
Leeuwarden
River Ems
Osnabrück
Munster
Arnhem
River Rhine
GERMANY
Düsseldorf

GERMANY

FRANCE

SWITZ.

ITALY

YUG

SPAIN

CORSICA

ADRIATIC SEA

BALEARIC
ISLANDS

SARDINIA

Taranto

Straits
of Messina

SICILY

Mount Etna △

Catania
Augusta

El Alounia
(airfield)

Skerki Channel

Tunis

Blida Algiers

Oran

Aumale

Constantine

Pantelleria

Enfidaville

Cape Bon

MALTA

Sousse

MEDIT

Djelfa

ATLAS

MOROCCO

ALGERIA

Laghouat

MOUNTAINS

Lampedusa

Gabes

Tripoli

LIB

STRIKE DEEP   IN VIA GLORIAE

PART I

HMS *Courageous*

1

The First Day

There was nothing unusual in the sight of one of His Majesty's ships lying at anchor in Plymouth Sound in the sunshine of an early September morning, even though she happened to be one of Britain's five big aircraft carriers. Her flight-deck was teeming with men falling-in for Sunday Divisions, and the small group of spectators lining the grassy banks of the Hoe were mainly the wives and children of the men on board. The ship had just returned to her home port after many weeks away, and the women were talking excitedly to each other, looking down at the ship in the bay just as sailor's wives and families have done since before the days of Sir Francis Drake.

That morning the excitement of homecoming was overwrought with heavy tension, which could be felt on the salt-laden air which blew in from the sea. It was 3 September 1939, and everyone knew that the years of uneasy peace were about to end, probably that very day. Hitler's invasion of Poland at five-thirty on the Friday morning was the final blow of many, and not even the most simple-minded person anywhere could still be in doubt that Britain's Prime Minister must now declare war.

On the flight-deck, leaning on my sword, dressed as a naval lieutenant in a frock coat, I stared over the heads of the squadron ratings and wondered which would come first, Chamberlain's declaration of war, or the Padre's final reading of my marriage banns. On the two previous Sundays the Reverend 'Brassbound' Beale had called out my future wife's full name, and the name of her parish, in front of the entire ship's company; and then mine, followed by the words, 'in the Parish of His Majesty's ship, *Courageous*'.

The Reverend Beale was known as 'Brassbound' because he was a very senior naval chaplain and considered that he was entitled to wear a senior officer's cap with gold leaf around the peak. He insisted on wearing it and nobody had bothered to tell him to take it off because it kept him happy, and everyone else amused.

This Sunday he would add: 'This is for the third time of asking,' and I was relieved that he was doing it for the last time; nothing could prevent us from marrying now – not even Hitler.

Standing amongst the wives on Plymouth Hoe, looking down at the ship, was my best man to be, Flight-Lieutenant E. L. 'Johnny' Hyde. He had driven round from the RAF flying-boat base at Mountbatten to join me for lunch on board and he had paused on the Hoe, on his way round to the dockyard, to see if we had begun to move.

Johnny and I had identical backgrounds: in 1930 we had left our minor public schools to go to sea as apprentices in the Merchant Service, I in the Clan Line. We first met in the West Indies when we were serving as RNR Midshipmen in different battleships. He was in *Valiant*'s gun-room and I was in *Rodney*'s. We had joined forces with another RNR, a South African named 'Sailor' Malan, also from the *Valiant*, and the three of us had gone ashore to London in 1934 to sit for our Board of Trade examinations. When we had passed, our brand new Board of Trade Certificates of Competence were useless. In the depression of the early Thirties there were so many ships laid up that jobs afloat were virtually unobtainable.

We discovered that we shared the same burning ambition to learn to fly, so we bearded the Admiral Commanding Reserves together, in person, to find out whether we could join the Fleet Air Arm. The admiral explained that the Navy's aviation was really 'The Fleet Air Arm of the Royal Air Force'. In 1918 the Royal Flying Corps had amalgamated with the Royal Naval Air Service to become the new third service, the Royal Air Force. He told us that in one day the Navy had lost control of all research and development into naval flying and naval aircraft. 'On that day – April Fool's Day – in 1918, fifty-five thousand officers and men transferred from dark blue uniforms to light blue, and grew hideous moustaches! They took with them two thousand five hundred aircraft which belonged to the Navy, and nearly one hundred airfields dotted about the world. Ever since then the Air Ministry have controlled our flying, and there is no scheme for naval reserves to be taught to fly, nor can we transfer you to the RN.'

He was very apologetic, but in 1935 this was the end of our hopes of being able to fly with the Navy, and so we walked across London to Aldwych and applied to the Air Ministry for short service commissions in the Royal Air Force. We felt rather guilty about this, but if the Navy didn't want us, and the Merchant Service couldn't continue to employ us, what else could we do? As Malan said, 'If you can't beat 'em, join 'em.'

Our applications coincided with the first great expansion of the RAF, sponsored by Winston Churchill from the back benches, when he was at last able to point out to Baldwin and Attlee that Germany had two thousand aircraft in comparison with our paltry five hundred. We were medically examined within a week and learning to fly within a month.

Three years after we joined the RAF the Admiralty won back the control of its own aviation: in 1937 Lord Chatfield demanded the return of the Fleet Air Arm to the Royal Navy, pointing out that research into the development of naval aircraft had been neglected to the point of insanity. As soon as the Government announced its decision I applied for a transfer to the new, naval-controlled Fleet Air Arm. The AOC Coastal Command was very cross and gave me twenty-four hours to 'make up my mind' so I sent a reply-paid telegram to my fiancée, who was lining her bottom drawer on the catering staff of Benenden School in Kent, asking her to make up my mind for me. She sent back a simple message: 'You must decide, but I do like sailors!'

I was granted a short service commission in the Navy's new Air Branch almost immediately, which explains why I was standing at Divisions on the flight-deck of HMS *Courageous* eighteen months later, at the outbreak of war. I did my best to persuade Johnny Hyde and 'Sailor' Malan to come back to the Navy with me, but Johnny was very happy flying his Sunderland flying-boats, and 'Sailor' had become one of the RAF's most expert fighter pilots. He was a 'natural' in every sense of the word, and always did everything better than anyone else without being aware that he was not as other men. It was a good thing from the country's point of view that he stayed where he was.

In 1938, when I put on naval uniform again, I was twenty-four. The four years I had spent at sea in cargo ships and my six months' training in a battleship's gun-room, followed by three years' flying with Coastal Command, had been tough, but Hyde, Malan and I had managed to extract a tremendous amount of fun from it all, despite the trade depression and occasional periods of bleak unemployment. As a Midshipman RNR I had boxed for the Navy in the Inter-Service championships of 1934 as a light-weight; then in 1936, after winning the RAF Officers' championship at the same weight, I did the same for the RAF; and in 1938, in the Navy again, I competed in the same championships against the Army and the Air Force. My constant reappearance on different sides caused a certain amount of caustic comment from the RAF and Navy coaches, who reckoned me a turncoat, each claiming to have taught me to box; but in fact I had learned when an apprentice at sea in a Mission in Buenos Aires, under the expert tutelage of a famous fighting Padre named Canon Brady, who once persuaded me to box in the professional ring under the pseudonym of 'Seaman Benson', on the grounds that I needed the experience and his Mission needed the money. I had to keep very quiet about this in the Services, because that one appearance would have disqualified me from amateur status.

Notwithstanding the wisecracking of the Service coaches, one man was really upset when I reverted to the Navy in 1938: he was the coach to the Oxford University team. In the week of my change-over I boxed against Oxford twice – for the RAF on the Monday, and for the Navy on the Thursday. Nothing could convince that Oxford coach that I had not shaved off my moustache and made the transfer merely to do him down. He was sure that there was some sort of fiddle going on somewhere.

After Divisions I was busy signing chits at the bar, buying drinks for the entire wardroom for not having objected to the banns, when there was a sudden hush, and I looked up to see the Captain and Commander walk into the ante-room. Captain Makeig-Jones was a very imposing figure, being well over six feet tall.

'Gentlemen,' he said, 'the Prime Minister is about to make an important announcement on the wireless, and the Admiralty has made a General Message to the Fleet saying that all officers and men are to be given the opportunity of listening.'

In deathly silence in that pleasant ante-room, with the sunlight streaming through the scuttles making round pools of light on the chintz-covered furniture and the polished tables, with a glass of gin in my hand which seemed as inappropriate to the occasion as the vase of flowers on the table beside me, we heard the tremulous voice of Mr Chamberlain, breaking with emotion, apologizing for the inevitable.

The attack on Poland had been the ultimate act of aggression which left him no alternative . . . 'so this country is now in a state of war with Germany.'

The shocked silence in the packed ante-room was beginning to break into a hum of conversation, but this was interrupted by the alarming sound of the ship's bugler sounding-off 'Action Stations', and we all stared at each other in astonishment thinking, 'So soon!'; then the Commander's voice came across on the tannoy, telling everyone to muster on deck and 'man the side'. We were to stand, side by side, right around the ship to watch for a possible submarine attack, and as we scrambled up the ladders we heard the sound of the first air raid warning, floating across the water from Plymouth. All over the country the sirens were wailing, for the first time, because of some foolish false alarm which sent people scampering for cover from Land's End to John O'Groats.

The all-clear sounded after a few minutes, followed immediately by the 'Secure' by the ship's bugler, and 'Special Sea Dutymen'; and we hurried to our berth in Devonport Dockyard where I found Johnny Hyde waiting impatiently.

In a very crowded bar in Plymouth's Union Street, shortly after we went ashore on that Sunday evening, we were startled when the naval patrol marched in through the doors wearing gaiters and armbands. The Petty Officer in charge called out: 'Anyone here from *Courageous*?'

We signed to him that we were, and he marched across to us and stood to attention. Being the first day of the war, it was our first time ashore in uniform and we were all feeling rather self-conscious, and were on our best behaviour.

'You've been recalled, gentlemen,' he said. 'You're to go back on board at the double.'

Jo would still be in church, and was expecting me to telephone during the evening. Now I had lost the opportunity. But there was no time to think about that. The blackout was so intense that the taxi-drivers who had brought us ashore had warned us that they were going off the roads for the rest of the night, and we would have to walk back. For the first few months of the war, before headlight shields were put on the market, everyone had to drive using sidelights only, and it made driving a nightmare.

The noise in the bar was uproarious, but we had to get back, and in the end I stood on a table and made my first public speech. The good people of Plymouth had seen the patrol stride in, and when I held up my hand they hushed very obligingly. I told them that we had been recalled to our ship and had to hurry. 'There are no taxis because of the blackout, and I am wondering whether there are any kind car-owners here, who would be willing to brave the darkness and take us back to the dockyard?'

There were so many volunteers that we were embarrassed. Every car-owner present insisted on taking someone, and in the end, rather than disappoint the eager volunteers, some of us went back in solitary state. My driver was a charming pork butcher, and on the way, through the impenetrable dark I explained my problem. I wanted Jo to know that our banns had been called for the third time, but was not allowed to tell her that we were sailing. He very kindly agreed to telephone her for me later, when the last hymn had been sung, to explain that I was unable to telephone for a day or so, but would do so as soon as I could.

As I climbed the brow on to the quarter-deck, I could tell by the hum of the engines that the ship was ready for sea. She was in total darkness but I could hear the voices of men taking in the warps, and I heard the Master-at-Arms reporting to someone that all officers and men were on board. I wondered how that had been achieved; it must have been a major administrative problem to round up the entire ship's company of a Fleet aircraft carrier, that evening, in the blackout. C-in-C Plymouth probably called for a naval patrol from the duty watch of every ship in the dock-yard, because they would have to call at every address written on every leave card, and visit every pub in Plymouth and Devonport. To make the men leave their wives and families after a reunion of only a few hours must have taken some doing too; but it had been done, and we sailed within an hour without a single absentee.

Standing out on a battery space, amidships, I watched the ship slip through the darkened dockyard and admired the way the Captain manoeuvred, with only the winking lights of the buoys to help him. It did not occur to me that it would be the last time that he would take a ship to sea, or that it was the last time the *Courageous* would leave her home port – or any other.

It had been a long day and I decided to turn in.

2

The First Fortnight

By Saturday, 2 September, all scheduled passages in ships bound for America had been cancelled, except one, the 13000-ton *Athenia*. On Friday, 1 September, she embarked about a thousand passengers in Glasgow, and then sailed for Liverpool and Belfast to cram in another two hundred. A substantial percentage of these were school-children, being evacuated by anxious parents who used all their persuasive powers, and pulled every possible string, to obtain a berth for their loved ones so that they did not miss this final scheduled crossing, away from danger, before the war began.

The parents could not have guessed that during that very week-end Hitler was to invade Poland; nor could they have any reason to know that on 22 August eighteen German U-boats had slipped out of harbour, to go to waiting positions on our shipping lanes in the Atlantic, and in the Western Approaches.

At four in the morning on Sunday, 3 September, the *Athenia* left Ireland behind, and headed out into the Atlantic swell, The Captain imposed strict 'darken-ship' routine because although the war had not begun he had no wish to advertise his departure. It was not until the afternoon of this fateful Sunday, when the war was only two hours old, that his ship was torpedoed by a German U-boat and ninety-three of his fourteen hundred passengers were lost. Sadly, there were many children amongst them. During the afternoon, reports from other ships under attack began to filter through to the Admiralty, and by the evening of the first day, the Battle of the Atlantic had begun in earnest.

The arrival of the U-boat at the beginning of the First World War had introduced a second dimension into naval warfare and, between the wars, the Admirals and the scientists had devoted the greater part of their time and effort to combat this underwater menace. The gradual arrival of a third dimension – the air – had crept upon the naval scene almost unawares. It appeared to have had little or no effect on naval planning, because the third horizon was thought to be mainly a matter of the air defence of our shores, and the development of a strike capability by Bomber Command. The role of the Fleet Air Arm had always been one of support for the big guns of the Fleet, plus reconnaissance and anti-submarine warfare, and it does not seem to have occurred to anyone that the next war would end with the aircraft carriers being the main striking force of the Fleet.

In September 1939 we had six old carriers, the *Eagle, Argus, Furious, Courageous, Glorious* and *Hermes*. Only one new carrier had been built between the wars, the *Ark Royal*, and she commissioned as late as 1938, and at the outbreak of war was operating in the North Sea. Four others, of the *Illustrious* class, were under construction: the *Illustrious* was nearing completion, and the *Indomitable, Victorious and Formidable* were scheduled for use as soon as their shipyards could launch them down the slips. Two others of bigger design with two hangars and with a capability of carrying bigger and better aircraft, were on the drawing-boards, and were expected to be built and launched in about three years' time. These were the *Indefatigable* and the *Implacable*.

When *Courageous* sailed from Plymouth under cover of darkness on 3 September, to go out into the middle of what we believed to be a pack of German U-boats, she was provided with an escort of four destroyers. It was anticipated that the ship would attract U-boat attacks, when the destroyers would achieve the miraculous results with their Asdic which were forecast so confidently. The presence of the ship would also serve to distract the attention of the enemy from the merchant ships and their valuable cargoes and their passengers, hurrying home to the British Isles in their dozens from all parts of the globe. The two Swordfish squadrons on board were expected to hunt the U-boats and harass them, and keep them down, and it was thought that it would be the presence of aircraft which would provide the major deterrent to the U-boats.

The fact that the twenty-four biplanes on board had a potential far beyond that of hunting U-boats, and were capable of attacking enemy ships with torpedoes at a range of nearly two-hundred miles, which later, with long-range tanks, was extended to over eight hundred, does not seem to have dawned on the planners, and it took at least two years of hard fighting at sea before this became obvious. Throughout the war the value of the aircraft carrier was in fact very considerable indeed, and to send *Courageous* out into that hotbed of underwater activity, to act as bait for enemy U-boats, might have been the right decision in the circumstances had there been an adequate escort, as would have been the case with a battleship, whose guns possessed a hitting range of only thirty-five miles at the most. If *Courageous* had been a battleship she would have been escorted by a small fleet of vessels, none of which would have been permitted to leave the screen except to hunt in the immediate vicinity. Our four destroyers were there to protect *Courageous*, but they also had to go submarine-hunting and answer calls for help from distressed shipping, and throughout those opening days of the war there were seldom more than two escorts within sight of the ship. *Courageous* presented an easy target.

On board, the attitude of everyone was carefree and casual. We carried no fighter aircraft, and hundreds of miles west of the Scilly Isles there appeared to be no need. We flew on various types of search in answer to the distress calls that came flooding in from all directions, but these calls only affected the ship's aircraft and aircrew, not the ship, where the atmosphere was beguilingly peaceful. The ship's company remained at 'cruising stations' during the day, and the scuttles remained open until 'darken ship' was piped, at sundown. Officers dressed for dinner each evening, and at times it was difficult to realize that the country was at war. The absence of two out of four of our escorts for the majority of the time did not seem to worry anyone because Asdic was thought to be infallible, and two ships ahead of the carrier were considered quite sufficient.

Our flying was not concerned with the safety of the ship. When not flying on searches in response to U-boat sightings, or distress calls, we had to stand by on board at immediate readiness, in case one was received. Later, no carrier would ever be under way again without her own anti-submarine patrol of aircraft, flying ahead of the ship – within sight – and at depth. Most of these sensible precautions came into being because of the lessons learned from *Courageous*.

Radio Telephony (R/T) had not then reached the Swordfish squadrons, and there was no radio link between the ship and her aircraft, though the telegraphist air gunners were able to make W/T reports in the air, which could not be answered. Strict W/T silence was in force. In the aircraft, our only means of communicating with the parent ship, if an answer was required, was with an Aldis lamp when she was within sight.

During a prolonged absence out of sight of the ship, it was seldom possible for the carrier to stick to her intended plan; but any alterations of course and speed would be adjusted to bring her back to the planned rendezvous with her aircraft within a mile or two. She could not inform her pilots because of W/T silence, and so we had to allow a safety margin of petrol by reducing our radius of action so that we could search for the carrier if she was not where we expected to find her at our estimated time of arrival. Even if she was in the right place it was possible to miss seeing her, if the visibility was bad. An error of a couple of miles in the navigation by the observer, or an error of one degree in the course-flying by the pilot, was sufficient to put one's heart in one's mouth in reduced visibility, when the ship failed to materialize when expected, at the end of a long flight; and on those occasions the sea looked very cold and unfriendly. But on board again, it was refreshing to find everyone relaxed and behaving quite normally.

On Sunday, 10 September, we lost our first aircraft and crew. The pilot was one of our flight leaders, a very experienced aviator named Bill Playfair. He was accompanied by a young sub-lieutenant observer named Woodhouse and a telegraphist air gunner named Frizell. When they returned after a patrol the ship was obscured by cloud, low on the water, and although they flew right over the ship and we saw them, they failed to see us. Searchlights were shone up into the clouds, and star-shells were fired, but there was no further sign of the aircraft.

I had an interesting conversation with our squadron CO, Pat Humphreys. 'Has it occurred to you, sir, that they might have been shot down?'

'Shot down! Don't be an ass! We're miles from anywhere out here.'

The tragedy had given me the opportunity of saying something that had been bothering me for a week.

'I know it's a very remote possibility, but it isn't impossible; and I think it is time we armed the aircraft guns.'

The Swordfish had a Vickers gun in front, which was fired by the pilot by pressing a button on the control column; the gun then fired through the propeller. We also had a Lewis gun in the rear cockpit, which was fired either by the observer or the air gunner – if one was lucky enough to be carrying such a luxury as a third member of the crew.

'You've been watching too many films about the last war!' said Pat Humphreys, scathingly. 'What on earth do we want bullets in our guns for?'

'Because they are more useful with them than without,' I replied, equally scathingly, and was rebuked for being impertinent.

The transition from peace to war takes time, and in HMS *Courageous* it wasn't until the following Sunday, 17 September, that the ship's company really woke up to the fact that we were at war; and even then we needed a German submarine's captain to bring the fact home. His demonstration was most convincing: at eight o'clock, on a warm Sunday evening, he fired two torpedoes at the ship, which struck us on the port side, almost simultaneously, and we sank in twenty minutes.

3
The Last Day

At three in the afternoon, on Sunday, 17 September, eight pilots and observers trooped into the wardroom for tea. We had been standing-by all day, in case of emergency calls, and there was only an hour to go before the other squadron took over the duty. As our Flight Commander pointed out, if we had to take off before our duty ended at four o'clock, it would be our last opportunity to eat or drink for many hours.

My observer brought his sandwiches to the place next to me, and we sat in silence, sipping our tea. Robert Wall was a very pleasant, wiry Lieutenant with thin features and wavy gingery hair, who had turned over from the RNR in 1938, after doing his apprenticeship in the City Line. Although this change-over had not been possible when Malan, Hyde, and I had applied in 1935, three years later in 1938 – when Lord Chatfield won his battle for the return of the Fleet Air Arm to the Navy – many RNRs accepted commissions in the permanent Navy, either as Seamen Officers of the Executive branch, most of whom specialized as submariners, or as pilots or observers in the Fleet Air Arm. Wall had opted to become an observer and we had been flying together for some months. By leaving the RNR and spending that intervening three years in the RAF I had lost three years' seniority in the Navy, but did not regret it because I gained far more experience of aviation than I would have done otherwise, and made some lifelong friends.

While we were sipping our tea our peace was shattered by the blare of the ship's bugler sounding off 'flying stations' on the tannoy, and then the Bosun's Mate's pipe, 'All stand-by pilots man your aircraft'; and I joined the general scramble out of the wardroom and up the ladders to the crew room in the island, where we kept our flying clothing. Clad in our overalls and helmets and goggles, we ran to our aircraft, which had been parked ready for take-off all day, armed with anti-submarine bombs, and ready for any emergency. While we ran up our engines and tested the magnetos, the observers were briefed by Commander Dan Baker, the Operations Officer, in the Operations Room in the island. They then sprinted down the deck to their aircraft, carrying their navigation instruments and Bigsworth Boards – a square wooden frame fitted with parallel rulers to which they clipped a plotting diagram, or a chart, so that they could navigate with the board resting on their knees in the confined space of the rear cockpit. Behind them, facing aft, sat the telegraphist air gunner, Doug Hemingway, who, as well as manning the Lewis gun when it was needed, also tuned the aircraft's radio to the ship's W/T frequency to keep a listening watch.

When Wall had climbed into the rear cockpit, and attached himself to the aircraft by the safety wire which clipped on to the harness between the observer and the air gunner's legs – obviously known as the 'Jockstrap' – he called me on the voice-pipe to tell me what we were about to do. Rubber voice-pipes between both cockpits connected to the earpieces of all three flying helmets, known as Gosport Tubes, and were very effective. It was surprising how clearly one could hear by this primitive method of communication.

We were the last of the eight Swordfish to take off and while we watched the others roll down the middle of the flight-deck and clamber into the air, Robert Wall briefed me down the voice-pipe.

'A big passenger liner, the SS *Kafiristan*, is being threatened by a U-boat on the surface. The German has ordered the crew and passengers to take to their boats, before he sinks the ship with his guns. The ship's radio officer managed to pass this information with his SOS, but only had time to give a rather shaky position. She's thought to be ninety or one hundred miles to the south, on the Atlantic edge of the Bay of Biscay, but she could be anywhere within fifty miles of the position he gave. We are to do a diverging search. We're the outboard aircraft on the eastern flank.

'Apparently there are a lot of other unconfirmed reports and we've got to keep a good lookout for other subs, there and back, and attack the first we see. The sea's alive with them!' He then told me the course to steer on take-off, and a few seconds later the seventh aircraft's chocks were waved away; and then mine, and we were off. When I opened the throttle that afternoon I was the last pilot to take-off from HMS *Courageous* and was to be the last to land.

After I had been flying the course for about fifteen minutes, Wall hailed me on the voice pipe. 'I've done all my sums,' he said. 'Is there anything you want to know? The ship's estimate of visibility distance is eight miles.'

We discussed the technicalities of the search. From our two ETAs – at the radius of action, and back at the rendezvous with the ship – it was clear that there wasn't going to be much of a margin of safety where fuel was concerned. We then discussed the reason for our search. I wondered how long it would take for a submarine to sink a ship with her guns, and how long a shipload of passengers and the crew would take to lower the boats and abandon ship. I put the question to Robert Wall and he said: 'Not very long, I imagine, if they've got a bloody great gun pointing at them!'

'I expect they will stretch it out as long as they dare in the hope that someone will turn up, having heard their SOS.'

I hailed the TAG on the pipe. Hemingway was a first-class chap. He had heard no sound on the W/T.

For the first half hour or so we could see the aircraft on our starboard beam but our courses gradually widened, and then we were out of sight of each other, but we had been able to see him for so long that I considered that the ship's estimate of visibility distance was much too low. The aircraft farthest away, on the other flank, was being flown by Neil Kemp, ninety miles away to starboard. He made the sighting report as early as 5 p.m. but we were out of range of his W/T transmission and heard nothing, and flew on.

Two of the ship's four escorts raced off at maximum speed to Kemp's position report, and the ship altered course in the same direction and increased her speed to 25 knots – almost the maximum for the old *Courageous* – but because of W/T silence she was unable to inform us. The slightest depression of a morse key by anyone on board the ship would have attracted the German U-boats from a radius of hundreds of miles.

I heard later that the destroyers recovered the passengers and the crew, but met another merchant ship and transferred them, and they all got home safely. Neil made his attack on the submarine, which was still on the surface, and succeeded in making it dive. Six of the aircraft heard his signal and altered course, though none of them could get there in time to join in with the attack. The alteration put them within range of the carrier's new position, and they had all landed safely before Robert and I, and the aircraft on our immediate right, had reached the furthermost point of our search.

When we returned there was no sigh of *Courageous*, and we began our square-search immediately. We had a questionable forty-five minutes of flying time remaining, but would almost certainly run out of fuel at a quarter to eight. I flew four minutes to the west, four minutes to the north, eight minutes to the east and then eight minutes to the south, and altered course to start the fifth leg – sixteen minutes to the west – with a sinking heart. At the end of that leg, if we reached it, we would have been searching for forty minutes, and might have four or five minutes' petrol remaining. Neither Wall nor I spoke. We were both thinking of Bill Playfair and his young observer, exactly a week before, and it seemed certain that like them, we too were to disappear without trace. It would be dark within an hour, and the mist which obscured the horizon was deepening with evening shadow. There was no possible chance of rescue out there, five hundred miles west of the Scilly Isles.

At the end of that sixteen-minute leg to the west, flying into the sun, which was only a few degrees above the hazy horizon, I began my turn to the north, cursing the lack of horizon which made accurate flying difficult. The blind-flying panel and artificial horizon had not appeared on the scene then, and all we had to guide us was a Reid and Sigrist Turn-and-Bank indicator, and some red mercury in a small thermometer tube, to tell the pilot whether he was flying nose-up or nose-down. As we began to swing, the setting sun rolled away over my left shoulder and its rays were reflected by something which glinted on the water for a split second, way out on the port beam; I checked the turn and steered towards it. Could it be the ship?

'It's the *Courageous!*' I yelled, and throttled right back.

When a carrier turns into wind to receive her aircraft, it seems to be a lazy, leisurely movement to the approaching pilot about to land. The bow starts to turn, imperceptibly to begin with, and then more emphatically in a graceful sweeping arc. The stern seems to kick the other way, as though resisting the motion, and then gives way in a rush, causing a mighty wash astern. While the ship is turning, the wind across the flight-deck can be violently antagonistic to a pilot who tries to land before the turn has been completed. Since we were about to run out of petrol, the turn seemed interminable, and after one half-circuit of the ship I decided to risk the cross-wind, and the violent turning motion, and get down before it was too late.

'Hey!' protested my observer. 'What the hell are you doing? She's only half-way round, and the batsman's waving us off like mad!' He could not know that the petrol indicator had been showing 'E' for Empty for the last ten minutes at least. The Swordfish has a Bristol Pegasus 111 M.3 radial engine which obscures the flight-deck – and the ship – in the very last stages of a deck-landing. Normally, by approaching in a gentle turn to port, right down to the deck, it is possible to keep the deck in sight until straightening up; then it is necessary to look between the engine cylinders, at 'eleven and twelve o'clock', when the yellow bats come into view for a split second as the deck swoops upwards at an alarming rate. This is fine by day, but at night the cylinders are always red-hot, and glow very brightly, and they can obscure the batsman's illuminated signals altogether. That afternoon he was being very helpful – by waving his bats around his head in a frenzied 'go round again' sign – and I could see him all the way down to the deck.

Fortunately, in 1939 the Deck Landing Control Officer's signals were not mandatory; they were intended as a guide. I was glad of that because I doubted whether there was anything like enough fuel to obey – which I had no intention of doing anyway. But he had every right to wave me off. Apart from the obvious danger of landing on a restricted area, which was swinging violently to starboard as the bow swung to port, I was much too high. In case my petrol gave out in the last few vital seconds, I had kept my height, to remain within gliding distance all the way down, intending to side-slip if necessary; or to ease the aircraft on to the deck in a stall by opening the throttle with the last few pints of petrol, once we were over the round-down. This is quite an effective method of deck-landing a Swordfish and is known as 'hanging on the prop'.

To the pilot of any aircraft, old or modern, height is like money: it is conceivable that too much might be an embarrassment, but too little is always fatal.

The Swordfish has a strong fixed undercarriage, an enormous rudder, and very good brakes. If our landing was rather like that of a clumsy seagull alighting on the water in a rush, it was nevertheless successful, and nothing broke. The hook picked up a wire and all was well.

'Christ!' said Wall. 'The ship's still turning into wind!'

We taxied up the deck and I applied the brakes when we got to the forward lift, and as the squadron ratings were folding the wings the engine stopped. There had been no need to pull the toggle which cuts the ignition. What little petrol remained in the carburettors had drained back into the tank as soon as my tail went down. The petrol had just ceased to flow. We walked through the hangar and down to the wardroom without knowing that my crab-like landing, which had caused so much indignation, was the last ever on that flight-deck. An officer on board HMS *Impulsive* – the escorting destroyer stationed on our starboard quarter – had taken a photograph of my landing. It appeared in many news-papers a few days later under the caption: 'The last plane to land on the deck of the *Courageous*.' He was also busy taking shots of the ship as she turned out of wind, and managed to get some magnificent pictures of her just before and just after she was torpedoed. As the ship turned out of wind she must have crossed the bows of the U-boat, providing the German with a straight-forward beam-on shot. His two torpedoes hit us almost simul-taneously, just as Wall and I were stepping into the wardroom. I had said to him: 'What are you going to have?' but he had no time to answer because at that moment there were two explosions, a split second apart, the like of which I had never imagined possible. If the core of the earth exploded, and the universe split from pole to pole, it could sound no worse. Every light went out immediately and the deck reared upwards, throwing me backwards, and the hot blast which followed tore at the skin on my face and plucked at my clothes. There was something Satanic about it, and unreal. In the sudden deathly silence which followed I knew that the ship had died.

In the wardroom passage the deafening silence was broken by the tinkling of glass, breaking somewhere; and the tiny sound of trickling water. There was also a persistent whisper of noise which at first I failed to identify. Then it dawned on me that it was the sound of men breathing.

The bulkhead behind me was now partly underfoot; and facing aft, I was standing with my left foot on the deck, which sloped upwards to starboard at an amazing angle. My other foot was on the wall. In this position it was obvious that the ship could not remain afloat for long. The silence was frightening. I supposed that the ship's engine had been blown to bits. All that remained was a great hulk, not a ship, lying on its side. The port side of the flight-deck was only a few feet above sea level.

The next few hours were unforgettable. Being torpedoed in a big ship, which had only fifteen minutes to remain afloat, is a strange experience. *Courageous* was the first ship of the Royal Navy to be sunk in the Second World War, and the events of the next twenty minutes, and the long night which followed, have made 17 September a date I shall never have any difficulty in remembering.

4
The Evening of the Last Day

When the torpedoes ripped open the ship's side and she rolled over to port at such an incredible angle it was obvious at once that she had been struck a mortal blow. In the first few seconds the whole length of the port side of the flight-deck hung suspended a few feet from the sea, crushing the ship's boats which burst through the sea up to the surface, swept from their stowages on the decks below. In those opening seconds, the aircraft in the hangar slid to port, crashing against each other and against the port bulkhead, adding greatly to the uneven top-weight and increasing the ship's list; furniture in the mess-decks broke from deck fastenings and slid crazily to port; petrol tanks burst, flooding down into the decks below, and an evil slick of oil and petrol quickly spread over the calm sea, surrounding the ship with an inflammable mixture which might have burst into flame – and a massive explosion – at any moment; hundreds of men were hurled into the sea from all parts of the ship, some being sucked from their underwater compartments on the port side when they were suddenly exposed to the sea, like pebbles under a heavy surf; a thousand things must have happened throughout the ship to make her doom inevitable. Two of them combined to turn the ship's last floating moments into a nightmare of contrasting silence and sound: the ship's ring-main was severed at once, extinguishing all the lights and cutting all power to every piece of machinery throughout her great length and depth, silencing the broadcasting system so that not even the essential pipe, 'abandon ship', could be made, and in one fraction of time a bustling community, humming with life became a silent floating tomb. The other event had no effect on the ship's diminishing seaworthiness but was perhaps even more of a blow to morale than any other single factor, for some object – probably a mast aerial – fell across the lanyard which operated the steam siren on the funnel, and as though to counteract the ghostly silence below, a long mournful blast, high above the tilted decks amongst the trembling super-structure, went on and on and on, as though the ship herself was crying out in her death agonies as her decks slowly filled, plunging her to the depths.

During the crowded twenty minutes in which she sank, over five hundred men lost their lives.

When a ship goes down there are always more relatives whose lives have been saddened by the tragic events than there are men drowned, and I have no wish to increase their sorrow by recounting all the horrors of that evening. In any case it was a time for action, not introspection, and one had to ignore the fearful things which were happening and concentrate on survival. For me the next few hours, and most of the night, were a jumbled mass of isolated and exhausting events, some of which were quite funny in a macabre way. When the ship heeled over and left me standing in that total darkness at an unnatural angle in the wardroom passage, I was shocked and frightened, but not really surprised. With some subconscious prescience – a boxer's sixth sense of trouble to come, perhaps – I had been expecting this knock-out punch ever since we were piped to action stations in Plymouth harbour after Chamberlain's declaration of war. Acting as bait for German submarines was tantamout to leading with your right, instead of your left, and my chin had felt exposed for a fortnight. Perhaps that was why I had brought my Mae West down from the crew room instead of leaving it up near the flight deck with all my other flying clothing. On my way down I had tossed it on the bunk in my cabin, which was just abaft the ante-room on the starboard side, before hurrying to offer Wall a drink, and have one myself.

When I had recovered my senses from the stunning blast, I remember thinking two things: 'The human frame was not intended to experience a sound like that,' and, 'I must get my Mae West at once.' But before I had moved from the darkness of the ante-room I heard a voice calling for help in a pleading tone which couldn't be ignored. Inside, by groping about, I found that a big, glass-fronted bookcase had been wrenched from the bulkhead by the blast and had fallen on top of the Principal Medical Officer, a huge pot-bellied Surgeon-Commander named Clifford-Brown. He was a very popular PMO, whose good humour was normally an even better tonic for his patients than his naval medicines; but under that bookcase he was feeling anything but jovial. With the strength born of the desperation inspired by his cries it did not take long to lift it – just enough for him to crawl out and up – and we both stood in the half-light, panting. Then he peered at me by the light from the scuttles – which I was horrified to see were open – and thanked me. I felt that there was no time for courtesy and said: 'We'd better go aft as quickly as we can. If the scuttles are open on the port side too, she'll sink at any moment,' and I propelled his colossal bulk into the passage, which led straight aft to the quarter-deck. A long way away, the doorway out to the deck was flooded with sunlight, like a bright light at the end of a long tunnel, inviting everyone to safety, and I left him plodding through the dark passage towards its salvation. I turned uphill, to starboard, into the intense darkness, to get my Mae West from my cabin. I had to clamber up the sloping deck. Fortunately the door was open and I congratulated myself on my carelessness: at that unlikely angle it might have jammed shut. I felt for the inflatable waistcoat on the bunk, and put it on. Then, standing in that unearthly silence in the pitch dark on that sloping deck, I tried to remember in which drawer the silver combs I had bought for the bridesmaids were lying; with them were two fivers and the wedding ring. But at that moment the deck under my feet gave a shuddering heave and lifted uneasily and the slope to port increased, and all the books from the shelves above my desk tumbled downwards, striking me on the head and shoulders. I panicked, thinking she was going to roll over, and before I knew that I had moved I was out in the passage again, the combs forgotten. It was a pity that she hiccuped at that moment because, as it turned out, there would have been plenty of time for me to find them and jam them into my pocket. The bridesmaids would have treasured them even more if they had been rescued from a sinking ship. Besides, although only about six inches long, their cases were embossed with naval crowns and they had been jolly expensive!

The silence and darkness of the passage were oppressive, and I could feel and hear the bodies of men stumbling past, breathing heavily. It was confusing being forced to walk with one foot on the port bulkhead instead of the deck. I joined the silent anonymous procession and someone's hand felt my shoulders from behind. Whoever it was must have been seeking physical assurance that he was upright. Reassured, he removed his questing touch and we plodded on, staring at the bright sunlight at the end of the tunnel –

which suddenly changed to a terrifying blood-red incandescence. With an involuntary spasm of fright I thought, 'The quarter-deck is on fire!' But when I stumbled out into the fresh air, I saw that it was only the setting sun. The stern was pointing due west and the door had been filled by the sun's vermilion, bloodshot glow. The contrast between the pitiless black-out of the cavern I had just left and the wide beam of sparkling light stretching across the sea from the horizon was quite incredible.

There was to be no let-up to admire the scenery. A little group of aviators were manning the starboard 4.7 gun, mounted on a pedestal by the guardrails on the quarter-deck, and I looked aft and saw a horrible sight: in the wide path of the shimmering light on the water, silhouetted against the sun as it sank below the horizon, were the twin periscopes of the U-boat which had just torpedoed us, pointing upwards. The thought that our hidden enemy was lying just under the surface, gloating at the sight of a great ship writhing in her death-throes, was obscene, and I hurried up the sloping deck to join the group. Lieutenant Ingram had taken charge. Assisted by the others he had wrenched a ready-use shell from its bulkhead stowage and rammed it into the breech. He was trying to train the barrel downwards, by the hand mechanism, which at first none of us understood; but eventually we succeeded.

'Do you know how to fire this bloody thing?' Ingram said fiercely. 'I'd like to blast him to hell . . .'

I had to admit that I didn't. The firing of ship's guns is not included in the Training Manual for Aircraft Pilots, and none of us knew what to do next. Pulling what we though was the trigger had no effect.

'I think they are operated by electricity,' I said, dumbly. It was just as well, in some ways, that we were unable to explode the shell, because at that moment the head and shoulders of an astonished stoker appeared, clambering over the stern, gazing straight into the barrel of the gun. He had been blown into the sea on the port quarter and was seeking temporary refuge, back on board, before being swept astern, and the prospect of being blown to pieces by a bunch of young lieutenants was not at all to his liking. He was about to drop back into the less unfriendly sea, when Kiggell and I dashed aft and dragged him on board. I think he thought we had all gone mad and were about to blow his head off.

The destroyer on our starboard quarter had spotted the periscopes, and suddenly leapt ahead, her stern packed down into the water with her violent acceleration; but the German U-boat skipper saw the move and the twin periscopes disappeared before the ship had moved a hundred feet. The destroyer dropped a pattern of depth-charges over the spot where the U-boat had been, killing all our men then in the water, but failed to damage the submarine. (Some weeks later the German skipper was given the Iron Cross for sinking the *Courageous*.) The intentions of the destroyer's captain were sound, but I was glad that I was still on board *Courageous* at the time. Then the Commander's face appeared above the quarter-deck, looking down from the seaplane platform, which protruded over the quarter-deck below, and shouted 'abandon ship' several times. His face was grey with anxiety. Men were diving into the water in all directions, some from the flight-deck which was fully seventy feet above sea level. The bilges, normally concealed below the water-line, were horribly exposed, and were quite ten feet farther to starboard than the edge of the flight deck. As I looked a man misjudged it and failed to reach the sea. I felt slightly sick at the sight and watched with my heart in my mouth as Sub-Lieutenant Oxley, one of our young pilots, made the same attempt. High above our heads he sprang out into the air, wearing his Mae West, his chest arched forward and his arms spread wide in a swallow-dive, and I grimaced with relief when he missed the bilges and plummeted into the sea.

Kiggell laughed. 'Typical!' he said. 'Only "Jumbo" Oxley would abandon ship with a swallow dive!'

'He was doing it to make sure that he missed the bilges,' I said. 'I would have done the same. I always turn over in the air if I try a high dive in any other way. With a swallow-dive you can see where you're going.'

There was now quite a little crowd of men lining the starboard rails of the quarter-deck. It was the nearest point to the sea and therefore the easiest place for disembarkation. A steady stream of men were climbing over the rails into the sea, but I noticed two or three, from the Reserve Fleet, standing together, looking gloomily over the side. Then my attention was diverted by a noise above, on the seaplane platform; and looking up I saw that the Royal Marines were falling-in neatly, as though they were attending some parade. A Corporal was in charge. I watched, expecting him to give them the order to abandon ship, but he stood them at ease and then stood at ease himself.

'Look at those Marines!' I said to Kiggell, who was standing beside me. 'They haven't heard the Commander and are waiting for the Captain Royal Marines to tell them what to do. He was blown over the side from for'ard some minutes ago. I saw him swimming to the destroyer, in his pink mess jacket. Perhaps they don't know.'

To remain in a neat assembly the Royal Marines were forced to stand at an angle to the deck of at least forty-five degrees. They looked like some comic turn on a music-hall stage.

'Silly buggers!' said Kiggell. 'They'll stand there until someone gives them an order and if nobody does, they'll all go down with the ship, still standing at that absurd angle!' He moved towards the starboard ladder leading up to the seaplane platform. 'Come on,' he said to me, and I scrambled up behind him.

Lieutenant (A) Lancelot Kiggell was the adjutant of the other squadron commanded by Lieutenant-Commander Simon Borrett, and was my 'opposite number'. He had turned over from the RAF after several years of flying in India on the North-West Frontier, and wore the green and black ribbon of that campaign. He was a fine pilot and a very efficient chap with a strong character. He suffered from one tremendous disadvantage: his very sensual face, with curling red lips and dark eyes, was a combination of Rudolph Valentino and Ronald Colman – two popular pre-war film stars – and his black hair curled in waves as though it had been set by some Mr Teasie-Weasie in a Bond Street salon. He couldn't help his appearance, but most orthodox naval officers shied away from him at first, until they discovered that he was a perfectly normal chap with a pleasant sense of humour. The effect he had on some females was remarkable, but he had very little effect on the Corporal Royal Marines, and neither did I. We explained that the Commander had given the order to abandon ship, and that his Royal Marine Captain had been blown into the sea and was no longer on board. The Corporal just gazed at our left sleeves and went pink with embarrassment. All Air Branch aviators, newly entered since 1938, were made to wear a little metal 'A', surrounded by an embroidered laurel leaf, above their wings on their left sleeve. Because the 'A' came unstuck after only a few days and fell off, and the laurel on its own meant very little, the 'A' was eventually changed to an embroidered letter sewn inside the executive curl.

The badge was designed to warn all beholders that the wearer knew nothing about the Navy, or about seamanship or navigation, and could not be expected to answer any question which was not about aviation. In other words it was the only badge ever worn by a naval officer to indicate that the wearer was *not* qualified to do something.

'You must hurry,' I said to the Corporal. 'The ship is down by the head, and the stern is now well above the horizon. See for yourself. At any moment she is going straight to the bottom.' But the Corporal's eyes were glued to the little 'A' on my sleeve. I could almost see the dotted lines bouncing back to the round-eyed stare of dismay with which he was gazing at it. Somebody must have briefed him to avoid all Air Branch officers like the plague. At this point Kiggell's experience of coping with natives on the North-West Frontier came to the rescue. He took a firm pace forward and with head thrown back and both arms rigid, he bellowed like a bull, his voice vying with the ship's siren.

'ROYAL MARINES – HUN! TURN FOR'ARD – DIS – MISS! ABANDON SHIP – OVER THE SIDE AT THE DOUBLE – EVERY MAN JACK OF YOU!'

It was the only language they understood and they reacted at once. Almost before the words had stopped echoing across the water there was a stampede of khaki-clad bottoms disappearing over the bulwarks into the sea, leaving the Corporal looking dejectedly after them. 'Go on,' I said, 'you'd better follow suit, and the best of luck to you . . .'

Back on the quarter-deck I saw that the stern had risen even higher and it was time to go. Only the three men from the Reserve Fleet remained at the rails, plus one Lieutenant (A) who looked as though he was going to be sick. He was one of Kiggell's squadron and I listened with horrified curiosity to their short conversation. The lieutenant said that he felt too ill to swim and was going down to his cabin for a bottle of brandy he had secreted in a drawer.

Kiggell told him not to be crazy. It was obvious that there was no time to go below quarter-deck level – or anywhere inside the ship – but the lieutenant refused to listen and disappeared through the doorway into the darkness. Perhaps he preferred to go this way. I have since wondered whether he was unable to swim and was too proud to say so, but have discounted that theory as too improbable. Perhaps he was just thirsty. Whatever his reason, he was never seen again.

We discovered that the three Reserve Fleet men were unable to swim and were just standing there, having abandoned all hope of survival, waiting for the ship to take them with her. We had a long argument, because I had no need of my Mae West – the destroyer lay such a short distance away that I could have swum to it many times. The sea was calm and would probably be pleasantly warm. None of the men would accept my Mae West – they said that they would only float about in it, and take longer to drown. So I offered to take them across, one by one, if there was time, and after a lot of silly argument one of them agreed and Kiggell helped him over the side as soon as I dived in. The sea was warm, and the Mae West was like an armchair. I had never tried one in the water before, and realized that I could have floated about in it for days. The man was wearing yellow braces and I clutched him by these, but was unable to prevent him from putting his face into the sea and making burbling noises. We reached the destroyer in a matter of minutes – ten at the most – by which time he was dead. A crowd of men on board *Impulsive* hauled him up the side, but shook their heads at me, sadly. This upset me, because he certainly hadn't drowned. He was just too old for the shock of the last twenty minutes and I felt angry with the Admiralty for dragging these old pensioners back to sea. We could have managed without them.

On my way back to the *Courageous* from the destroyer, the carrier's stern suddenly rose in the air until the ship was vertical. The quarter-deck was pointing at the sky and it seemed to be hundreds of feet up. Then she was gone.

The sea all round me was a mass of heads, all bobbing about in the calm water. As the ship plunged downwards a great cheer went up from the sea's surface and someone started to sing 'Roll out the Barrel', which seemed rather a waste of breath. It was dark a few minutes later and I had a long swim before I found the destroyer and was very glad when I did. An American liner appeared on the scene at the same moment and picked up hundreds of survivors.

Robert Wall was one of the first people I saw on *Impulsive*'s upper deck when I climbed on board. He had swallowed a great deal of oil during his swim and was looking exhausted. Later he discovered that he had damaged one lung by absorbing so much oily water, but at the time he assured me that he was okay. I was very relieved to see him. I remarked that it was odd that we had not seen the American passenger boat during our square search, but he pointed out that we had been searching to the south-west, whereas the ship had come from the east. We wondered if she would have seen us if we had ditched, and were encouraged because, at a time when so many needed aid, ships could appear from nowhere, like policemen at an accident.

The next two hours, until midnight, searching for survivors were very uneasy; the destroyer had to stop engines while each swimmer was recovered, and when stationary she presented an easy target for the U-boat, which we all suspected was still in the area watching our manoeuvres (and there might have been other submarines in the vicinity). As each body was hoisted out of the water we moved away quickly, as a precaution against attack, to search in other areas, and this made survival doubly difficult for the swimmers.

Those who were fit enough were kept very busy helping *Impulsive*'s men deal with the half-drowned men who were hauled on board. There was a lot to do. We applied artificial respiration to those who needed it, and then put them into a hot bath and gave them some fire-water to drink. By the time I arrived on board all the normal spirits had been drunk and all that was left was neat Pimm's; but it was a wonderful reviver after the taste of that oily sea-water. Everyone needed clothing and the destroyer's ship's company had made a great pile of everything they could spare on the deck of the lobby above the wardroom ladder. I grabbed a pair of rugby shorts, a Maltese steward's jacket and a pair of gymshoes, and as I put them on it suddenly dawned on me that I had just lost everything I owned in the world! Tails, dinner-jacket, all my civilian clothing and uniforms, which I had spent years acquiring. A pair of twelve-bore guns in a leather case lined with red velvet, golf clubs, boxing trophies . . . it didn't bear thinking about, and I made some remark to that effect to Neil Kemp, who was dressing beside me. 'Never mind – we've survived!' he said. 'And those rugby shorts are a beautiful fit.'

I asked Neil if he had any news of Simon Borrett, the CO of the other Swordfish squadron, and it was a strange coincidence that when we had dressed in our makeshift clothing we walked out on deck and saw him going past, stretched out on a Carley float. His body was rigid and he was unconscious. Fortunately the ship was stationary at the time and it took only a few minutes to get him on board. I carried him down the deck and was shocked by his lack of weight: I might have been carrying a boy of ten. We put him into a hot bath but his eyes remained closed. I tried to persuade him to swallow a little neat Pimm's but he was an abstemious chap and resisted, even though unconscious.

'Try again,' Neil said, 'that little drop almost brought him round.'

I tilted the bottle against his teeth; his eyes opened for a fleeting moment, just long enough for him to say: 'I – don't – think – I'll – have – any – more – thank – you,' before he lapsed into a coma again.

I said to Neil: 'Even when out for the count, Simon still behaves like a gentleman! Anyone else being forced to drink against their wishes would have been far less polite!' Together we carried him down the ladder and stretched him out on the wardroom settee, lying head to toe with the Commander, who was looking awful. His face was a stricken grey, but when I asked him if he was all right he nodded. I could see something was wrong and put my hands under his blanket and found that he was soaking wet and shivering with cold. So I rubbed him down with a towel, ignoring his protests, and was greatly helped by a young Midshipman named Andy Aitken, who was also from our squadron in *Courageous*. We wrapped him in a dry blanket and stretched him out on the settee again. Then Aitken and I found a number of empty bottles and filled them with hot water and stuffed them all round the outside of the blanket. During the night I looked at him occasionally and saw that his colour was returning. He seemed much better in the morning.

There were others not so fortunate, and a number of men died during the night. Some of those deaths were unnecessary – one in particular.

When a man is feeling low, and is cold and dispirited, and has been subjected to shock and perhaps injury, it is easy for him to drift into a torpor from which he may not wish to recover, unless something is done to jerk him out of his apathy. I learned this simple fact of life that night, but at the expense of a man's life. He was stretched out on deck by one of the hatches leading down to the wardroom flat. From one direction he had to be stepped over, and since men were carrying comatose bodies down the ladder, he provided a dangerous obstruction. I knelt down beside him and asked him if he would mind moving, thinking he was only asleep, like hundreds of others strewn about the ship's decks. He said 'Bugger off,' without opening his eyes, so I left him in peace for a while. Later I tried again, but he said: 'For Christ's sake leave me alone!' He was there all night and I spoke to him several times, and asked him if he was all right, or needed anything, but always received the same brusque reply. In the morning he was dead.

With so many men lying about on the decks, it was difficult to discover who was sleeping and who was *in extremis*; but I have always felt guilty about that man because I should have realized that he was dying.

At midnight the Captain of *Impulsive* decided that all survivors had been recovered and that it was time to start for home. We were all very relieved to hear the ship's engines open up to full speed, putting an end to all fear of further torpedoes. We arrived in Devonport early the following evening, on Monday, 18 September, and as we went alongside we saw that there was a big crowd on the jetty, mostly doctors, nurses and sick berth attendants, who were standing beside ambulances.

There was also a sprinkling of senior officers, and one of them called out to us as the heaving lines were being thrown: 'You will all be going on survivor's leave tomorrow.'

We gave a little cheer at this and he held up his hand for our attention. 'All ratings are to go to the canteen, where you can have hot baths and showers, and where there are tailors waiting to fit you out with new clothing. You will be given some ready-use money in the form of "casual payment". All officers are to report to the wardroom at HMS *Drake*, where the same facilities are awaiting you.'

The RN Barracks at Devonport are inside the dockyard and have always been called HMS *Drake*. It was only a short walk, but it was very nice to feel solid earth underfoot.

5
Survivor's Leave

The wide stone steps leading up on either side of the front entrance to the stately barracks wardroom at HMS *Drake* are very dignified; and in my gymshoes, bare legs, rugby shorts and Maltese steward's jacket I was glad that all my companions were as scruffy. When we walked inside I was even more glad, because in that panelled hall we found ourselves facing the Commander-in-Chief. The gold braid on his arms seemed unending and behind him, peering over his shoulder, were his Secretary and Flag-Lieutenant, their aiguillettes dropping from their shoulders in a cascade of gold. A team of officers was spread on either side in the background and we were touched that all these people had turned out to receive us. By the appearance of the assembly we might have been attending some civic reception.

White-coated stewards moved round us while we waited our turn to be interviewed by the great man himself. A member of his staff stood at his side with a navigator's notebook, noting down names, ranks and answers. Until each of us had undergone this interrogation we were kept apart from the crowd of spectators who were waiting to escort us to bathrooms, and to the tailors upstairs.

When I walked past the line of spectators, known as 'goofers' in the Service, one of them sprang out and threw a jocular punch at my chest.

'That's one fight you lost!' said Lieutenant-Commander Cecil John 'Gresham' Grenfell, RN, who had been a Lieutenant in *Rodney* when I was a Midshipman RNR. We had swopped punches so often that we were close friends.

From that moment onwards my problems were over: he took me under his wing and completely organized my immediate life – and my wedding. First of all he rushed me up the stairs to a big room where Gieves and Bernards were standing behind trestle tables which were piled high with civilian clothing ready for immediate purchase. 'You must do this before you have a bath or all the best suits will be snapped up,' said Gresham.

At first it seemed that the tailors had assumed that the only people who could be expected to survive such an ordeal would be giants, because all the clothes were too big for me, until Gresham spotted a grey-checked suit under a pile of jackets. It was a perfect fit, but a trifle loud for my taste, so I bought some plain shirts and ties to tone it down. Ever afterwards my wife, Jo, referred to it as 'your bookmaker's suit'. Because my feet are enormous I had little choice there either, and in the end had to buy a pair of brown brogues with pointed toes and a fancy pattern in the leather. 'Goes rather well with the suit,' Gresham remarked. Then I remembered, and asked Gieves' representatives if they had any full-dress uniforms for hire in Plymouth, and Gresham exclaimed: 'What on earth for? We've been told to put them away for the duration. The only uniform needed now is an ordinary reefer and a sword.'

'I want to hire a cocked hat, and buy a sword, too,' I said to the representative. Gieves never employ 'salesmen': they are always 'representatives'.

I explained that I was about to be married and told Gresham about the banns, and he volunteered to drive me home in the morning.

'My dear chap, you must get married tomorrow!' he said. 'Don't waste a minute of your leave – it may be your last! We'll go and ring up now.' He rushed me off to a cabin with a phone extension and said: 'Help yourself, while I run a bath for you.' When I dialled the dockyard the operator said: 'Are you from *Courageous*? Then your calls have priority over ordinary calls,' and I was astounded how quickly I got through. Jo's mother answered the phone and I was expecting her to be a bit shattered that I was able to ring so soon after being sunk, but she sounded quite normal.

'I am so glad you have been able to telephone,' she said. 'Jo will be pleased. We had a very nice message from a kind person in Plymouth a fortnight ago, and guessed you had sailed.'

I was very relieved. So, they didn't know! I thought that it would have been on the radio and in all the papers, but, of course, it was less than twenty-four hours ago!

'Obviously you haven't heard the news. I hope Jo hasn't either. I'm afraid the ship was sunk yesterday, but I am perfectly all right and back on dry land in Plymouth and am just going to be given some leave.'

There was only a slight pause while she assimilated this rather startling information.

'Were you hurt in any way?' she asked anxiously. I told her that I had never felt better.

'I'm all ready for a snap wedding and a snap honeymoon.'

'Of course,' came the reply, without hesitation. 'When are you coming on leave?'

'Tomorrow,' I said. 'I understand that it is for three weeks. But there's no point in waiting for the thirtieth' – which was the date we had planned to wed.

'Of course not, we'll organize the wedding this week.'

What a wonderful woman! 'What about tomorrow?' I asked.

'Too soon,' she said 'We'll arrange it for Wednesday.'

The day after tomorrow! Splendid! All those tales about mothers-in-law were poppycock.

An hour or so afterwards Gresham drove me towards the gate by the Commodore's funny house, which looks as though it had been designed by Emmet. Outside the gate I saw a huge crowd of women standing in the road, and my elation evaporated. They were standing very still, in silence, in the shadow of that high grey wall which reeks of history. New history was in the making – a terrible, tragic page of it. Over 300, at least, of those women were going to discover that they were widows that night. Some of them knew already, and were being comforted by the others. It was a tormenting spectacle. Just fifteen days before they had been standing on Plymouth Hoe, with Johnny Hyde, waiting to welcome their husbands home – and what a short reunion that had turned out to be. But how much worse it would have been, when their husbands were dragged away in the evening, had they known that they would never meet again. I felt a great ache in my stomach for them all, and longed to be able to leap out of the car and say something which would make them less sad. But there was nothing – nothing that anyone could say, or do. I caught Gresham's eye and blew my nose.

The village of Charlton All Saints in the county of Wiltshire is a small collection of farms, houses, and cottages surrounding a large parish church. It is spread out on the banks of the River Avon beneath the wooden hill which leads up to Nelson's estate, and the stately Trafalgar House on its summit.

The inhabitants of the village had acquired a proprietary interest in HMS *Courageous*: for three Sundays, from his pulpit in the parish church, the Canon had called out the ship's name when publishing our banns.

On the Tuesday morning, when the news of the sinking was on the front page of every newspaper in the land, there was a feeling of shocked sorrow in the farmhouses and cottages for miles around; but in the afternoon, when it became known that the wedding was to take place the very next day, sadness changed to jubilation and, without being asked, many of the local housewives decorated the church with flowers in readiness. The headmistress closed the village school for the day and equipped all the children with little Union Jacks, and when I arrived at the church on Wednesday morning the children were lining the path from the lychgate to the porch, standing on either side, waving their flags. It was all so spontaneous and unexpected that I found it a heart-warming spectacle.

At the altar, standing beside my white-veiled bride, a delayed reaction set in which I tried hard to control. The events of the last three days crowded into my mind and made concentration difficult. I kept seeing mental pictures of those women standing outside the dockyard gates; then the Reserve Fleet Chief Petty Officer who kept putting his face into the water; and the other one later, lying on deck at the top of the ladder spurning all help, though on the point of death; the terrible picture of the ship's stern, rearing upwards just before she sank. So much tragedy had taken place in such a short space of time, and yet that fearful event had brought me happiness. I felt that I had no right to be there, in that peaceful church. But perhaps those women outside the dockyard would be glad that someone was achieving happiness even if it blossomed alone, like a flower growing from a heap of manure.

PART II

The Phoney War

6

The Birth of a Squadron

The Hampshire village of Crawley, near Winchester, is composed of exquisite 'olde worlde' cottages, neatly thatched, facing either side of the only road which leads down from the main road at the top of the hill to the Fox and Hounds Inn and a circular pond at the bottom. It is very beautiful. Most of the officers who had survived the sinking of *Courageous* were appointed to Worthy Down, a nearby naval airfield, to form a new Swordfish squadron; and somehow we managed to rent many of the cottages in Crawley. For the rest of that bitterly cold winter of 1939 the village became the domestic headquarters of Number 815 Squadron.

My wife and I rented an enchanting cottage called Little Thatch in the precincts of the village. It was supposed to be the house in which Thackeray had written *Vanity Fair*, though I have never been able to discover how that rumour began. The cottage next door to Little Thatch was called Thackeray Cottage and still is. Whether or not he gave birth to his great work in our first married home, the thought added to our pleasure in its beauty, which had a natural undisturbed serenity. Even the icicles hanging from the thatch in the mornings seemed attractive.

For our formation period 815 Squadron was commanded by Lieutenant-Commander Simon Borrett. He had recovered from his immersion in the sea sufficiently well to nurse us through our teething stages, but looked pale and very thin. Nevertheless he led us in the air, tightening our formation flying, and leading us out over the Solent for dummy torpedo attacks, and dive-bombing rushes to earth, which must have been a great strain for him. Whenever possible Neil Kemp took over command and persuaded him to stay on the ground. As second-in-command, and a Flight Leader, Neil was very efficient, and could be much ruder to us than Simon.

The Swordfish was a sturdy aircraft, and its robust qualities were proved almost beyond credulity by our CO, one bleak November afternoon in 1939, when he was leading us back from the target ranges in the Solent. Over Southampton we ran into low cloud, and when we emerged, Simon had disappeared. We flew back to Worthy Down and waited for him. Unbeknown to us balloons had been hoisted over Southampton and Simon had led us right through them in cloud. He was the only one of us who was unlucky: his port wings had struck a balloon cable and without warning he was swung round, one hundred and eighty degrees, in a turn of startling velocity, which must have frightened him out of his mind. When he recovered he found that he was flying in the wrong direction and had lost his squadron. When he landed at Worthy Down we saw that his port mainplanes were partially severed and were holding together by the flying and landing wires between them, and a few feet of the trailing edge of both wings, which was still intact.

The remarkable qualities of the Swordfish were the product of the genius of Marcel Lobelle, the chief designer of Fairey Aviation Company. In 1933 the Admiralty asked Sir Richard Fairey to design an aircraft which would fulfil every naval requirement except the air defence of the Fleet. They listed six for a start: reconnaissance, at sea and over the land; shadowing, by day and night; 'spotting' the fall of shot from ship's guns; convoy escort duties such as anti-submarine searches and attack; torpedo and divebombing attacks against shipping; minelaying – and the carrying of other heavy loads – which in the Second World War varied from searchlights to rockets, plus depth-charges, bombs and flares.

To combine all these varied functions in one aeroplane was a revolutionary concept. There were other complications which had to be embodied into the design: the aircraft had to be capable of landing in small areas, and on pitching decks at very slow speeds. It also had to be able to carry heavy loads of nearly 2000 lb in a dive attack at speeds not far from 200 knots, if it was to survive. Therefore a low stalling speed when carrying all this weight was essential.

Lobelle produced the prototype in 1934, called the 'TSR', which stood for Torpedo Spotter Reconnaissance. It was test-flown successfully and renamed the Swordfish; but when trying it out with all those different loads some wag remarked that 'No housewife on a shopping spree could cram a wider variety of articles into her stringbag.' The name stuck, and from that moment the pilots always called it the Stringbag when talking about it amongst themselves.

Of all its many weapons the most devastating was the aerial torpedo. This weighed 1610 lb and was capable of sinking a 10 000-ton ship within minutes of the moment of impact. To deliver this weapon in the face of intense opposition in daylight, pilots were taught to attack from a steep dive, at speeds of 180 knots and more. They have been known to reach 200 knots in that dive – *in extremis* – but there was then a real danger of the wings folding back, or tearing off. In that headlong rush to sea level, the pilot had the impression that he was standing on the rudder bar, looking over the top of the centre-section of the upper mainplane. His face was only partially screened, so that a helmet and goggles were a 'must' for all normal individuals. Those dives had to be very nearly vertical. Any modern clean-surfaced aircraft needs many thousands of feet to pull out of a dive, but the Swordfish could be eased out, with a pull-out of less than five hundred feet. After straightening out and throttling back, the forward speed came right down to 90 knots very quickly, because of the drag provided by the fixed undercarriage, and all the struts and wires between the mainplanes. This violent alteration in speed made the aircraft a difficult target for the gun-aimer on the ground, or in the ship being attacked, and the sudden deceleration helped the pilot to deliver his weapon very accurately. Nevertheless there was never any doubt that the Stringbag was a very slow machine, and a vulnerable target for all, especially in daylight.

There was a well-worn jest amongst Swordfish pilots that the enemy had no speed settings on their gunsights as low as the Stringbag's cruising speed of 90 knots, and therefore a Swordfish could only be hit by shells aimed at a flight astern. This was an exaggeration, of course, yet there was an element of uneasy truth in the statement. But the lumbering old ladies were an easy prey for a capable fighter pilot, providing he appreciated the remarkable manoeuvrability of the old biplane he was attacking.

Its defence armament was a pathetic hangover from the First World War: the Vickers gun in the front cockpit was fired by the pilot through the propeller, and was all of one stage more advanced than a bow and arrow. The Lewis gun, in the rear cockpit, fired by either the air gunner or the observer, had been very successfully used in the First World War, but was quite valueless in the Second. The sensible Swordfish pilot ignored these weapons and put his faith in his own ability to outmanoeuvre the other man. Given enough height and space in which to throw the aircraft about, the Stringbag could outfly almost every other aircraft – with the possible exception of the Gladiator.

The Stringbag could be very roughly handled in incredible attitudes without stalling, providing the pilot knew what he was doing. To stall a Swordfish by mistake was almost an impossibility. Marcel Lobelle had given the aircraft a stalling speed of 55 knots, and no pilot, however ham-handed, could allow his speed to drop to that extent without noticing. To induce it into a spin was quite hard work: the aircraft could be stood on its tail in mid-flight so that it became almost stationary, before it would drop into a stalled turn, and then recovery could be instantaneous. Quick application of throttle and opposite rudder, and a speedy lowering of the nose, would provide almost immediate stability, when the manoeuvre could be repeated without fear.

There were no refinements to bother with, such as flaps or a variable pitch airscrew, and the undercarriage could not be retracted; but the aircraft had one very special asset which, like everything else in the machine, was simple and most effective: its torpedo sight was foolproof if used with care. Whoever designed it was as much a genius as Marcel Lobelle. Two rods, one on either side of the front cockpit, fixed to the trailing edge of the top mainplane, displayed a neat little row of electric light bulbs, spaced equally far apart. The distance between each bulb and the next represented five knots of enemy speed.

By arriving over the sea at right-angles to the enemy ship at a range of about two thousand yards, the pilot would steer towards the ship with the correct light bulb in line with the ship's bow. For example, a ship doing 20 knots needed four light bulbs between its bow and the nose of the aircraft. In a daylight attack, because the aircraft was most vulnerable during this breathtaking run-in, and the time spent low on the water had to be reduced to seconds if the pilot was going to be able to deliver his weapon and survive, the assessment of enemy speed had to be made before the pilot started his dive. Last-minute yawing – by use of rudder – to keep the bulb in line, only served to throw the torpedo out of true when it was released, and then it might run in circles.

Torpedoes were temperamental weapons which required

accurate flying if they were to run properly. They had to be dropped from a height of sixty feet, no more and no less. At the beginning of the war we had no sensitive altimeter, or 'blind-flying' instrument panel, and could only read our height above sea level to the nearest one hundred feet, so this dropping height required accurate judgement by the pilot.

The torpedo, or magnetic mine, slung under the fuselage, was released by an electric firing-switch on top of the throttle, operated by the pilot with his left thumb. Because the weapon was so heavy, the moment it was released the aircraft's nose would surge upwards, and so with his right hand the pilot had to hold it down and keep the aircraft in level flight, otherwise the torpedo would 'porpoise'. If the nose of the aircraft was allowed to rise the torpedo would be tossed in the general direction of the target so that it entered the sea with a splash, like a diver doing a belly-flop; but if the aircraft was kept level and steady, the 'fish' entered the sea at the correct angle, without a splash, and sped smoothly towards its target.

All these complications were simplified if the attack could be made at night. There was then no need for a dive approach, and one crept towards the enemy ship at half-throttle in a long glide. Because the Stringbag was a spidery silhouette it was most difficult to see at night when coming in low on the water, and one could approach to very short range so that the torpedo was certain to hit the target. When it did, the first sign to the attacking pilot was a small puff of smoke bursting upwards from the ship's funnel, as she belched from this tremendous blow in the stomach. Then it was time to turn and get to hell out of it in case the ship blew up and took the Swordfish up with her.

It could be very cold in those open cockpits, strapped to one's parachute, but I always felt the deepest respect for the observer and air gunner, exposed in the rear cockpit, sitting with their heads lowered away from the slipstream, concentrating on their exacting but less exciting task of navigating, or tuning the radio. They were entirely in the hands of the man in the front seat and had to rely on him to get them safely there and back. He had the excitement of delivering the weapon and avoiding the flak, while they sat helplessly in the rear cockpit, praying that he would not make a mistake. They were brave men indeed, and I would not have changed places with them for all the inducements on earth.

In the 'Rolls-Royce' days of the early stages of the war, each pilot had his own 'fitter' and 'rigger', and they looked after his aircraft only. It was at Worthy Down that I first met Burns and Brown. To them I owed my life over and over again. In 815 Squadron my aircraft was always 'Q' for 'Queenie' and after a while the three of us thought of each other as a part of 'Q'. They were both very efficient men. Burns was the fitter and cherished my engine, and was very rude to me in a jocular way whenever he thought I had abused it. Brown, being the rigger, looked after the airframe; he was a round-faced, cheerful individual. Burns was thin-faced and pugnacious, but they were both extremely good-natured, and intensely loyal. They balanced each other perfectly, and I could not have been blessed with a better team. Later in the war it was necessary to introduce the centralized maintenance of aircraft, and pilots seldom flew the same aircraft a second time, except by chance, and the maintenance crews looked after the squadron machines as a whole. With more advanced aircraft this had to come, and it made sense, being more economic; but I am glad that in the Swordfish days the air and ground crews were part of the same aircraft, because it worked in a way that was unbelievably sound. Without Burns and Brown, 'Q' for 'Queenie' would never have remained the same wonderful old aircraft through all adversity; nor would I have been able to fly secure in the knowledge that there could be nothing wrong with its airframe or engine that was controllable by human hands.

Although living at Crawley and flying from Worthy Down was extremely pleasant, and there was a great deal of other activity at the station which was most interesting, we all began to feel restless after 17 December 1939, when the German captain of the *Graf Spee* finally scuttled his pocket battleship outside Montevideo. For four days we had listened to the inspiring news of three British cruisers fighting a running battle with a ship which could fire a broadside half as powerful again as their total fire-power, and which greatly out-ranged them; yet they emerged the victors. In the saloon bar of the Fox and Hounds in Crawley, on that quiet Sunday evening, Neil Kemp voiced the opinon of us all. 'It's time we got back into the war,' he said. 'All we've succeeded in doing up to date is to be sunk!'

We could only wait for orders, and in the wardroom and on the hilly airfield we were merely a small part of a big community. Dozens of RNVR pilots were based there, employed in collecting new aircraft from factories and delivering them to new units which were forming all over the British Isles. Amongst them were two famous actors who were Lieutenants (A)RNVR, Ralph Richardson and Laurence Olivier. There was also a hush-hush experimental unit commanded by Robin Kilroy, a famous man who had the reputation of being one of the Fleet Air Arm's most skilled pilots. As well as being in command of a fascinating unit doing secret trials, he managed to find time, occasionally, to exhibit some of his paintings in London's West End, where they were drawing big crowds. He was a small tough bachelor, with a quiet friendly manner, and when we told him how restless we were all becoming at not being an operational squadron, he smiled gently and said, 'I should enjoy it while you can,' in a significant way, as though he had private knowledge of our future movements. 'You'll be in the front line when you're needed, and once there you'll find it difficult to get back to your wives.'

After Christmas we were moved to Cardiff airport to chase German U-boats reported in the Bristol Channel. We were told that we would not be returning to Worthy Down, so we loaded our stores into railway containers and flew to Cardiff, leaving our wives to pack up the cottages in Crawley and follow us by car. Flying on dawn patrols, out past Lundy Island, was getting us a little closer to the war; but Cardiff airport was below the water-level of the Channel and though surrounded by a dyke-like wall was more often than not under water, when we were unable to fly at all.

Simon Borrett grew noticeably thinner week by week and we were all beginning to worry about him. Flying a Swordfish involved a certain amount of physical strength, and the effort was beginning to tell on him. Because of the absence of any control in the aircraft to counteract torque, the only solution was to experiment with sticking-plaster and gum, in order to rig a 'jury-rudder' down the side of the big rudder itself, to relieve the pressure on the rudder bar. With Brown's aid I experimented between flights and eventually ironed out the bias in 'Q' for 'Queenie' altogether. Without this there was constant pressure on the rudder bar and one suffered from what was known as 'Swordfish leg'. Being the CO, Simon had no time to spare to fuss about his own aircraft, and because nobody could do it for him his aircraft remained uncorrected. Rudder bias is personal to each pilot, and it cannot be corrected for one pair of legs by the owner of another. Apart from that, the exposure to slipstream in an open cockpit was in itself exhausting after a few hours in the air. We were all relieved for his sake when one afternoon he addressed us in a subdued voice and said how sorry he was that he could no longer continue. With much regret, he had informed the Admiralty that he was not strong enough to continue as our leader. He was handing the squadron over to another Lieutenant-Commander much more capable of the task than himself.

'Robin Kilroy arrives tomorrow,' said Simon. 'I can think of no one I would prefer to hand you over to.'

7

Kilroy is Here!

The next morning we were addressed by our new CO, sitting on a table on the stage of a lecture room. He was a small man who looked younger than his age. In his early forties, his features were youthful and very tanned, and his brown hair had fair streaks in it, as though he was just home from the tropics and it had been bleached by the sun.

After saying some nice things about Simon Borrett he startled us all by dividing the squadron in two, and sending one half away. He explained that we had a special job to do which required a minimum number of hours' flying experience.

'I know very little about your flying ability and nothing at all about you as individuals, so there is nothing personal about it. But as there is some urgency I am sending away all those with less than a thousand hours' flying by day, and a hundred hours by night. They will go on immediate leave.'

When their names had been read out and they had left, he asked us for our undivided attention. It was an unnecessary request. We were all agog. He spoke without notes, and with his hands in his pockets.

'When you were at Worthy Down you may have noticed that I sometimes flew a Swordfish with a strange object sticking up in the air in the rear cockpit, where the observer usually sits. I'm sorry to disappoint the pilots – it was not a replacement for the "looker" – it was a long-range petrol tank.

'In that tank, gentlemen, there was nearly one thousand pounds' weight of petrol, which, when added to the Stringbag's normal fuel, gave me a total of three hundred and thirty-six gallons. Carrying a dummy torpedo, weighing one thousand six hundred and ten pounds, I managed to stay in the air for nearly nine hours, and flew a distance of nearly one thousand miles!' He paused to allow time for this information to sink in.

'You will have realized, of course, that under normal conditions, flying against the enemy, I would not have had to carry that load for more than half the distance because, had it been for real, I would have dropped it when I reached the target. So the nine hours is not an arbitrary figure. Under real conditions we can fly even farther than one thousand miles. On our way back from wherever we have to go, there will be no load, so we can probably stay in the air for about nine and a half hours, perhaps ten, with safety.

'This extra fuel has given us the opportunity of striking a really telling blow at Germany. It has brought into range a multitude of targets which haven't been considered by the Fleet Air Arm before, nor have they been within our range, except from a carrier. With our accurate navigation we can fly to the German coast and lay magnetic mines in a prescribed pattern; we can dive-bomb German shipping and harbours when they least expect it. There is almost no limit to our new-found versatility. You should be proud that this outfit has been selected as the vanguard of all the others which will follow.

'There is one target which has been brought within our reach which no aircraft other than the Swordfish could possibly attack with the same chances of success – and that's the German port of Wilhelmshaven. As you know, it's the enemy's main harbour, because it is defended on either flank by land masses, and to get there by sea entails negotiating the Weser, an open stretch of water which is heavily defended from surface attack. An attack from the sea by shipping is out of the question, and the only attack they will be anticipating from the air is high-level bombing. We are going to give them an unpleasant surprise,' he said, cheerfully. 'Naturally we shall only attack when the harbour is bulging with ships, but there is enough water inside most of the locks for a torpedo to run. Some pilots will torpedo the ships, inside; others the lock gates; and some will lay magnetic mines inside the locks when there is insufficient water for a torpedo. In short, we are going to make an unholy mess of Germany's main maritime stronghold, and we can do it without much difficulty and – if we are skilful – perhaps without loss.

'The Navy School of Photography has made a scale model of Wilhelmshaven, from accurate charts and from photographs taken for us by pilots from RAF Benson. From these we have been able to pinpoint all the ack-ack positions, and the position of all the balloons; the model is a beautiful piece of work, but it is rather substantial, and it's being taken in a covered lorry to our new base this weekend. We are moving to the RAF Coastal Command station, Bircham Newton, near The Wash, in Norfolk, within the next forty-eight hours. The rest of the squadron will follow shortly. Some are already there. Lieutenant-Commander Chapman and I have already visited the station, and called on the Group Captain, an excellent chap named Primrose, who is expecting us. His adjutant has a list of houses in the vicinity which can be rented by the married officers. Single officers like me will live in the officers' mess.'

I wasn't surprised when Kiggell interrupted.

'The rest of the squadron, sir?' he interjected, in a puzzled voice. 'But we are all here?'

Our new CO smiled at him benignly. 'While you were swanning about at Worthy Down I spent quite a long time at the Admiralty selecting the right chaps to come and join you. You will find some very old friends awaiting you at Bircham Newton. They are the pick of the Fleet Air Arm.

'To revert to Wilhelmshaven; at Bircham Newton the model will be kept out of sight, under lock and key, available to us only; but I expect every officer to familiarize himself with it at least once a day, until he knows every building surrounding the harbour, every lock entrance, and the position of every balloon cable. I have decided on our way into the harbour, and our way out. I will show you this in due course. We shall have surprise on our side because the Hun won't know that a torpedo aircraft like the Swordfish has suddenly acquired the range to fly into the harbour, so it won't have occurred to him to put out anti-torpedo nets. I have already mentioned that some of the locks are too shallow for a torpedo and that we are going to lay mines in those; but gentlemen, by the time you have blown up some of those lock gates there will be enough water in Wilhelmshaven for you to torpedo the town hall!

'Before we go there is one important item – security. I see no reason why the wives shouldn't come with you to Bircham Newton, because I have one more rather startling piece of information for you: in the summer, this squadron is going to embark in the new aircraft carrier, *Illustrious*, as soon as she is ready, and it will be a long while before you see them again, once you have embarked, so make the best of it while you can.

'Although the wives can come with us, let it be clearly

understood that this is not to be discussed – not even between yourselves outside this room – and certainly not with your wives. You can tell them that we are going to do some flying over the North Sea, which is true, but our ultimate target, of Wilhelmshaven, is not to be mentioned to another living soul.

'Don't be too alarmed at all this. It will be some time before you are ready for Wilhelmshaven and I have arranged that we shall be allowed to stay at Bircham Newton for a month or two so that we shall have plenty of time to acquire the necessary skills. What you need is plenty of experience of flying in the dark over enemy territory, and some experience of being shot at, so we are going to do plenty of minelaying and dive-bombing attacks before we think about Wilhelmshaven.' He grinned at us disarmingly. 'The Germans are very poor shots at anything as slow as the Swordfish. I can vouch for that from personal experience, during my trial flights from Worthy Down! And of course, we shall only attack at night. Let's go and have a drink in the airport bar. The bar in the RAF mess won't be open yet.'

8
Baptism

When we flew to Bircham Newton there were only two pilots in the squadron who were junior to me, and they had been allowed to stay only because they had protested at being sent away. The dividing line had come immediately after my name in the squadron's seniority list. They were two Sub-Lieutenants (A), RN, in their very early twenties: Julian Sparke and Douglas Macaulay. When their names had been called, instead of going to pack they waited for Robin in the ante-room in the RAF officers' mess, where we lunched.

I suspect that Sparke had summed up his new CO very accurately, and refused to go on leave; that would have appealed to Robin, since it is precisely what he would have done himself in the same circumstances. They won their appeal and remained with the squadron, and our history would have been very different had they not done so.

Of all the flying I had to do during the war, I disliked our twenty-nine Bircham Newton operations the most. Each trip across the North Sea was as frightening as the last. On the first occasion I struggled with butterflies in my stomach and a perpetual dry throat all the way across the North Sea, trying to take encouragement from my knowledge that they were old friends. I always suffered from them before going into the boxing ring, and knew that they would disappear with the first gong. Unfortunately, I lost the battle on that first attack from Bircham, because they failed to depart until it was too late. Creeping up the Frisian Island channel at 85 knots, past the black silhouettes of the islands rising from the sea, in the cold dark hours before dawn, I was flying right behind Robin, at about one hundred feet above sea level, concentrating on his dim blue formation light which we all carried on our wing struts on either side of the aircraft facing aft.

They were very difficult to see unless one flew close to the aircraft ahead. A flak ship, anchored in the middle of the channel in preparation for just this sort of attack, suddenly opened up with a stream of coloured shells which looked just like the rockets in the annual firework display at the end of Cowes week. They were streaking upwards, pointing directly at my aircraft, from very close, and I had stuffed my nose down and to port and away from them before I knew that I had done it. It was instinctive, but I had broken formation – the one thing that Robin had warned us not to do – and from then onwards, for a terrifying few minutes, I was an isolated aircraft, flying very low, right over a group of those little ships, providing them with an excellent target. It may well have helped the squadron, because I attracted all the fire, and the Swordfish formation flew on, past the islands of Ameland and Schiermonnikoog, to lay their mines off the entrance to the River Weser by the island of Wangerooge, as planned. By some miracle my aircraft wasn't shot down, but there were some very nasty holes in both mainplanes when I landed at Bircham Newton, after somehow managing to put the island of Terschelling between me and the flak ships. I then flew back with my tail between my legs and my magnetic mine still under my fuselage. I apologized to my observer, Dick Janvrin, and he was very sympathetic about it. He was an easygoing six-footer, and nothing ever seemed to disturb his equanimity.

When the rest of the aircraft returned shortly after daybreak, I stood on the tarmac and waited for my expulsion from the squadron. When they landed, I was astonished to see that my aircraft was the only one to have been badly hit.

Robin climbed out of 'A' for 'Apples' and strolled across. He put his arm around my shoulders, reassuringly.

'You will always draw the enemy's fire if you break formation,' he said, as calmly as though he was discussing the tactics of a game of cricket. 'Quite honestly, the only answer is to "stick close to Father". Then your chances of being hit are less certain, I promise you.' He gave my shoulder a little squeeze, and said: 'You and I, and our observers, will go back tonight, and fill in the hole in the minefield. Right?'

All that day, Burns and Brown supervised the repairs to 'Q' for 'Queenie' with fabric and glue, and I was surprised at what little damage had been done. It had looked much worse than it was. Brown's workmanship was beautiful, and in the morning, before driving home to turn in, I watched him with admiration.

'Bit careless, weren't you, sir?' he grinned. 'You shouldn't have drunk all that brandy from your flask!' My father-in-law had given me a silver hip flask encased in leather, and I flew with it full of neat brandy, resisting the temptation to take a sip until on the way back from the target.

It was something to look forward to, on the way there. It kept out the cold, but occasionally a quick sip took the dryness out of one's throat before turning for home, when the immediate future looked appalling. Once Brown had discovered it, in my map-case between my knees, it became public property between the three of us, and when I landed, Brown would climb up on to the stubplane and lean down into the cockpit and extract it. He would then hold it up to the light to see how much I had drunk, take a swig and pass it to Burns, who always emptied it. It became a daily – or nightly – routine, which would have shocked most naval officers, because if it was empty Brown would say, in a voice of unqualified admiration: 'You bastard, sir!'

That evening the rest of the squadron was stood down, but we had to go back to the minefield. I was given another aircraft to fly while my repairs had time to set. Dick Janvrin was again in the back seat, and I apologized for being the cause of an extra flight for him, in a strange aircraft, but he was as benign as usual. He said: 'I suspect that we are being taken back on the principle of "the hair of the dog".'

'You mean in case we get cold feet?' I asked, and he nodded.

'Christ, I'm sorry!' I said. 'Your feet must have been frozen last night, after my fiasco!'

'I don't blame you in the slightest,' he said calmly. 'I'm sure that I would have done the same if I'd been driving.'

Lieutenant-Commander Chapman, the Senior Observer, was very good about it too. He and I, and our wives, who were both called 'Josephine', were sharing the same comfortable country mansion near Hunstanton, called Woden House, and so he had plenty of opportunity to tell me what he thought of me, as we drove back to the house after breakfast in the officers' mess. He said. 'Don't tell the girls that we are going back tonight without the rest of the Squadron. They might be very cross.'

'Aren't you?' I asked, rather apprehensively.

He laughed. 'Of course not. Frankly, I don't think it is at all necessary to go back, because those bloody mines were well and truly planted, and I doubt whether any ship can get past them, down that channel, without blowing itself up. But Robin is a perfectionist and if he wants to return it's okay by me.'

We filled in the gap, and I 'stuck close to Father' and came to no harm. Laying those enormous mines required very accurate navigation, which was Chapman's responsibility. When laying them, the squadron always flew in line astern, and on arrival off the island of Texel he would make Robin lead us round in a wide circle at our dropping height of sixty feet, until he was quite sure that he had plotted an accurate fix. Sometimes, if the weather was bad, and he wasn't sure, he would make Robin take us round again, and as we knew that the telephones would be ringing from Texel to Borkum, alerting all the flak ships and all the defence posts ashore, this was extremely irksome. But he was quite unmoved at our protests. 'We're not a lot of bloody chickens, dropping our eggs indiscriminately all over the bloody shop,' he drawled. 'We've got to put them in the right place or there's no point in going.'

He was right, of course, because they were laid to a careful pattern, and an error of a hundred yards could be enough to provide a loophole in the minefield. The method of laying was simple but practical. A few moments before reaching the beginning of the area to be mined, standing up in his open cockpit and facing aft, Chapman would flash a series of dots at us with a blue shaded torch, meaning 'stand by', which would be repeated all down the line by the observers in the rear cockpits. The mines were dropped by the same push-button on the pilot's throttle used for dropping a torpedo, and we would sit with thumb poised, eyes glued to the aircraft ahead. I was always immediately behind Robin – a position for a junior pilot – and when 'Chappers' flashed his light again, I would drop our mine, Janvrin would count ten, and then flash his torch, and the aircraft astern would drop theirs; and so on, right down the line. The interval between drops varied with the size of the minefield, but it was usually about ten seconds. We had to stay in careful formation even after we had planted our mines, to ensure that the 'tail-end Charlie' aircraft were following the right pattern; it was sometimes difficult to ignore the flaming onions and other unfriendly greetings which were hurled at us.

We began these long flights at the end of March and continued them through April and into May. At the very beginning, as the squadron stores officer, I had drawn a score or so of RAF flying jackets from the Bircham Newton clothing store. They were lined with fur, and were called Irvine Jackets. Because we were not entitled to them I signed for them on 'temporary loan', and they were to bedevil my life for nearly a year until I found a way of striking them off my charge. Everywhere I went, afterwards, the naval paymasters chased me for their return, to clear their books; but many of the jackets ended up in the sea, or in prison camps or officers were appointed to other squadrons and took them with them. It was impossible to return them and I ignored all these demands. We wore these jackets on top of our flying overalls, and with fur-lined flying boots which were naval issue, fortunately, and with leather fur-lined gloves, we managed to keep fairly warm. But even when wrapped up like that it could still be bitterly cold in those open cockpits, which was partly why I carried the brandy, and why we were always puzzled by Robin's stoicism, which seemed quite unnecessary, and quite mad, to us. He was delighted to wear the Irvine Jacket I presented to him, but this was the only concession he made to the weather. He always flew in the same inadequate rig: with the collar of his jacket turned up he wore a helmet without goggles, a pair of gymshoes on bare feet – he never wore socks or gloves in the air – and a pair of grey flannel trousers. He must have been freezing most of the time, but he seemed quite impervious to the weather. Under the Irvine Jacket, he wore an old uniform reefer, but only because he would have been shot without it had he been taken prisoner.

April passed and the spring weather was with us. Taking off and flying across the lovely English scenery, the old biplanes would grumble their way over meadow and wood, on their way to the dreaded German or Dutch coast, flying over village cricket matches, and groups of people enjoying the evening sunshine. The smell of grass wafted up to us in the open cockpits. Nobody ever seemed to look up, and if they did they probably assumed that we were some training squadron. I doubt whether anyone ever realized that we were off on a flight which would probably end the following morning, when they were all getting out of their beds.

9

Bircham Newton

The Station Signals Officer at Bircham Newton was Acting Squadron-Leader Darby Welland, a swarthy Australian pilot with a raucous sense of humour. We had done the RAF's first Astro-Navigation course together at Manston in 1937, and he was an old friend. After we had exchanged greetings at this unexpected meeting in Bircham's officers' mess, he came down to the hangar with me to look at our aircraft. He admitted that he had never seen a Swordfish, and was curious. The spectacle of the big biplanes, parked outside the hangar on the grass, with their enormous long-range petrol tanks sticking up out of the rear cockpits, reduced him to silence. He turned to me in obvious disbelief.

'You fly with that thing full of petrol sticking up between you and the navigator?' He shook his head doubtfully. 'I mean – don't you feel a bit vulnerable with a bloody great magnetic mine strapped to your belly, and that thing towering over you, behind your neck?'

'I don't think it makes us any more vulnerable,' I said ruefully. 'The whole aircraft is a conspicuous target when we are charging up that channel past the Frisian Islands at sixty feet, in formation!'

'How long does it take you to get there and back?'

'It depends on the wind, of course, but each passage across the North Sea takes a minimum of two and a half hours. The time over the target, within range of the flak ships and the shore batteries, is seldom more than half an hour, but it seems longer. With that tank we can stay in the air for about nine hours if necessary!'

His curiosity was aroused at the sight of a cork and a piece of string protruding from a little pipe on top of the tank.

'What's that?' he asked. I explained that the pipe was an air vent, to allow the petrol to flow into the main supply.

'It points down, straight at the observer. When we take off with a full tank, the petrol has a nasty habit of slopping out on to the observer's head. So we have stuck a cork in the pipe on the end of a piece of string, and when we are airborne, flying straight and level, the observer merely pulls the string – and out comes the cork!'

For some unaccountable reason this sent Darby Welland off into a paroxysm of uncontrollable mirth. I was accustomed to this behaviour from him, and stared at him coldly, which made him laugh even more. I protested that it was a simple and very effective cure, and he gasped, 'Oh yes – I agree!' When he had recovered he stood staring at the aircraft, shaking his head.

'It's typical of the bloody Navy!' he said admiringly. 'You would expect an old biplane like the Stringbag to be operated by corks and bits of string!' He grinned at me in approbation. 'I must admit that you couldn't find a better cure. It has the Nelson touch. In the RAF we would've grounded the aircraft for an expensive modification!'

For the next few weeks we were kept hard at it. We sat in the sunshine outside the hangar, or, when it was raining, in the crew room, playing cards in our flying clothing, at 'immediate readiness'. On the grass beside each aircraft there was a selection of weapons on their trolleys, waiting to be loaded when the target was known. Torpedoes, mines, six 250-lb bombs per aircraft, incendiaries, and flares. When the phone rang, Robin would dart off to the Ops Room to be briefed, but the message about which weapons to load would be rung through before he returned, and from this we could guess where we were going. We knew that the day the squadron armourers started loading a mixed bag of torpedoes and mines would be 'the day', and Wilhelmshaven would be the target, but during April and May nine out of every ten trips were minelaying.

On 9 April, Germany invaded Denmark, and our minelaying was in nightly demand, generally at the request of sinister little men in bowler hats, carrying dispatch cases, who arrived by rail from London to tell Robin which of our mines had been touched off. We would then have to return to the minefield to fill in the gaps caused by the successful sinking of some ship. It always puzzled me how these little men knew, only a few hours after a ship sank. The lines of communication between that stretch of enemy teritory and this country seemed more swift and accurate than the GPO.

When these messengers arrived in the middle of the night – which appeared to be their habit – the Duty Officer would ring round all the houses and we would kiss our wives good-bye and drive to the airfield in the dark. Waking in the middle of the night to the noise of the telephone, knowing that one faced at least six hours in an open cockpit in the cold and the dark, and that in about three hours German guns would be doing their level best to put that connubial bed out of reach for ever, was altogether too shattering to be sustained for long. The contrast between a sleepy wife and what lay ahead was too marked; and each time the phone rang one couldn't help thinking, 'I wonder if it's Wilhelmshaven tonight?' We knew, without discussing it, that when we did eventually fly into that harbour, some of the wives would be widows, or their husbands would be prisoners of war. I found myself wishing that the wives could be sent away. If we lived in the officer's mess, the exchange of a warm but empty bed for a Swordfish's cockpit would have been far less intolerable.

Our arrival at the airfield after driving from Hunstanton often coincided with German raids on Bircham Newton, when we would see the flames and flashes exploding in the distance as a friendly greeting before we took off. The Coastal Command Ansons and Hudsons took a great deal of hammering during the phoney war.

On 10 May, Germany invaded Holland, Belgium and Luxembourg, and on 14 May, parachute troops landed on the airfield at Rotterdam, and we were sent across to dive-bomb them the moment that they captured the airfield. Our timing was a little too exact: when Robin led us down through the clouds, the German aircraft were still attacking, and so he took us back above the clouds again until they had finished. Then we sailed down with our six 250-lb bombs per aircraft, and splatted the new arrivals before they had time to unbutton their parachutes. It made a splendid change, to be sitting peering over the top mainplane in a vertical dive instead of creeping along under fire in tight formation, laying mines. There was a feeling of abandon about it, and satisfaction in dishing out the punishment instead of being on the receiving end at Bircham Newton, or off the Frisian Islands.

Afterwards, reports from the Dutch confirmed that our timing had been perfect and the attack very successful, which was reassuring. A number of us were worried, when we saw the German attacking, that we had got there too soon, and had assisted the Hun in capturing the airfield.

The situation became very confused as May passed. The British Expeditionary Force were suffering terrible losses in France. We were enormously cheered by the arrival of Winston Churchill as Prime Minister on 11 May, and felt that his new National Government would be a great improvement. Twice during this period we had to fly to Detling, a field in Kent, to operate across the southern end of the North Sea to lay mines off the Dutch and Belgian coasts, and each time we were given the impression that we would not be returning to Bircham Newton, and so all the wives drove south, to await us at Ford, near Arundel; but each time we were recalled to Bircham, presumably to do the Wilhelmshaven attack. The first time the target had been changed at the last minute and we had to lay mines again; and the second could have ended in disaster had it not been for Robin's strength of mind. We were told that a number of German capital ships had moved from their various harbours and were anchored off Borkum, and we were to attack them with torpedoes. Our departure was delayed while RAF reconnaissance flights were sent across to confirm the enemy reports, and so much time had elapsed before we were given the order to take off that it would have been impossible for us to attack in the dark. We would have arrived at Borkum long after dawn, and our chances of delivering the weapons were minimal. Robin protested that it was suicide, and that the entire squadron would be written off for no purpose; but the Controllers at Group Headquarters had no alternative torpedo-dropping aircraft to send, and somebody had to be the scapegoat.

A white-faced Kilroy briefed us. Because of the time factor he wanted us to form up in line astern over the airfield, in our attacking formation, instead of changing formation on arrival at Texel, before flying up the channel past the Frisian Islands. We were puzzled about this, because there seemed little point in crossing the North Sea in line astern. There was only an hour of darkness left, and because we had to form up on him, Robin was the last to take-off. As soon as he was airborne he switched off all his lights and headed out to sea on his own, leaving us circling the airfield searching for him. In the end the ground controllers at Bircham fired green Very lights at us, indicating that we were to land.

Being the senior officer amongst us, Neil Kemp answered the urgent summons to telephone the station Ops Room as soon as he had landed. Kemp was then ordered to telephone Group at once, and when he did so, the Controller demanded to know what had gone wrong.

'I have no idea,' said Neil, quite truthfully. 'We have been playing "hunt-your-leader" for the last thirty minutes without success . . .'

'Who is the idiot who has flown out to sea on his own?' was the next question.

'I'm afraid I can't answer that either. We have no idiots in the squadron!'

We sat in the crew room all night – or what was left of it – waiting for Robin to return. After a couple of hours, Neil and one or two of the senior lieutenants strode off to Bircham's Ops Room to talk to Darby Welland, who was highly amused by the whole incident. He was entirely on Robin's side. Apparently Group had demanded the Group Captain's explanation, and Welland had had to rouse him from his bed. Primrose's side of the conversation on the telephone was recounted to me by Welland.

'What sort of chap is Kilroy?' repeated Group Captain Primrose. 'There is none finer. I would support any action taken by Lieutenant-Commander Kilroy to the hilt.' He then replaced the receiver and asked Welland for a 'sit-rep'. He was horrified to learn that Robin was on his way across the North Sea, apparently determined to attack the German ships single-handed, and ordered Darby to recall him at once.

'That means breaking W/T silence, sir,' Darby pointed out.

'Then break it,' said the Group Captain. 'And let me know when the signal has been passed and acknowledged.'

Lieutenant-Commander Chapman, the Senior Observer, told me the rest of the story as we drove back to Woden House.

'When I received the recall,' he said, 'we were just approaching Texel, and the sun was over the horizon. I passed the message to Robin down the voice-pipe, and he said, "Have you acknowledged it?" When I said that I had, he said: "Pity," and turned for home. I'm sure that he would have had a bash at them on his own if I had not acknowledged the message.'

'You were bloody lucky, sir,' I said, when he told me this.

'So were you,' he retorted. 'If it hadn't been for Robin we'd all be feeding the fishes now!'

After the second abortive drive, down to Sussex and then back to Norfolk, the wives were all rather relieved when Robin suggested that they should go home. So were we. We moved into the officers' mess ready for the Wilhelmshaven attack, and although it was a heartrending parting, from our point of view – and we had the mother and father of all farewell parties in Woden House before they left – we were relieved that they had gone.

All that time at Bircham Newton we were under RAF operational command, and could not select our targets ourselves, otherwise we would have done the attack on Wilhelmshaven long before May. Robin had admitted that we had acquired the necessary skills and the passage to the Weser had become our back-alley. We knew where to expect flak from ships and shore batteries, and under Robin's expert leadership I am sure that some of us would have returned. On 27 May we flew back to Detling to cover the evacuation by the little ships at Dunkirk, and our association with Bircham Newton was over.

It had been a most effective baptism, and nothing I was ever required to do in the air, thereafter, was as unpleasant. Some flights were more frightening, but in a less nightmarish way by comparison. It had also shown us that, although obsolete in appearance, the old Stringbag was a very effective means of transport when flying on these ghastly operations.

The final words about that short period in the history of the Swordfish were written by the late C. G. Grey when founder-editor of *The Aeroplane*, a magazine of high repute in flying circles. His praise was all the more convincing because he had been fighting a single-handed duel with the Admiralty about aviation matters ever since the First World War. In 1937, when the Admiralty recovered control of the Fleet Air Arm, he opposed the First Sea Lord vigorously, and was acknowledged to be the most anti-Navy correspodent in Fleet Street.

In the spring of 1940, under huge headlines in the *Sunday Express*, his article took up three whole columns. His words have been condensed and reproduced here because they represent the unbiased opinion of a famous man with vast experience of writing about aircraft and the men who flew them; and they are a most suitable memorial to Robin Kilroy as well as to the Swordfish.

'Just when the Blitzkrieg on Norway had started I was staying at a Coastal Command station of the RAF . . . which was a regular aeronautical menagerie. The day I got there our newspapers had published maps of our new minefields . . . blocking the German and Danish harbours in the Baltic, from which ships had to take troops to Norway.

'Very rightly our people said: "Wonderful thing the British

Navy. But how did our minelayers or submarines get through the German minefields and past the German submarines and destroyers and air force to lay those mines?"

'That evening about cocktail time into the ante-room of the mess came half a dozen young officers in naval uniform, led by one who was himself led by an amiable but terrific-looking bull-terrier. Man and dog were much the same shape and ever so English.

'My host told me that they were part of a Fleet Air Arm squadron which was at the station on a special job. Later I was shown what it was, and how they did it.

'On the airfield was a squadron of Fairey Swordfish . . . the machine was built for Fleet reconnaissance and as a torpedo-dropper, so it is a weight-lifter, and its best cruising speed is about that of the trainers which one sees floating around the sky. These Swordfish were different. Where the navigator ought to sit was an enormous petrol tank which stuck up between the pilot and the after cockpit. It took up all the second seat and ended in a blank wall, high above where the second seat should have been. There, beneath it in the third seat, the navigator had to sit with his legs underneath a mass of petrol, all ready to drown him in flames if an incendiary bullet caught it. At bombing-up time, just before dark, instead of the normal torpedo or bombs, huge flat-ended barrels were rolled out on trolleys and fixed between the wheels. These were our magnetic mines, far more powerful and more magnetic than the German mines of which we heard so much at the time. These barrels brought the flying speed of the Swordfish down to about 80 knots.

'That night, as the rest of us were going to bed, we heard the growl of the Bristols starting up, and a few minutes later the drone of the heavy stuff taking off, circling the CO's house and heading seaward. Next morning they all came back – bar one – and reported results, had their suppers at a late breakfast time, and went to bed, all ready to do it again the next night.

'Now figure to yourself that sort of courage – the "three o'clock in the morning courage" which Napoleon admired in our people – the machine outrageously overloaded, carrying a mine which would leave nothing to pick up if it exploded in a crash, and carrying a truck-load of petrol to give it the thousand-mile range; its speed such that the worst anti-aircraft gunner or search-light operator could hardly miss it; its only protection against fighters the fact that it was too slow for them to stay with it and shoot at it;

pilot and navigator without the companionship of a cabin, lonely all night on the end of a voice-pipe.

'They had none of the excitement of the single-seat fighter or his interval for refreshment after a three-hour patrol, and none of the crewmanship, as it were, of the big bombers or flying-boats. If ever there was a "solitude à deux" the minelayers in the Swordfish had it – for most of ten hours at a stretch.

'They were the bravest men I have met. I have known a good many vcs and plenty of dsos. None of these FAA lads had any decorations then. I hope they have got them since. Nobody admires our bomber crews and coastal reconnaissance people, and our fighter pilots, more than I do. But those couples in the Swordfish deserve to be recorded in history for they made so much history themselves.'

10
Dunkirk – From the Air

In Chamberlain's time as Prime Minister there seemed to be a dearth of news and it was his resignation on 10 May that brought it home to everyone that all was far from well with our Army in France. On 28 May King Leopold startled the world by surrendering, and although the BEF's war had already been lost, the capitulation by the Belgians left them completely exposed over an area of thirty miles to the sea.

We arrived at Detling on 27 May, the day before King Leopold surrendered, and the next day the evacuation began in earnest. It went on until 4 June, for an historic nine days and nights.

When it was over the situation was summed up for the whole free world by Winston Churchill, in his electrifying speech when he said: 'We shall fight on the beaches, we shall fight on the landing grounds, we shall fight in the fields and in the streets, we shall fight on the hills; we shall never surrender.'

A great deal has been written about Dunkirk but very little about the battle in the air, and on the beaches our war-weary soldiers felt that British aircraft were conspicuous by their absence. At a time when the remnants of the British Army were being subjected to continuous and seemingly undefended attacks from enemy aircraft, that is understandable. In his speech to the House of Commons on 4 June 1940 Churchill did his best to explain. He said: 'They [the Germans] sent repeated waves of hostile aircraft, sometimes more than a hundred strong in one formation ... the Royal Air Force engaged the main strength of the German Air Force, and inflicted upon them losses of at least four to one; and the Navy, using nearly 1000 ships of all kinds, carried over 335 000 men, French and British, out of the jaws of death and shame ... We must be very careful not to assign to this deliverance the attributes of a victory. Wars are not won by evacuations. But there was a victory inside the deliverance, which should be noted. It was gained by the Air Force. Many of our soldiers coming back have not seen the Air Force at work; they saw only the bombers which escaped the protective attack. They underrate its achievements . . .'

As well as being able to watch the little ships save an army, from my Swordfish I was also able to watch the RAF do the same from the air, out of sight of the beaches. Armed with bombs we ranged from the Dunkirk beaches in the smoke and flame of the battle down to Calais and up to Ostend, and then out into the North Sea, attacking the pockets of E-boats wherever we could find them, before they could close in on the floating armada for the kill. In the air we saw the RAF facing overwhelming odds, and emerge the victors. On 29 May I saw a squadron of Defiants attack a formation of bombers escorted by ME 109s and 110s. The formation was so vast that it was impossible to count the number of enemy bombers. I heard that night that the Defiants had shot down eighteen bombers in the morning, and twenty-one in the afternoon, and this was only one squadron within sight of my cockpit. Hurricanes and Gladiators and every possible type of aircraft which could be used as fighters flung themselves at the German bombers with increasing success, day by day. On 1 June they shot down seventy-eight German bombers on their way to slaughter the soldiers massed on the beaches, attacking without pause from dawn until 7 p.m.

Although they came from bases all over the country, they used Detling and Manston to refuel and rearm, and I have no doubt whatever that had it not been for the superb efforts of the RAF – out of sight of the men they were fighting to save – the 335 000 men who were safely rescued would have perished on the beaches, as Hitler planned.

Perhaps it should be remembered that three years before Dunkirk Great Britain could boast only 500 aircraft altogether. During the phoney war RAF losses were such that without Churchill's emphatic urging from the back benches in 1936, there would have been no aircraft to defend the army at Dunkirk at all. It is a sobering thought.

Our own flying was intense throughout those nine days and nights, because we had to continue to chase the E-boats at night as well as by day. We snatched sleep whenever we could, while our aircraft were being refuelled and rearmed, stretched out on the grass in the warm summer air, using our parachutes as pillows. We subsisted on a diet which was to become very familiar throughout the war – corned beef sandwiches, innumerable cups of tea, and the occasional gin. 819 Swordfish Squadron joined us, and 806 Squadron, flying naval Skuas, arrived from the Orkneys to help the RAF fighters, and this was my first proper glimpse of the red-bearded Charles Evans, their CO, whom I was destined to accompany for most of my life. His piratical appearance put heart into Burns and Brown who were great admirers of his. Desmond Vincent-Jones, his observer, was several inches taller than six feet, and his enormous figure stuck out of their Skua like one of our long-range tanks. Whenever they took off he waved to us as though he was thoroughly enjoying himself.

It was at Detling that Sub-Lieutenant Sparke emerged as the man of the moment. He was indefatigable, and seemed to be able to smell out the E-boats in the dark. Afterwards Robin told us that he had been allowed to forward one name for 'meritorious service' and he had had no hesitation in recommending Sparke for an immediate DSC. It was the first honour to be received by 815 Squadron and it was especially pleasing that it had been awarded to the youngest man amongst us. But the one form of recognition which pleased us most occurred during our last week at Bircham Newton. Robin was suddenly promoted to Commander, out of the blue, and this was something which delighted us all.

Something about the magnificent spectacle of those columns of ships, to-ing and fro-ing endlessly between Dunkirk and Dover or Ramsgate, so that from the air it looked as though it would be possible to use them as stepping-stones and walk across the Channel, fired the imagination of all of us who had the amazing experience of looking down from the air at history in the making. From above, the pattern of little ships, nose to stern – so close that it was difficult to see any water between them, and so small but so steadfast – were packed tightly together into parallel lines stretching right across the Channel and back – a distance of forty miles. The homecoming ships were the centre columns, protected on their flanks by the outgoing ships; but on the outside, on both sides, crammed with soldiers on their homeward run, were destroyers, minesweepers and every possible type of small ship able to fly the White Ensign, acting as guards for the lines of little ships inside them. Whenever possible the naval craft on their way to Dunkirk took station on the outer flank of the rescuing craft on their way home. But it was the armada of little ships of all shapes and sizes forming the inner lines which made such an incredible spectacle. Below my wings was the biggest collection of privately owned vessels which had ever sailed in company, without being asked. Yachts of every description, fishing vessels, oyster smacks, dredgers, Thames barges under full sail – but keeping up with the others – lifeboats, paddle-steamers, ferries – even one Thames fireboat, the *Massey Shaw*, belonging to the London Fire Brigade. An inexorable phalanx of marine craft, bent on rescue or bust, as many of them did. They appeared at Ramsgate and Dover and other channel harbours, from all over the country. The British Army was in peril, and therefore the safety of the country was at stake. There was no need for a clarion call, nor for any appeal to their patriotism. Quietly, from almost every port and harbour and seaside town in Great Britain, men who owned boats put down their fountain pens, or their tools of trade, hung up their bowler hats, kissed their wives good-bye, and then sailed to one of the two Kentish harbours. Never in maritime history, throughout the centuries, in any country in the world, has such an armada put to sea, spontaneously, without instructions, and without sailing orders of any kind.

After Dunkirk we flew along the south coast to Ford, near Arundel, in Sussex. The squadron ratings wanted a few days to service the aircraft and give them a thorough overhaul in the vicinity of full naval workshops before we embarked in the *Illustrious* at Plymouth in a day or two: and Robin decided that we all needed an opportunity to catch up with our sleep.

Bachelors often have these mistaken notions, and place far too much emphasis on the importance of sleep. The married officers all persuaded Chapman to ring his wife, who was living in an hotel in Littlehampton, and ask her to reserve enough double rooms for us all.

It was a pleasant break but all too short. A group of us went to a Littlehampton cinema to see *Snow White and the Seven Dwarfs*, and Jo and I were haunted by the music of that enchanting film – mainly because it was the last show we were to go to, together, for some years. Our shared pleasure in the film's music was to have rather silly consequences for me later in the war.

On 8 June we flew to Roborough, near Plymouth, to await a

signal from *Illustrious* telling us to fly out into the Channel, to land-on. When we parked our aircraft on the little grass airfield, we found a sombre Commander Kilroy and Lieutenant-Commander Chapman awaiting us. They told us that they were leaving the squadron shortly for new appointments – before we embarked in the ship.

'That's not why we are looking gloomy,' admitted Robin, 'though we are both sorry to be going,' He then broke it to us that the *Glorious* had been sunk, with only three survivors. She had been returning from Norway with some naval and RAF pilots on board, who had been flying from the frozen lakes, trying to stem the German advance. On her way across the North Sea the *Glorious* had been sandwiched between the *Scharnhorst* and *Gneisenau*, without an adequate escort. Because the airmen on board were all completely exhausted, no flying had been taking place from the ship, otherwise the two German battleships might have been sighted, and other ships informed so that they could intercept. As it was, the old aircraft carrier had no chance of survival.

It looked as though our stay at Roborough and our departure to the ship was going to be shrouded in gloom; and, perhaps to dispel this, Robin and Chapman did something which was incredibly foolish, but which cheered us up enormously. They were very lucky that their adventure was not discovered, because they would have incurred a court martial apiece.

Robin had some French friends who owned an inn by the coast, just beyond Cherbourg; there was a handy field close by on which he had often landed. While we were awaiting the signal from *Illustrious* and had to remain on the airfield, because they were not coming with us they decided to take a chance and fly to that inn and try to discover how far the German occupation had penetrated. They were going to have a drink with the innkeeper and pick his brains.

It was a warm day, and they flew without overalls, in their uniform jackets. Robin's brand-new Commander's rings were shining very brightly.

When he landed, as an ordinary matter of routine airmanship he taxied down-wind, leaving the aircraft parked into wind, ready to take off. They then sauntered across the field and pushed open the door of the tavern. The bar was crowded with German soldiers.

'I said "Pardonnez-moi!" in my best French, and shut the door,' said Robin. 'Then we sprinted like mad, and leaped into the aircraft. "Chappers" had to wind the inertia starter, and then plunge head first into the rear cockpit, still holding it in his hand. We just managed to get off the ground in time, with a lot of German goons taking pot shots at us with their revolvers and rifles!'

They left us the next day and when they had gone some of the sparkle seemed to have disappeared from the squadron. Fortunately the embarkation signal arrived soon after their departure. *Illustrious* was off Land's End, and we were to rendezvous 'forthwith', to make our first deck-landings on her flight-deck.

We had already seen some history in the making, but there was plenty to come.

PART III

HMS *Illustrious*

11
Working-up

When we stepped out of our aircraft, off Land's End, we had been struck down into the hangar. I stood by the forward lift looking aft, conscious of my own unimportance in the midst of this huge complex of machinery. I was looking through the folded wings of thirty aircraft, all stacked together very tightly, according to some preconceived plan, so that they could all be stowed down below. The wings were almost touching. On the bulkheads, brightly coloured markings indicated fuel points, or connections for high pressure air, oil, water, electric power – all vividly painted in clearly defined colours, so that there could be no mistake. Overhead, metal firescreen curtains were rolled and stowed, ready to be dropped in an emergency dividing the hangar into three separate compartments. The whole deck-head was a series of overhead stowages containing spare aircraft engines, airscrews, long-range tanks, and all manner of objects: but the whole of the hangar deckhead was bristling with little sprinklers a few inches apart, so that in the event of fire at the turn of a switch the curtains would fall and the entire hangar would be sprayed with jets of salt water.

Everything looked brand new and beautifully clean. It was exciting to be back at sea in a new ship. The deck underfoot was throbbing. We were on our way to anchor for the night in Plymouth harbour.

I joined a little group of 815 Squadron pilots and went up on to the flight-deck. We were astonished at the amount of space available. It had not looked particularly large from our cockpits a few moments earlier, but flight-decks never do look very large from the air. As we strolled down the deck admiring the great *Illustrious* we were joined by Captain Denis Boyd, who surprised me because of the informal way he greeted us and welcomed us on board. I was intrigued to meet him at long last. He was a famous man, with a great reputation. Nobody ever mentioned his name without saying something complimentary, and I studied him with great interest. Although his face was sensitive his whole appearance exuded determination, and I noticed that when he smiled his lips remained tightly shut, and his face lost none of its rather grim resolution. Yet somehow he managed to convey a relaxed good nature at the same time. He shook hands with each of us, and when he turned to go aft, he made a very nice remark. He said: 'I have been standing-by this ship at Vickers-Armstrong's yard in Barrow-in-Furness for many months, while she has been building; but now that you have embarked, the ship has come alive for the first time. It is a moment I have been looking forward to for a long while. An aircraft carrier without any aircraft or aircrew is like an unfurnished house!' He then gave us another grim smile and walked away.

The Commander Flying of *Illustrious* was Commander J. I. Robertson, a tiny little man who looked like a bird. Because of his prominent nose and sharp features he was known as 'Streamline'. The ship was hurrying off to Plymouth and we were startled to learn that we would be flying the next morning, early, before the ship weighed anchor. Flying from a stationary deck was a new concept to us, and we were surprised to discover how straightforward it was. The Swordfish needed very little space to take off, and with a reasonable wind down the deck, when we landed we were entering the wires at a net speed of about 50 knots, which was quite acceptable for the Swordfish's sturdy undercarriage.

I had never been on board a purpose-built aircraft carrier before, and was most impressed. I could only make comparisons with the old *Courageous*, but everything in *Illustrious* was so much bigger and better that the comparison was absurd. *Courageous* had been converted into a carrier from the hull of an old cruiser, but this ship had sprung into life from the combined skills of many marine architects. The result was not just a masterpiece of planning and design, but a mighty ship of great beauty. Comparing her with *Courageous* was tantamount to comparing her with Noah's Ark.

Illustrious had two Swordfish squadrons and one Skua squadron on board, and I was tickled to find that they were the squadrons who had also been flying from Detling. I was interested to realize that our flying over Dunkirk had also been part of our work-up for the ship: one of the most important aspects of this period is for everyone to get to know everyone else, as quickly as possible, and thanks to Dunkirk this had already been achieved for the pilots and observers and air gunners.

The first ship of a new class is liable to take longer to work-up than her successors, especially if she is fitted with a lot of new gadgets. There were so many on board *Illustrious* that Captain Boyd had obtained authority to take the ship away so that we could fly around the clock if need be; and the ship's company could be exercised without restraint, and without fear of enemy interference. We were to be based on Bermuda.

The period needed for a work-up depends on the time it takes every officer and man on board to be brought to such a knife-edge of efficiency that they could do their work automatically and competently in the most difficult circumstances. During the work-up these conditions had to be reproduced, and the obstacles intensified, and the time allowed decreased, so that she became a first-class fighting ship before we left.

Although we were flying almost every day, and on some nights, the ship's company had an exacting time too. They were at action stations most of the time, practising fire drills, damage control, abandon-ship, and all the emergency drills in the book. The ship's weapons were fired daily, and this, combined with the noise of the aircraft being catapulted and flown off, and the constant roar of engines as we circled the ship, made conditions exhausting for everyone.

The success or otherwise of this important period is almost entirely dependent upon the personality of the captain; and in Denis Boyd we had a man who was always friendly, yet in complete control.

Flying from *Illustrious* was unlike anything I had experienced before. The most startling innovation in the ship was the new 'safety barrier' across the flight-deck. This was a heavy wire net suspended between two hydraulic arms which could be raised or lowered. It was half-way up the flight-deck, abreast the bridge structure known as the island, and it divided the deck into a landing and a parking area. In the past we had only been able to land with a clear deck, so that we could open the throttle and go round again if our arrester-hook bounced over all the wires. The interval between landings had been conditioned by the time it took to taxi the aircraft on to the forward lift, fold its wings, strike it down into the hangar, and bring the lift up to deck-level again. With practice this could be reduced to two minutes, but when a carrier is receiving aircraft she must steam into wind, and the direction of the wind might be diametrically opposed to the direction of the Fleet, or the eventual course which the ship has to take. To land-on twelve aircraft, at two-minute intervals, meant steaming into wind for twenty-four minutes at least, which is a long way to steam, if it is in the wrong direction. With the introduction of the 'safety barrier' (which was always known as the 'crash barrier' of course), instead of striking aircraft down after they had landed, they were parked on the foredeck. If a pilot missed all the wires he floated into the barrier instead of into the deck-park, forward. The netting had a long pull-out, like the arrester-wires, so that it stopped the aircraft's nose with a cushioning effect. The propeller would break into little pieces, of course, and the engine had to be carefully inspected afterwards for shock loading, but it was often surprising what little damage had been done.

With the use of the barrier the interval between landings then became the time that it took for an aircraft to land, taxi forward over the lowered net, and into the deck-park, when the barrier would snap up into its upright position again. With the combined efficiency of 'Streamline' and the Deck Landing Control Officer with his yellow bats, the interval between our landings was reduced to ten seconds, or twenty at the most. So, instead of taking twenty-four minutes to land a squadron of twelve, it took less than five.

The DLCO, or 'Batsman', was Lieutenant-Commander D. McI. Russell, known as 'Haggis'. For the first time, his signals were mandatory and had to be obeyed. The barrier was also a 'first time ever', and to begin with there was a certain amount of toothsucking about these two introductions to naval life until we became worked-up, that is to say, expert at our jobs, and friendly with our shipmates.

Working-up in Bermuda was a wonderful break. Nearly every evening we anchored in Hamilton Bay and went ashore to that tropical paradise; and to be swimming in a warm transparent sea and basking in sunshine amongst beautiful girls made Bircham Newton and the blackout seem a long way away. It was all so unexpected that I had a sense of unreality all the time we were there.

The Captain made sure that the ship's company had a clear day or two at weekends to relax ashore, and they returned on board refreshed and ready for anything. Bermuda was a wise choice for a work-up – particularly in wartime.

With Janvrin in the back I was sent off one afternoon, in company with a Skua pilot, to work out the best defence for Swordfish from fighter attack in daylight. I expect a number of other pilots were sent off to do the same. We climbed to ten thousand feet and then the Skua pilot flew off into the sun to begin his first attack. He was a friend of mine whose wife had just had their first baby.

When he dived out of the sun on my port quarter, I did what I had always planned to do if I was caught by an enemy fighter: I wrenched the aircraft into a violent stalled turn towards him, i.e. to port, and stood the aircraft on its tail. When his target suddenly stood still – right in his path – he tried hard to keep me in his sights but spun over on to his back in the attempt, temporarily out of control. As he was heading for the sea in an inverted loop I was relieved to see him roll out, and climb safely away for his next attack.

The moment that he spun over, I jammed the stick forward, putting the Swordfish in a near-vertical dive to lose as much height as I could before his next dive.

'What are you doing?' Janvrin asked, politely. Even when being thrown about in the back his urbanity never deserted him, and his voice was only expressing mild curiosity. He was taking an interest in my method of defence and was not complaining. I tried to explain as we hurtled towards the sea.

'If you can keep an eye on him and let me know when he starts his next attack I'll be grateful. If I can get down to sea level before he comes in again he will have to break off the dive at about five or six hundred feet or he will run out of air. As soon as he starts to attack I'll stall the aircraft so that his shots would miss ahead. If he tries to do a dive attack he is bound to roll over on to his back. So, to get us in his sights he'll have to throttle back and approach us as slowly as he can. Then we shall be on equal terms and you can take a pot-shot at him with your Lewis gun. We should be able to see him off, because I reckon a Swordfish is every bit as manoeuvrable as a Skua . . .'

In 'Q' for 'Queenie', Janvrin and I and Pat Beagley, the TAG, were only about fifty feet above the sea when the fighter pilot began his second attack, from two or three thousand feet.

The Caribbean is translucent, and its surface is sometimes so still that in some angles of light all one can see is a vague shadowy panorama of the bottom – coloured sea-urchins and seaweedy rock – as though there was no water in between at all. In the excitement of the chase I can only imagine that the pilot of the Skua omitted to glance at his altimeter, and had no idea that I was down at sea level. To my horror he did another dive attack and instead of breaking away at a safe height he kept coming, trying to keep the Swordfish in his sights, and when he spun over on to his back there was no room to recover, and he plunged into the sea upside down.

There was no chance of his survival after entering the water in an inverted dive, but in the hope of a miracle we flew around the spot for quite some time. The only thing to come to the surface was the Skua's tail wheel. Janvrin dropped a smoke float, and plotted an accurate fix, and we hurried back to the ship to raise the alarm. *Illustrious* searched the area but my friend was never seen again.

Many German pilots made the same error of judgement later, and only discovered the weird manoeuvrability of the Stringbag with their last conscious thought. His death was not wasted because that method of defence from daylight attack by fighters was used by Swordfish pilots throughout the war with tremendous success. Every Stringbag pilot made the same discovery without help from me, but at least the death of that young father had succeeded in making that method of defence the one which was officially recommended to Their Lordships of the Admiralty by the Commanding Officer of *Illustrious*

Our brief glimpse of paradise and our plans to go straight out to the Mediterranean from Bermuda, were both interrupted by a minor catastrophe: in one short holocaust, amounting to about twenty minutes, the ship lost all her fighter aircraft and we had to return to the United Kingdom for replacements. It proved to be a multitude of blessings in as many disguises, but at the time we were dumbfounded.

Our zealous and very popular Commander Flying could never resist the temptation to exercise his pilots and observers in all reasonable conditions of flight. He was a man of great personal courage, as he had proved to our concern after a pilot had been catapulted into the sea; when the fault with the machinery had been repaired 'Streamline' insisted on being the next pilot to be 'squirted off', in case there was a repetition of the failure. He was always prepared to do anything he demanded of us, and we respected him for it.

He had not been able to fly us off in Bermuda harbour when the ship was at anchor, because there was seldom any wind at all. But one morning he awoke to the unmistakable sound of a tropical storm. Looking out of his scuttle he saw that the wind was dead ahead. The ship had swung around her cable and was lying bows-on to the weather. He roused the Met Officer and demanded to know how long the gale was going to last; on being told that it might last all day, he insisted on flying off all three squadrons. Meteorology will never be an exact science, and when we returned to the ship, which was at one hour's notice for steam, there was a flat Bermudan calm, and not a break of wind anywhere to be seen.

In 1940 cars were not allowed on the island, and there was nowhere to land an aeroplane. The nearest airfield was in the United States, six hundred miles away.

The use of the 'safety barrier' was considered, but with no wind down the deck even the Swordfish might have torn out their hooks, and it was out of the question.

All the Swordfish landed safely, with the barrier down in case their hooks tore out. Each landing extended the arrester-wire to the maximum. As each pilot climbed out of his aircraft in the hangar, he made straight for the 'goofer's platform' on the island to watch the rest. The Skuas were in a tough spot: there was nowhere for them to land ashore, and it was clear that none of them was going to be able to stay on the flight-deck after touching down at their high speed of entry.

Being the CO, Charles Evans landed first. The deceleration caused by his hook tearing away from the fuselage was insufficient for him to remain on the flight-deck, and so he applied right rudder and slammed his nose into the island. Needless to say he did this with great panache. The second Skua to land also tore out his hook – as did all the others – but he was travelling much too fast and managed to clamber into the air again, and for the next twenty minutes he circled the ship and watched his co-pilots come to grief one by one. Either they followed their CO's example and smacked their noses into the island, or they trickled up to the bows after their hooks had torn out, and fell into the Bay with a splash. There was one exception: the departing storm had left one recalcitrant gust of wind scudding about somewhere in that colourful bay, and it chose to make its dying appearance just as one of the Skuas touched down. After he parted company with his arrester-hook he managed to pull up in the eyes of the ship where for a breathless moment he teetered in a cliff-hanging manner until his tail dropped on deck, and he was safe. At this there were loud cheers from the 'goofer's platform'.

Nobody was hurt, but the air gunner in the back of the Skua which had gone round again had found the strain too much. His pilot was instructed to find somewhere to force-land ashore, and he selected the seventeenth fairway of the Belmont golf course. This was a narrow strip of sandy grass hedged in on either side by pine trees; the fairway was so narrow that, the day before, my ball had bounced off the trees from tee to fairway. The Skua did the same, but the trees succeeded in removing both his wings, and he ended up on the green having done a hole in one.

The air gunner leaped out of the rear cockpit and burst into tears. Nobody blamed him for this, but as he was a man who boasted an enormous black beard we all felt that his behaviour would have been less incongruous had he been clean-shaven.

The ship returned to the Clyde to re-equip with Fairey Fulmars, which were much better than Skuas. There was a delay of several weeks to collect the Fulmars, and to give Charles Evans a chance to work-up his squadron with their new aircraft, and so 815 Squadron was disembarked to Donibristle, near Inverkeithing, in Fife. Jo came hurrying up to Edinburgh with all the other squadron wives, but a few days later we were moved to Campbeltown, in the Mull of Kintyre and as the journey by rail and boat would have taken the wives many days, Admiralty flew them to Campbeltown in an old Dominie, which was incredibly kind. We suspected that Denis Boyd and 'Streamline' had something to do with that decision.

The squadron took off for Campbeltown a few minutes after the Dominie, and ahead of a warm front which closed down behind them. Unfortunately I was delayed by an irate paymaster-commander who wanted to know what had happened to twelve Irvine Flying Jackets, the property of the RAF at Bircham Newton, and after a long argument about that, when I tried to depart I was stopped by Instructor Commander McKay, the Met Officer. He was a big man with an imperturbable manner and a superb sense of humour, but I am afraid I put both into jeopardy that day. In 1940 a pilot could fly if he wished, no matter what the weather. Pre-flight briefing consisted of a glance at the met report, and then at the map, to choose a route.

'I shall fly down the Stirling Valley,' I said.

'Steady, laddie!' said 'Schoolie' McKay. 'When the communications pilots have grounded themselves that's the time to pause and think carefully. 781 Squadron have stopped flying today . . .'

781 Squadron was a famous naval transport squadron who guaranteed to get their passengers anywhere in any weather.

'Yes,' I said, 'but they haven't a wife waiting for them at the other end.'

As a final resort 'Schoolie' McKay used a phrase I have never forgotten. I have never been able to find it in the Manuals, but it does describe certain flying conditions very adequately.

'My dear chap,' he said, 'even the birds are walking!'

In fact the Stirling Valley is safe in almost any weather – in Swordfish. I enjoyed a pleasant if rather low flight up the Firth of Forth to Stirling, and then under the clouds through the valley to Loch Lomond and the Clyde, after which it was plain sailing. The beautiful Kyles of Bute were disappearing into grey clouds, but there was enough room underneath to nip across to Rothsesay and then fly down the Kilbrennan Sound, leaving the high hills of Arran on my left. Campbeltown looked very pretty, nestling at the top of a little bay.

Machrihanish was a delightful spot but we were only left in peace for a few days. On 11 August *Illustrious* was off Ailsa Craig, and we had to fly out to join her. The same Dominie aircraft arrived from Donibristle, to fly the wives back to Edinburgh, and my last glimpse of Jo was through the little window at the back of a van when they were driven to the airfield. Her face was rather sad and wistful. We had been able to enjoy only a few months together out of the eleven which had elapsed since we married, and they had been under rather strained conditions one way and another. The vivid memory of her face framed in that little rear window was to accompany me through many trials and tribulations during the two and a quarter years which were to follow before I was able to see her again. It was a vision which was a tremendous help at all times.

12
Mare Nostrum

We had enjoyed an uneventful passage to Gibraltar escorting a convoy for the Mediterranean, in company with the battleship *Valiant* and the two anti-aircraft cruisers, *Calcutta* and *Coventry*. Just before we sailed, on 22 August, Rear-Admiral Lumley Lyster embarked, to fly his flag on board as Rear-Admiral Aircraft Carriers, Mediterranean. He had been in command of the *Glorious* in the Mediterranean before being promoted and his expert knowledge was going to be invaluable.

We were to take the convoy through 'bomb alley' – that narrow strip of water which starts at the Skerki Channel to the north-west of Malta and encircles the island to the south, past the enemy strongholds of Pantellaria and Lampedusa, well within range of Sicily – joining up with Cunningham's fleet on 3 September. In a talk to all officers before we sailed from Gibraltar Captain Boyd outlined the tactical picture in the Mediterranean, and explained our future tasks.

Two months previously, on 5 June, Hitler had declared a war of total annihilation on all his enemies.

'Since the tenth of June,' said Captain Boyd, 'Italian aircraft have been used in an all-out attack on the Fleet. They are using Cants, Savoia-Marchettis and Breda 88s. They occupy the Dodecanese Islands, north of Crete, and have been able to harass our ships at both ends of the Mediterranean. Invasion of Greece is inevitable in time, and in 1939, when Italy invaded Albania, we signed a guarantee to help Greece against aggression. Although they are strictly neutral at the moment, and General Metaxas, the Greek leader, has renewed his declaration of neutrality, the Italians have adopted an attitude of distinct truculence against her little neighbour. We must support Greece to our maximum capability. When we leave Gibraltar tomorrow we shall be escorting a convoy bound for Malta and Greece and the Middle East. This will be the first of many.

'In Egypt the British Army of the Middle East is under the command of General Sir Archibald Wavell. The Italians occupy the whole of Libya and their General, Marshal Graziani, has sixty-two thousand troops under his command, and they represent a direct threat to Egypt and the Eastern Mediterranean Fleet.

'For the next few months there will be no shortage of targets for the Swordfish squadrons. We shall be attacking the enemy from the Dodecanese to Libya. On this passage we are to do a surprise raid on their airfield in the island of Rhodes, called Calato. From that airfield the Italians have been plaguing the Fleet for the last two months. The *Eagle's* Swordfish will be attacking Maritza at the same time – their other base in the Dodecanese Islands.'

He explained that on our way through 'bomb-alley' we had to ferry new aircraft and equipment to the Swordfish squadron based at Hal Far, in Malta, and he gave us the squadron's background. Since Italy had declared war in June, 830 Squadron, at Hal Far, had been almost the only striking force against Italian shipping, and their losses had been heavy. 'We are landing long-range petrol tanks for them, and blind-flying panels. Up to date they have been flying with the old instrument panel.'

Our new panels had been fitted while we were in Scotland and they had made a tremendous difference.

'The Italian bombing is very inaccurate because they bomb from great heights, to keep out of range of the Fleet's guns. The radar at present in use in Cunningham's ships is not as modern as ours, and with our new fighter-direction we hope to alter the whole tactical picture. *Eagle* has had three Gladiators on board, flown by Swordfish pilots whom Commander Keighley-Peach has taught fighter techniques, and up to date they have shot down eleven enemy aircraft, which is incredible when you remember that their radar is inadequate and they cannot detect the enemy aircraft until they are overhead. It is my guess that 806 Squadron from this ship is going to give the Italians the surprise of their lives in the next thirty-six hours.'

Later that day he spoke to the ship's company over the tannoy, and told them much the same. He ended with a stirring forecast:

'Because of their apparent immunity from attack in the air, and because they have been able to bomb from out of range of the Fleet's guns, Mussolini has become boastful; he has got into the habit of referring to the Mediterranean as "Mare Nostrum" which means "our sea". We are going to change all that; by the time we have reached Admiral Cunningham's fleet the Italians will have learned a lesson that will make them hesitate to attack the Fleet in the future. Instead of "Mare Nostrum" we are going to change it to "Cunningham's Pond". I tell you that with no uncertain voice, which, as you will know, is the ship's motto . . .'

On 2 September our fighters taught the Italians a sharp lesson. In their first attack three were shot down by the ship's Fulmars and the others fled in disorder. In the Dodecanese we wreaked a terrible toll, and when we flew back to the ship the whole of Calato airfield was a mass of flame. We had left our visiting card 'with no uncertain voice'. To be blasted to eternity by waves of elderly-looking biplanes must have caused the Italians an uncomfortable bewilderment.

In comparison with those mine-laying flights off the Frisian Islands it was simple, and Burns and Brown were delighted with me: I forgot to take a single sip from my brandy flask.

On our way through bomb alley, wave after wave of Italian aircraft tried to reach the convoy, but 806 Squadron was working in three watches, patrolling at their maximum ceiling, and these flights were vectored on to them by the ship's fighter-direction team. Every single enemy aircraft was chased away, but our fighter pilots were so extended that Robin Kilroy volunteered to fly a Fulmar. He was taking passage on board *Illustrious* on his way to command Dekheila, the naval airfield in Alexandria, and Charles Evans accepted his offer with gratitude.

Towards the end of his sortie Kilroy was vectored on to a Cant which was shadowing the Fleet. I had just returned from an anti-submarine patrol ahead of the convoy, and was flying around at two or three thousand feet in the 'waiting-position' off the ship's port quarter, and I watched Robin shoot down the Cant. Suddenly, a Royal Air Force Hudson crossed ahead of me, flying straight towards Robin's Fulmar, and I could see what was going to happen. The RAF aircraft was beam-on to me and its roundels were very clear, but from Robin's vulnerable position ahead of it, the aircraft must have looked very sinister, and although the Hudson had no idea that it was blundering into a combat zone at the height of a battle, it certainly looked as though it was about to attack Kilroy. There was no time for him to do anything other than to put one burst of .303 bullets into its fuselage.

When he climbed away for a quarter-attack and saw the RAF roundels, he broke away in horror, but the damage had been done. The Hudson limped away to North Africa where the crew of four spent the next two and a half years in a series of very unpleasant Vichy-French prisons.

In fact, the Hudson should not have been there. Before we sailed from Gibraltar we had been assured that any strange aircraft would be hostile. The crew of the Hudson, flying from Malta, had also been told that any shipping or aircraft they saw would belong to the enemy. No blame could be attributed to either crew, but in retrospect it seems amazing that the Navy and the RAF, in War Headquarters at Malta, could have had no knowledge that the whole Mediterranean Fleet was escorting an important convoy through bomb alley and that the aircraft from *Illustrious* would be dominating the sky to the south and west.

Between anti-submarine patrols ahead of the convoy the Swordfish of both squadrons from *Illustrious* made a total of thirty ferrying flights to Hal Far, in Malta, carrying blind-flying panels in wooden boxes in the rear cockpit, and long-range petrol tanks slung under the fuselage, to 830 Squadron, which was based on the island. We took off in flights of two or three at a time whenever we could make ourselves available. There were twenty-four of each to be flown ashore, plus six new Swordfish straight from the factory.

830 Squadron had only been in existence for two months. In June, when Italy declared war on Britain, the pilots had been in a training squadron on board the old deck-landing training carrier, HMS *Argus*, which had been built in 1917. When the Italians began attacking the Fleet, the *Argus* was steaming along off the French Rivera and was ordered to return to the UK 'with the utmost dispatch'. All twenty-four Swordfish were flown off the ship, landing at Hyères, and on 14 June they attacked Genoa. France was about to surrender and did so on 22 June. The CO of the training squadron, rather than be incarcerated for the duration, took all the aircraft to Bone, in North Africa. Some of the pilots had only just learned to fly, and he sent them home via Oran and Gibraltar, and the rest of the instructors and crews, who were capable of operational flying, took off for Malta on the day the French capitulated. On arrival at Hal Far they were renamed 830 Squadron and began their operational life on 30 June with an attack on Augusta, in Sicily.

Their task, signalled to them by the Fifth Sea Lord, was to sink

Italian shipping plying through the Straits of Messina to Tripoli and Benghazi for Marshal Graziani and his army in Libya. The transition, from the immaculate parade-ground atmosphere of a training squadron, to a front-line task which was perhaps more vital than that of any other squadron in the Mediterranean, was violently abrupt, and for the first six months of the squadron's history their losses were very heavy. In the early stages this was thought to be because of lack of fuel for the extended flying that was necessary in those high temperatures. Also, the absence of a proper instrument panel when creeping into enemy harbours at night, or when attacking convoys with torpedoes, must have accounted for the loss of quite a few, who simply flew into the sea. When we took these instrument panels and long-range tanks to them we hoped that their problems were over.

During the next eight months the squadron flew almost nightly and was the only night-striking force based in Malta with a capability of attacking shipping from the air, at night, with torpedoes. They had no respite and were bombed every day, when trying to sleep in readiness for the next night's attack. It was a squadron with a very proud history.

13
Cunningham's Pond

For the next five months *Illustrious* was the work-horse of the Mediterranean fleet. From the moment of our arrival the Commander-in-Chief seized every opportunity to sail his armada of battleships, cruisers, destroyers, and two aircraft carriers as provocatively as he could, often within sight of Italy, hoping to entice Mussolini's fleet to come out and do battle. Inside Taranto harbour the Italians had far more warships than we could muster, and heavily outnumbered us; but I am sure that their admirals appreciated that with *Illustrious*, and *Eagle* perhaps, steaming about outside, the odds were more than balanced against them. They had no method of launching seaborne aircraft and would have to rely on air support from the shore , with consequent delays when their shore-based aircraft would have to fly to and from the battle area to refuel and rearm. They knew that Cunningham could launch at least three squadrons of torpedo-carrying Sword-fish at their ships, backed up with our own fighter defence constantly in the air. And so they remained in harbour – very wisely, in my opinion.

No Fleet Commander can go into battle without his own air defence on the spot. A man without belt or braces can hold up his trousers for only a limited time; sooner or later his hands will be required for some other purpose and the resulting exposure could be fatal when fighting defensively, at close quarters. Without their own aircraft carriers, the Italian admirals were in that position precisely: their trousers were well and truly down.

Many senior Italian officers had represented this to Mussolini, but with supreme egotism, and without really understanding the problem, he replied: 'Italy is one big aircraft carrier!'

While Cunningham steamed up and down, rattling his sword, the Italians did everything in their power to redress the balance by sending wave after wave of aircraft to attack *Illustrious* and *Eagle*. Eventually, because of this, *Eagle* was kept out of range of Italy. During July she had been subjected to some savage bombing, and although the worst she experienced were near-misses, they had damaged her fuel systems. It was considered wise to keep her at the eastern end of the Med, within reach of Alexandria. Occasionally the Italian bombers condescended to drop their bombs in the general direction of the battleships and cruisers, but only when our fighters had prevented them from striking at *Illustrious*. The musical noise of our multiple pom-poms and sixteen 4.5-inch anti-aircraft guns, and the voice of the Reverend Henry Lloyd giving his incomparable commentaries from the bridge, which was his task when the ship's company were at action stations, would be drowned by the roar of the Fulmars taking off to assist the airborne flight. Without much surprise we found that we could take-off and land with all the ship's guns firing; in many ways it was reassuring to know that they were firing at someone else and not us, which sometimes happened when we returned to the ship at night in ones and twos.

The Italian attacks continued unabated despite heavy losses inflicted on them by Charles Evans and his squadron, but towards the end of September we noticed that although the attacks were less frequent, a greater number of enemy aircraft were taking part, which showed that they had acquired a healthy respect for the ability of the Fleet to defend itself. The Med was not yet 'Cunningham's Pond', with the Italian fleet dominating the tactical picture from Taranto, but it was far from being 'Mare Nostrum'.

During one of the dog-fights we were standing on the 'goofer's platforms' watching, when the Fulmars succeeded in setting a Cant flying-boat alight. Two of the occupants baled out of the burning aircraft, but they had only one parachute between them, and the sight of those two wriggling bodies, like worms impaled on a single fisherman's hook, plunging to their deaths from ten thousand feet, was something I would rather not have seen. The mind boggles at what the rightful owner must have been saying to his unwelcome passenger.

In October Mussolini invaded Greece, and Cunningham's problems were increased. Arms and equipment had to be taken from Egypt to the Piraeus. To begin with the Greek soldiers were able to repel the Italian attacks with the aid of arms and supplies brought to them by the Fleet. They did not ask for the support of British armed forces to help them against Italy alone, because they feared that Germany would then join in with the Italians and a joint attack by the Axis powers would be more than they could withstand. The Italians were able to harass the Greeks from both flanks, across the Ionian and Adriatic seas in the west and from the Dodecanese islands in the east. They began to bomb Greece and Crete daily, and our attacks on their bases in the Dodecanese were stepped up in frequency and intensity. Flying over roof-tops on warm moonlit nights, dodging the trees surrounding the white-portalled buildings which were military depots or officers' messes, we could see the buildings disintegrate before our eyes. Our agents infiltrating amongst the Italians, dressed as fishermen, or in other inconspicuous attire, passed accurate information back to Egypt which gave us the exact details we needed. Once, I was sent to bomb an Italian Admiral's headquarters in the island of Leros at midnight, and when I swooped over the building, I saw the faces of the startled occupants who were standing outside on a veranda, gazing upwards in alarm. The spectacle of a noisy biplane suddenly appearing over the trees, its fixed undercarriage giving the impression that it was about to crash-land, prior to the explosion of six 250-lb bombs, bust have been very frightening.

Returning to the ship at dawn, after such an attack on islands with glamorous names like Stampalia, or Scarpanto, while all was still dark, the sea and the silhouetted islands were sinister and unfriendly, and the whole surrounding atmosphere was hostile. Then, like magic, the sun would appear over the horizon, turning the islands into havens of green and gold, and the sea into a sparkling vista of bright blue. On those dawn flights the first glimmer of sun revealed a very beautiful world. But more often than not we flew back in total darkness and were denied the sight of those lovely islands. In September, when entering my flying times in my pilot's log, I was not surprised to discover that I had done more deck-landings at night than by day.

In many ways I preferred landing-on in the dark, because the sea was then invisible, and just part of the surrounding night; by day it could look vast and unfriendly. After a long flight, which always included a short period of intense excitement, one was tired when approaching to land, and although deck-landing can be more simple than landing on an airfield's runway (because on deck the ship's wires grab the aircraft and hold it securely), it was just one more hazard which had to be faced. From astern of the ship the neat lines of dimmed pillar lights, indicating the landing area, were a welcoming sight. Just seeing them in line was reassuring, because they were only visible if the pilot was flying along the correct approach lane. They were so clear, even though dimmed right down by rheostat, that the brightly lit Lucite wands of the Deck Landing Control Officers were scarcely necessary. But even they were a help, too, to a tired pilot. Although I often disagreed with the batsman's interpretation of the best method of approach, I knew that if I obeyed his signals and relaxed I would eventually arrive on the flight-deck in one piece.

Accidents were bound to occur, but the Swordfish was so easy to land that in *Illustrious* they happened very seldom, and then only when an aircraft or pilot had been damaged in the air. On those occasions we all ran to the crash to help clear the deck quickly. On one pitch-dark night, the last remaining Swordfish to land kept circling the ship to indicate that something was wrong. The observer had been wounded and was unable to operate the Aldis lamp. When the pilot eventually touched down, the aircraft somersaulted, and we saw that his undercarriage had been shot away. We had just pulled the pilot and observer and air gunner from the overturned fuselage, and were standing in line beside the wreckage waiting for the mobile crane, when I saw the portly figure of Admiral Lyster approaching in the dark. Because it was the last aircraft to land there was no great panic, and he was strolling across the deck to see what had happened. In a roll-necked pullover and an old yachting cap he could quite well have been mistaken for Churchill.

In fact, in that tatty old rig, he might just as easily have been mistaken for a petty officer, which is the mistake that Lieutenant Swayne made, and probably never forgot. Even in the dark the Flag Officer's profile was unmistakable, especially below the waist, and I was very surprised at Ian's careless lack of recognition.

The Admiral fell-in beside Ian Swayne, and stood looking down at the wreckage.

'Anybody hurt?' he asked in a gruff voice.

When studying a wrecked aircraft all pilots think, 'There but for the grace of God go I!' and this thought can make them testy. It was evident that Swayne was not in the mood for light chatter.

'For Christ's sake!' he expostulated. 'We've only just hauled them out, and sent them off to sick bay. How the bloody hell do you expect us to know whether they are hurt or not? If you must ask damnfool questions go and ask the PMO.'

I waited with bated breath for Ian to be blasted to the high heavens for impertinence, but at that time I had no knowledge of Rear-Admiral Lumley Lyster.

'All right – all right!' he grumbled – but in an amused voice. 'Keep your hair on!' Then he shuffled off into the dark.

When he was out of earshot I took Ian to task. 'That was no way to speak to the Admiral, Ian! You should be ashamed of yourself!'

'What!' he gasped. 'For Christ's sake! I thought it was some dumb Seaman PO!' He looked nervously in the direction of the Admiral's departure. 'What shall I do? D'you think I ought to go and apologize?'

'I shouldn't if I were you. If you do he'll know who it was. At the moment he hasn't a clue!'

Right from the beginning of our time in the ship I was used as a guinea-pig, much to the indignation of Burns and Brown. One morning, I was sent for by Commander Flying. It was a quiet day, with only a few routine patrols, and we were out of range of any hostile airfield. I was looking forward to writing some letters. Whenever these occasions arose 'Streamline' could be relied upon to think up something devilish. This time it was simple: he wanted to know how many Swordfish he could range on deck in front of the Fulmars for a free take-off when fully loaded: so, 'Q' for 'Queenie' was ranged, armed with six 250-lb dummy bombs, and full long-range petrol tanks, and I was made to take off with a gradually reducing amount of deck. On the fifth take-off there was so little flight-deck left that the aircraft dropped over the bow, and I had to fly along at wave-top height with maximum throttle for almost half a mile before I had enough air-speed to climb, clawing my way into the air with my heart in my mouth, expecting a cold bath at any moment. From this experiment it was discovered that in certain winds both squadrons could be ranged ahead of nearly half the fighters. But after the fifth landing, with a full load of petrol and bombs – which no aircraft should have to do once, let alone five times – the strain was too much for my undercarriage, which splayed apart and fractured, and I ended up skidding along the deck into the barrier. Strangely enough the damage was only superficial, but the damage to the tempers of Burns and Brown was inestimable. They helped me out of the aircraft, cursing all senior officers without restraint.

'I could have told the silly bastards what would happen,' said Burns, bitterly. 'No aircraft would ever have to land with that load. Normally either your petrol or your bombs would have been used up, probably both. There isn't an aircraft in the Fleet Air Arm that's designed to deck-land with all that weight!

'Every time you touched down, sir,' he went on, 'your undercart was spreading apart like an old sow giving birth. What did they want to go and pick on this aircraft for?'

Brown answered that question, and his reply gave me much food for thought.

'Well,' he said to Burns, with a sly grin in my direction, 'they wanted to know how much deck the worst pilot in the ship would need with a full load! It's the old business of the lowest common denominator; it wouldn't have been much of an experiment for the masses, if they'd used a good pilot!'

I made a suitable comment which cast some doubt on his possession of a birth certificate, but I had to admit to myself that his remark contained a certain amount of unanswerable logic.

The two men ensured that the aircraft was repaired in time for me to be sent on another unforgettable mission. Because of an intelligence report that he had received, Admiral Lyster required an immediate attack on the island of Rhodes, to be done that night; but *Illustrious* was operating off Tunisia at the time, and it was entirely beyond our range. *Eagle* was in the area, but wireless silence was in force and so the instructions could not be signalled. Janvrin was given a despatch in a sealed envelope, and we were flown off, to land-on the *Eagle* at the other end of the Mediterranean. This would take most of our petrol, even with a long-range tank, and many hours of flying, and we would have to stay the night. After a long flight we found the *Eagle* south of Crete. Her flight-deck looked very small in comparison with *Illustrious*, and her Gladiators were protruding on to the deck on outriggers, reducing the landing area even more. I circled the old lady, seeing her for the first time from the air. She had been built for the Chilean navy in 1913 as a battleship, to be called 'Almirante Cochrane'; but all work on her had to stop during the First World War and in 1917 the Admiralty bought her back from the Chileans for over a million pounds, and turned her into an aircraft carrier. As I flew round her, the thought that pilots had been landing on that small area for twenty-three years was rather sobering, and I hoped that I wouldn't make a cock of it.

All aircraft carriers had an automatic signalling device mounted on the after-end of the island, clearly visible to the pilot about to land; this was a big shuttered screen which displayed the affirmative on one side and the negative on the other. It was operated by Commander Flying himself from his little bridge. When the affirmative was displayed in *Illustrious* it meant that 'Streamline' wanted us to land at once, at the double as it were. There could be no confusion between the signals and they were common to all aircraft carriers. I was surprised to see that *Eagle* was displaying the affirmative, and I did two circuits waiting to see if it had been left out by mistake, because from the smoke from her funnel it was apparent that she was going quite fast down-wind. I hailed Dick on the voice-pipe and put the problem to him.

'Surely they can't expect me to land on that tiny deck with the ship steaming down-wind?'

'I should wait for a bit,' said Dick cautiously. 'We've got enough fuel for another half an hour, haven't we?'

We circled the ship several times, but she showed no inclination to turn into wind, and yet the affirmative was still being firmly displayed.

I hailed Dick again. 'There's no batsman,' I said, 'but maybe this old steamer hasn't heard about DLCOs! She's been in the Far East for donkey's years.'

Dick was still hesitant so I decided to make a slow pass at the ship, above the flight-deck, to see at what speed we would be touching down if we did land. Flying just below the bridge, but well above the flight-deck, all I succeeded in doing was to scare the officers on *Eagle*'s open bridge out of their minds; going down-wind it was impossible to fly slowly, and I had to lift my starboard wings to avoid removing the caps from the startled heads of the Captain and Commander Flying as we flashed past. Hurriedly, the ship turned into wind and I landed-on.

On the bridge Commander Keighley-Peach had the grace to apologize, but I could see that he thought I was quite mad.

'I suppose that was partly my fault,' he said. 'Our affirmative always jams on when we fire the guns abaft the island, but surely you didn't think that I meant you to land-on when the ship was going down-wind, did you? Any bloody fool knows that that is impossible!'

'Not in *Illustrious*, sir,' I said. 'If the affirmative is out – we land – no matter what. Even if the ship is going down-wind and the Royal Marine band is playing Hearts of Oak on the forrard lift and all the ship's guns are firing. If we don't we are liable to be logged for disobeying an order!'

When the *Eagle*'s pilots and observers came out of the ship's briefing-room I could see from their white faces that the orders we had flown to them from the Admiral were very unpleasant. Apparently, since our attack early in September, Rhodes had been heavily defended, and there were now two squadrons of Breda 88s based on the island; which is why Lumley Lyster wanted the attack, before the arrival of a convoy for Greece. Although the *Eagle*'s Swordfish would be attacking in the dark their return flight to the ship would include some daylight, because there would be insufficient time for the ship to be close enough to Rhodes to land them on before daybreak. The Bredas were capable of flying more than a thousand miles, and being fitted with twin Piaggo engines they could do more than 300 knots. They were heavily armed, too, with two 7.7 mm cannon and three 12.7 mm machine-guns.

At about half past three in the morning we were within the Swordfish's range of Rhodes and I climbed out of my bunk to watch them fly off. One of their aircraft skidded into another on taking off and nearly overturned – I couldn't see what was happening in the dark – and because I belonged to *Illustrious* it had nothing to do with me, and I was afraid of being thought a snooper, so I kept out of the way. I saw that the bombs from one of the damaged aircraft were rolling about the flight-deck, which caused a minor stampede. By the time the bombs were rounded up, and the damaged aircraft had been struck-down into the hangar, the take-off of the majority of the strike had been delayed by nearly an hour, and they had to attack in daylight. There were few survivors.

One observer was picked out of the sea some weeks later. His body was easily identified because he had his name and rank stamped on the back of his Mae West, which had carried him right across the Mediterranean. He was found floating along face upwards off the coast of Egypt.

14
Preparations for a Battle

In October the situation in the Mediterranean changed for the worse: while the British fleet was busy escorting convoys to Greece from Gibraltar and Egypt, the Italians were equally busy ferrying vast supplies of arms and ammunition and troops into North Africa, through the Straits of Messina, past Malta, to Tripoli and Benghazi. Our submarines and aircraft in Malta did their best, but the enemy convoys were succeeding in getting through with very little damage or loss. By mid-October Graziani's forces had dug themselves in at Sidi Barrani, on the Egyptian coast. In Greece, despite the initial success of the Hellenic army, the Italians were advancing. With only two aircraft carriers, one of which was damaged and worn out and had to confine its activites to the Eastern Mediterranean, we could not be at both ends of the Med at once. Cunningham was beset by problems on all sides, and not least of these was the constant need to keep Malta supplied from Egypt.

Although they had not yet been persuaded to put to sea, the Italian fleet, comprising six Italian battleships, nine cruisers and seventeen destroyers, which were the main units amongst many other types of warship lying in Taranto harbour, represented an overwhelming threat every time our fleet approached Malta. The only way that this problem could be solved became increasingly clear to us in *Illustrious*. The Senior Pilot in 819 Squadron, a tall Northern Irishman named Torrens-Spence, put the problem very clearly when a group of us were sitting round the bar in the Cecil Hotel, in Alex. 'I'm afraid that Cunningham will have to do a "Nelson",' he said, and we all knew what he meant.

On 2 April, in 1801, Nelson sent his ships into the harbour at Copenhagen to sink the ships at anchor. In 1940, instead of sending surface ships, which would have been annihilated had they tried to enter Taranto through the narrow, heavily defended harbour entrance, Cunningham had to send his Swordfish aeroplanes, whether he liked it or not. We all knew that the attack was inevitable and throughout October were just waiting for the day; which was rather like waiting for the attack on Wilhelmshaven, at Bircham Newton.

The plan for this attack had been in existence since 1935, when Italy invaded Abyssinia. The British C-in-C was then Admiral Sir William Wordsworth Fisher, a fearsome man, whom I had met when I was a Midshipman RNR. When Italian bombs were rained on the heads of the defenceless Abyssinians, very naturally he assumed that Britain would declare war at once. On board HMS *Glorious* the plan to attack the Italian fleet in harbour was made immediately, at Admiral Fisher's instigation. But in 1935 our politicians wanted peace at any price, no matter how shameful that price might be; and not only did they hold back 'in fear and trembling', but they refused permission to the C-in-C to take any action whatsoever, other than to apply mild recriminatory sanctions to Italian shipping. Even those were faint-hearted. 'Do nothing,' implied Mr Stanley Baldwin, the Prime Minister of Great Britain, 'which might aggravate Germany. You may prevent Italian shipping from supporting the invasion if you can, by applying peaceful sanctions, but you must not interfere with their oil supplies. Their tankers must be allowed to pass unhindered.'

Without oil the invasion would have failed, and that might have made Hitler very cross indeed!

In my opinion this shameful episode in British history was largely responsible for the Second World War. In 1935, had Admiral Fisher been allowed to spread his fleet across the entrance to the Suez Canal at Port Said, the Italians would have turned tail and fled, without a shot being fired. There would have been no subsequent invasion of Abyssinia, and Britain would have been respected throughout the world. All that was needed then, when Hitler was a newcomer on the political scene, was a show of strength and determination, to put him and Mussolini in their places. But these were characteristics which were alien to British politicians at the time, and indeed to the whole nation. When we did nothing, Hitler and Mussolini – and the Japanese – were convinced that Britain was no longer an influential power to be reckoned with, and in Italy and Germany we were often described as 'degenerate'. Being fair, the foreign powers were given every encouragement by the British to come to that conclusion: a couple of years earlier, in 1933, Professor Joad won a much-publicized debate at Oxford University passing a motion that 'This house . . .' [the Oxford Union] 'will in no circumstances fight for its King and Country.' To a delighted Hitler and Mussolini, Baldwin's pussy-footing reaction to Italy's one-sided bullying attack, proved that Professor Joad and his students represented the thinking and behaviour of the youth of this country. 'In future we can ignore them,' said Adolf Hitler, in a speech to the Germans; and ignore us they did.

Three years later, in March 1938, when Hitler annexed Austria , the C-in-C Mediterranean was Admiral Sir Dudley Pound. Like his predecessor he, too, assumed that war was certain; and thinking on exactly the same lines as Admiral Fisher, he sent for the Captain of *Glorious* – who was his air adviser – and told him to draw up plans for an all-out attack from the air on the Italian fleet in Taranto. He was gambling on a quick offensive by the British, but expected the attack to be done by shore-based aircraft. It had not occurred to him that it could be done by naval aircraft. His small fleet was barely half the size of the Italians', and he wanted to arrange a telling blow before it was sent to the bottom.

On board *Glorious*, the Captain was Lumley Lyster, who had discovered the 1935 plan amongst the secret papers which were locked up in his safe when he first assumed command of the ship. He had read this plan with very great interest. His immediate reaction, when receiving the C-in-C's directive, was to send for his two senior aviators, Commander Guy Willoughby, and Commander Lachlan Mackintosh of Mackintosh, the head of the clan of that name and the Senior Observer in the ship. Between them, these three men revised the 1935 plan and brought it up-to-date. The three Swordfish squadrons in *Glorious* (812, 823, and 825 Squadrons) were given an intensive work-up in night deck-landings and night flying generally, including constant dummy attacks on the British fleet in the Grand Harbour at Malta, in darkened-ship and blacked-out harbour conditions. At the end of these realistic rehearsals Lyster made his report to Admiral Pound, who was by no means convinced.

Admiral Pound had no belief in the Swordfish as a weapon of attack, and no understanding of how devastating it could be.

Despite Lyster's conviction that casualties would be slight, Dudley Pound held to the belief that the casualties would be too heavy, and the results too insignificant, to make the attack by Swordfish worthwhile. Nevertheless, there was no alternative, and he had to accept the plan. He wrote to Lyster saying that he did so very reluctantly, and he hoped that shore-based aircraft would be available to do it. 'Only sailors who live in ships should attack other ships,' he said, which was a real contradiction in terms if ever there was one! How he could reconcile that remark with a request for an attack by shore-based aircraft is difficult to understand.

15
Judgement Day

The attack had been planned for Trafalgar Day, but by 21 October two calamities had occurred which made postponement essential. First of all we had a fire in the hangar, caused by a spark from a metal hammer in an atmosphere drenched with petrol vapour. (Thereafter, when refuelling was in progress, only rubber hammers were allowed.) The fire was quickly brought under control, but not before two Swordfish had been burnt out. The hangar sprays proved most efficient, but all the aircraft were saturated with salt water and every machine had to be stripped, washed in fresh water and oil, and then reassembled. It was a mammoth task. I helped Burns and Brown with 'Q' for 'Queenie', and eventually she was none the worse for her bath.

The second calamity was discovered on board HMS *Eagle*. The original plan was for the two carriers to sail in company, but the severe bombing in July had so shaken the old lady's hull that her fuel systems were now entirely unreliable, and she had boiler trouble. The result was that she was unable to come with us, and five of her Swordfish and eight of her experienced crews were transferred to *Illustrious* before we sailed.

On 8 November *Illustrious* sailed from Alexandria in company with the four battleships: *Warspite*, *Valiant*, *Malaya*, and *Ramillies*. With them was a most reassuring screen of cruisers and destroyers. On our way towards Malta, the Fulmars shot down two shadowing aircraft; and on 9 November Cunningham sent a force of cruisers and destroyers ahead, to search the waters surrounding Sicily for enemy surface vessels. I suspect that he was hoping that at the last moment he could entice the Italian fleet out of harbour, for a 'major fleet engagement', before the Swordfish had the opportunity of making such a battle an impossibility. The weather was poor and only one shadowing aircraft ventured in our direction. This was good news because the Italian pilot would report the entire armada sailing towards Malta, and not in the direction of Taranto.

The *Illustrious* was to be detached on the evening of the 11th, with the cruisers *Gloucester, Berwick, Glasgow* and *York*, and an escort of four destroyers, to make for the island of Cephalonia, opposite the Gulf of Corinth, and about seventy miles south of Corfu. We were then to steam to the north, towards Corfu, and the two squadrons were to take off to attack the Italian fleet in their harbour, at intervals of an hour. Each squadron was reinforced by the aircraft and crews from 813 and 824 Squadrons, from *Eagle*. 815 was to lead the first attack, followed by 819. As the first strike, we were scheduled to take off at 8.30 in the evening and attack immediately on arrival, with 819 Squadron, the second strike, following an hour afterwards. We had 170 miles to fly, across the Ionian sea; and the second strike an hour later, would have 150 miles of sea to cross.

Tension was running fairly high on our way westward for the great day. The attack had been given the code name 'Operation Judgement', and we all hoped that it was the Italians who were about to meet their Maker and not us. The name was singularly apt. On the morning of the 10th I was piped for, by name, to report to Commander Flying at Flying Control; and sped up the ladders to the bridge with my heart in my mouth, wondering what I had done wrong. With everyone in a highly-strung state, surprises were not welcome; but I found 'Streamline' Robertson sitting on his high stool, looking quite cheerful.

'The Admiral wants you to report to him on his bridge,' he said, pleasantly. Then he laughed. 'There's no need to look so alarmed; he only wants you to fly to Hal Far today, to collect the reconnaissance photographs for tomorrow night's party. He will tell you all about it.'

Captain Boyd stepped out on to Flying Control and leant with his back to the bulkhead, his hands in his pockets. 'You may be surprised to hear that you are the assistant flare-dropper tomorrow night. Not a very glamorous job, and I expect you would rather drop a torpedo?'

I shook my head – hastily. 'We have a superstition in the "Branch", sir,' I said. 'It is supposed to be very unlucky to volunteer. We all feel that to volunteer is asking for trouble. If we are told to do something, no matter what, that's okay; but volunteer – never.'

Denis Boyd nodded. 'I can understand that outlook,' he said. 'Well tomorrow night you have a roving brief. You can do as much or as little as you think necessary. Kiggell and Janvrin will be dropping the main flares, but we want you to follow along behind them and fill any gaps, or lay a line in another direction – to help the strike-pilots down below, in the harbour. In other words, use your own judgement and make yourself useful.'

Admiral Lyster was standing with his two operations officers, Commander Charles Thompson, a tall, very serious, dark-haired man, and the Assistant Operations Officer, Lieutenant David Pollock, RNVR, a young solicitor from an eminent London firm. (They were the legal advisers to the Bank of England.) Pollock had specialized in photographic interpretation, and his acute brain had been responsible for much of the detailed planning from the earlier photographic efforts by Glenn Martin pilots. He had discovered that some lines of white blobs on the photographs, which were thought to be blemishes, were almost certainly moored balloons. Although he was nearly sure that he was right, the photographs which had been taken daily for the last ten days, which I was being sent to fetch, would either confirm this or refute it. They would also show the latest disposition of the ships in the harbour.

It seems incredible that on a matter of such urgency inter-service and departmental regulations could not have been waived. Although all the photographs had been taken at the request of the C-in-C of the Mediterranean fleet, they were RAF property; and after development in Malta they had been flown to the RAF intelligence headquarters in Cairo, where Pollock had been allowed only to look at them. When studying them under a stereoscope he recognized the barrage balloons, and asked permission to take the photographs back to Alexandria to show to his Admiral; but Flight-Lieutenant Idris Jones, in charge of the intelligence headquarters in Cairo, was not allowed to part with any of the contents of the headquarters, and had to refuse. So Pollock plotted the position of the gun emplacements and anti-torpedo nets, and when Idris Jones wasn't looking, showed the intelligence one might expect of a graduate of Cambridge university, and purloined them. He returned them the next day, by which time they had been copied by the photographic department on board *Illustrious*, and seen by Admiral Lyster, and by the C-in-C. Their temporary absence was not noticed in Cairo.

Admiral Lyster explained to me what I had to do. 'The latest photographs are vital,' he said, 'and you are not to come back without them. They will be delivered to you at Hal Far as soon as they have been developed, which may not be until tomorrow morning. Bring them back as soon as you can, but by noon at the latest.' As I was leaving his bridge he halted me. 'By the way,' he said, as an afterthought, 'if you happen to see any potatoes lying about in Malta bring some back for the cuddy, will you please?'

At Hal Far, the station commander was a Wing-Commander Allen, from Coastal Command, a neat, good-looking man with a thin black moustache and penetrating eyes. He had been one of my instructors at the RAF School of Navigation at Manston in 1936. He explained that the photographs would not be available until 8.30 the following morning.

'What about a game of poker this evening?' he said. We had often played at Manston, and I agreed, but asked him what I could do about the Admiral's request for spuds. He looked doubtful, and then explained that there was a shortage in Malta too, but they were obtainable through the black market.

When I flew back to the ship the next morning I was feeling very pleased with myself. The cost of the potatoes had been added to my mess bill for the night at Hal Far, but my winnings at poker had cancelled the whole bill, leaving me a small amount of change; so I had made a profit on the deal – out of the RAF – which was very satisfying.

David Pollock took the photographs from me, and the Admiral fixed me with an inquiring look.

'Get any spuds?' he asked.

'They are being taken down to the cuddy now, sir,' I said. 'One hundredweight of the best potatoes available on Malta's black market.'

'How much?' he inquired gruffly, but I could see that he was pleased.

'A fiver, I'm afraid sir, but there's no need to worry – they were paid for by my poker winnings last night. If you agree I will enter it as a credit to me in the wardroom card-book.'

'Don't go putting me down for a loss in your bloody card-book!' the Admiral snorted. 'Put it down to Flags and I will settle with him.'

I had had much experience of trying to extract money from flag-lieutenants but I accepted this solution with good grace.

The photographs established that the barrage of twenty-one balloons were flying from moored barges, three hundred yards apart. As the Swordfish has a wing-span of 45 feet 6 inches there was plenty of room, but it would be a case of flying in and out very low indeed, at water level, so that there would be less danger of hitting the balloon cables secured to the barge decks. There would have to be enough harbour illumination to make sure that the pilots could see the barges and the cables as well as the battle-ships and cruisers they were attacking, and our job as flare-droppers was going to be very important.

As new people arrived in the squadron to take the place of pilots and observers who were either lost or taken prisoner, there were many changes, and after our long flights to HMS *Eagle*, Janvrin and I never flew together again. He was moved up by seniority to the back of Kiggell's aircraft and from then onwards my observers changed with almost every flight. I was sorry to lose Dick Janvrin, but he had always been my senior by about seven years and I was lucky to have had him in the rear cockpit for so long. As we were both the sons of clergymen we had a similiar outlook. Being a big chap with fair hair he had a quiet, almost placid temperament, and he was a comforting person to have in the back seat.

Because of the transfer of a number of pilots and observers from *Eagle* before we sailed from Alexandria, many of us were to fly with strangers in the rear cockpit, on our way to Taranto. My observer was Lieutenant Ken Grieves from *Eagle*. We had never met before, and I doubt whether two men have been together for such a concentrated period with less opportunity of getting to know one another. We exchanged not more than half a dozen sentences there and back.

There were other adjustments, too, made necessary by the third calamity which struck us on our way there. The fire in our hangar and *Eagle's* boiler trouble were the first two, and we were all wondering what the third would be when it began to happen. Probably as a result of the fire in the hangar one of 819 Squadron's refuelling tanks had become contaminated and for three days running the squadron lost an aircraft per day, all three ditching in the sea. At first this was thought to be some inexplicable engine trouble, until reports came through from the destroyers which picked them up, and it was realized that it was a case of dirty petrol.

Lieutenants Clifford and Going, who were in the third Swordfish to ditch, were able to take part in the Taranto raid after yet another accident, when their aircraft collided with another on the flight-deck that evening. Owing to the three ditchings, and the collision, the total number of Swordfish able to take part had been reduced from twenty-four to twenty, in the short passage to the Ionian Sea.

At the final briefing in the wardroom a large-scale map of Taranto and a magnificent collection of enlarged prints of the photographs I had brought out from Malta were pinned to cardboard backings and were on display. It was possible to study every aspect of the harbour and its defences, and the balloons; and, of course, all the ships in detail. In the outer harbour, called the Mar Grande, there were six battleships moored in a semi-circle: four of the *Cavour* class with ten 12.6-inch guns, and two *Littorio* class, with ten 15-inch guns. All these ships were protected with weighted anti-torpedo nets, suspended from booms, which reached down into the water as far as the ships' keels; but the Italians had a shock to come, because our aerial torpedoes were fitted with Duplex Pistols, a magnetic device which exploded the torpedo's warhead when it passed underneath the ship, being activated by the magnetic field set up by the ship. These attachments had been invented at HMS *Vernon* when Captain Denis Boyd had been in command. They were called Duplex because they performed a dual function: the 'fish' would explode either as it passed underneath, or on contact, if it struck the ship's hull. Neil Kemp whistled appreciatively at this news, and said: 'Heads I win – tails you lose!' The eleven torpedoes which were being used that night were set to pass under the hulls, to avoid the nets.

To seaward of the six battleships, and between them and the harbour entrance, were three 8-inch gun cruisers, the *Zara*, *Fiume*, and *Gorizia*; and stretching right across the harbour, from side to side, were eleven moored ballooons. Another eleven encircled the harbour to the south and east.

In the inner harbour, called the Mar Piccolo, were two 8-inch cruisers moored in the centre, the *Trieste* and *Bolzano;* and alongside each other, stern-to, in true Mediterranean fashion, were four 6-inch cruisers and seventeen destroyers.

Promptly at 8.30 in the evening Williamson, the CO of 815, and Scarlett our Senior Observer, took off, followed by the rest of the first strike of twelve Swordfish. The second strike, led by

Lieutenant-Commander 'Ginger' Hale, the CO of 819 Squadron, and a Navy and England rugby player as unshakable as the Rock of Gibraltar, were due to take off an hour later. Owing to the ditchings and the collision, Hale's flight had been reduced to eight aircraft. Six in our flight and five in the second were armed with torpedoes, and the remainder with six 250-lb armour-piercing bombs. Kiggell and I, the flare-droppers, were armed with sixteen parachute flares apiece, and four bombs.

Almost as soon as we were airborne we had to climb through heavy cumulus cloud, and when we emerged into the moonlight at 7500 feet, only nine of the twelve aircraft's lights were in sight. When the others were unable to find their leader they flew direct to Taranto. One of them was Ian Swayne, who flew at sea level and reached the target area fifteen minutes before anyone else. He had no wish to be the first uninvited guest of the Italian navy in Taranto, and for a quarter of an hour he flew to and fro, keeping the harbour in sight, waiting for the main strike. There was nothing else he could do, but of course his presence had been detected by the Italian listening devices, and as a result all the harbour defences and the ships had been alerted. For the last fifteen minutes of our passage across the Ionian sea Scarlett had no navigational problem, for Taranto could be seen from a distance of fifty miles or more, because of the welcome awaiting us. The sky over the harbour looked like it sometimes does over Mount Etna, in Sicily, when the great volcano erupts. The darkness was being torn apart by a firework display which spat flame into the night to a height of nearly 5000 feet.

'I think our hosts are expecting us,' I said to Grieve down the tube.

'They don't seem very pleased to see us,' said Grieve, and it was the last thing he could say for some time to come, and for what must have been a very uncomfortable interval as a passenger in an open cockpit above a volcano. As he spoke 'Blood' Scarlett's dimmed Aldis light flashed the break-away signal to Kiggell and me, telling us to start adding to the illuminations over the crowded harbour, and, once again, for an unforgettable half an hour, I had a bird's eye view of history in the making.

The harbour defences at Taranto were designed to protect one of the biggest fleets in existence, if not the biggest. The Italians possessed all the necessary skills to make it into the impregnable fortress that it should have been: the guns, placed at strategic points on all the breakwaters, and all over the harbour, were expected to safeguard all the ancillary installations ashore which combined to make this their most important port. It had to be impregnable for a huge fleet to be able to rest, and to carry out repairs in complete security. Dotted around the dockyard there were machine workshops, a floating dry dock capable of accommodating a 35 000-ton battleship, and several armouries stacked high with weapons and spare shells. Then there were the vast docks themselves to be defended, with cranes and loading bays, and slipways and railway sidings and engine sheds. It was no wonder that there were hundreds upon hundreds of anti-aircraft guns and multiple pom-poms and close-range weapons mounted all over the harbour. The anti-torpedo nets and the balloons were only the 'belts-and-braces' which helped to make this one of the most heavily defended harbours in existence.

During the final briefing Commander George Beale had drawn our attention to all these installations in infinite detail when outlining the methods of attack, and when he said, 'And now for the return trip,' 'Blood' Scarlett's rough voice boomed out, 'Don't let's waste valuable time talking about that!' and we all laughed. It was a typical 'Blood' Scarlett remark; but as it turned out he was to be one of four present who were destined not to return.

Cruising along quietly at about five thousand feet, waiting for Kiggell to begin the flare-dropping, I realized that I was watching something which had never happened before in the history of mankind, and was unlikely to be repeated ever again. It was a 'one off' job. 815 Squadron had been flying operationally for nearly twelve of the fifteen months of war, and for the last six months, almost without a break, we had attracted the enemy's fire for an average of at least an hour a week; but I had never imagined anything like this to be possible. Before the first Swordfish had dived to the attack, the full-throated roar from the guns of six battleships and the blast from the cruisers and destroyers made the harbour defences seem like a side-show; they were the 'lunatic fringe', no more than the outer petals of the flower of flame which was hurled across the water in wave after wave by a hot-blooded race of defenders in an intense fury of agitation, raging at a target which they could only glimpse for fleeting seconds; and into that inferno, one hour apart, two waves, of six and then five Swordfish, painted a dull bluey-grey for camouflage, danced a weaving arabesque of death and destruction with their torpedoes, flying into the harbour only a few feet above sea level – so low that one or two of them actually touched the water with their wheels as they sped through the harbour entrance. Nine other spidery biplanes dropped out of the night sky, appearing in a crescendo of noise in vertical dives from the slow-moving glitter of the yellow parachute flares. So, the guns had three levels of attacking aircraft to fire at – the low-level torpedo planes, the dive-bombers, and the flare-droppers. The Swordfish left the Italian fleet a spent force, surrounded by floating oil which belched from the ships' interiors as their bottoms and sides and decks were torn apart.

In those two strikes a total of twenty Swordfish dropped eleven torpedoes and forty-eight 250 lb semi-armour-piercing bombs, right in their very midst; and all but two aircraft escaped without so much as a burst tyre from a stray bullet on their old-fashioned fixed undercarriage, and without a single sparking plug faltering. They left one battleship sunk, another sinking, and a third so dreadfully crippled that four years later, when the war ended, she was still being repaired. But that was only what happened in the outer harbour, called so pompously, the Mar Grande; in the inner dock, the Mar Piccolo, much damage was also done at the seaplane base.

It seems incredible that only two aircraft were brought down in exchange for that extensive damage, because in opposition to this achievement the 'lunatic fringe' of the harbour defences fired a total of 13 489 rounds of high-angle anti-aircraft shells at the flare-droppers; 1750 rounds of four-inch, and 7000 rounds of three-inch shells, at the eleven torpedo-droppers and the dive-bombers. There is no record of the amount of armament expended by all the ships, but this greatly exceeded the flak put up by the harbour defences. All this was aimed at twenty slow-moving, elderly biplanes, dancing a stately minuet in their midst, and performing feats of agility which no other type of aircraft could attempt without falling out of the sky.

The arrival of the first aircraft at the harbour entrance coincided exactly with Kiggell's first flare bursting into a yellow orb of light, which seemed to be hanging quite stationary in the still night air. The guns at the entrance were throwing long streaks of flame across the harbour entrance, spitting venom out to sea, and the shells of these tracer bursts illuminated the first Swordfish so brightly that from above, instead of appearing a bluey-grey, it seemed to be a gleaming white. I watched it wing its way through the harbour entrance five thousand feet below and disappear under the flak, and imagined that it had been shot down at once. Then I saw the lines of fire switching round from both sides, firing so low that they must have hit each other. The gun-aimers must then have lifted their arc of fire to avoid shooting at each other, and I saw their shells exploding in the town of Taranto in the background. The Italians were faced with a terrible dilemma: were they to go on firing at the elusive aircraft right down on the water, thereby hitting their own ships and their own guns, and their own harbour and town, or were they to lift their angle of fire still more? Eventually they did the latter, because all the other five attacking Swordfish managed to weave their way under that umbrella to find their targets. Had the arc of fire been maintained at water level, all six would have been shot to pieces within seconds, instead of two; but the guns would have done even more extensive damage to the ships and the harbour itself.

The anti-aircraft high-angle guns were concentrating on Kiggell's flares, sinking gently to earth in great pools of yellow light which lit up everything above the curtain of flame shooting to and fro across the harbour. The guns followed each flare in turn, wasting all their ammunition trying to hit these small elusive bundles of incandescent flame. Each flare had a delay action of one thousand feet before it ignited, so the high-angled guns achieved nothing but target practice, which they appeared to need rather badly. When they fired at his first flare Kiggell was busy dropping the third and when they switched to the second Kiggell was happily releasing the fourth, and so on, all around the harbour. They succeeded in shooting down neither the flares nor the flare-dropping aircraft.

The Italians were criticized afterwards by our own pilots because they failed to use searchlights. Ian Swayne remarked that had they done so they would have succeeded in shooting down every single aircraft, but from above I could see that the opposite was the case; because the aircraft were only a few feet above sea level, the use of searchlights would have floodlit the six battleships and the harbour defences, and greatly assisted the attacking aircraft in selecting their target. In the second strike Torrens-Spence admitted to having bounced off the water as he came through the harbour entrance, and I am convinced that it was the low height of the attacking machines which enabled them to fly in and out with scarcely a scratch, under that umbrella of flame. Somebody was bound to be hit, of course, and poor Lieutenant Bayley and Lieutenant Slaughter from HMS *Eagle* disappeared in flames to their deaths, on their run in. 'Hooch' Williamson and Scarlett managed to put a fish into one of the *Cavour* class battleships before they were struck, and then plummeted down into the sea on their way to a prisoner-of-war camp for the next four and a half years.

From my position astern of Kiggell and Janvrin I was in no danger whatever and could watch proceedings at leisure. I have never been in less danger in any attack than I was that night, when the rest of the squadron were flying into the jaws of hell. I was convinced that none of the six torpedoing aircraft could have survived.

I have always been very grateful to the Italians for favouring the tracer-type shell, which streaks upwards in flaming balls of fire, known as 'flaming onions'. It is possible to see them coming from the moment they leave the gun's mouth until they soar past. Admittedly they streak upwards at an alarming rate, but there was always time to dip a wing and swerve out of their path. In the dark there was plenty of time to dodge, and in any case they were firing at the flares, not the aircraft.

With my bird's-eye view it seemed that the harbour was more brilliantly lit than the attacking Swordfish could want – if any of them were still in the air, which seemed unlikely . There was no point in adding to their vulnerability by lighting them up further. After one complete circuit of the harbour I found myself on the western side looking down on the Mar Piccolo, and had to make my way back, across the Mar Grande, to reach the oil refineries which I had been ordered to bomb. I took a last lingering look at the cruisers and destroyers alongside in the inner harbour, but the whole of the Mar Piccolo was in shadow, and they were not easily distinguishable. I toyed with the idea of swooping low, after illuminating them with a flare or two, and scattering my bombs across their decks, but as I hesitated I saw the white wings and fuselage and tailplane of a Swordfish, two or three thousand feet below me, doing that very thing, and realized that all I would achieve was to illuminate the dive-bombing aircraft from above, silhouetting them for the guns below. Without being able to see them in that dark corner I might well endanger them if I were to follow them down and drop my bombs too. In any case, 'Streamline' had been emphatic about my obeying orders, so, reluctantly, I sped across the harbour for the oil refineries. Grabbing the voice-pipe I sang out to Grieve: 'I'm about to attack, so try to see if we score any hits,' and off we went in our dive to earth. I saw no results, but as the bombs were semi-armour-piercing any explosion would be internal, probably after they had buried themselves into the earth, and there was no point in hanging about. On my way upwards again I turned steeply to port towards the harbour to see if there was anything else I could do with my remaining flares, but the firing was still intense, which puzzled me; either all the Swordfish would have been shot down, or they would have gone home by now, and I could not imagine why they were still blazing away so ferociously, until it dawned on me that my engine was roaring away above their heads. On our way across the harbour and out to sea, I released the remaining flares, squirting them out behind me in a rude parting gesture, one by one, to encourage the Italians to expend some more useless but expensive ammunition. It was a gesture which only needed the action of pulling the plug to round it off. Then I climbed out to sea over the breakwater, and upwards into the dark, to the peace of the passage home.

All the way back to our rendezvous with the ship off Cephalonia the moon was on my starboard bow, which helped me to relax. The clouds had all dispersed and the shimmering path of watery gold, lighting up the sea's surface from the horizon to the water below us, made night flying simple. When he passed me the course to steer, Grieve asked me to leave him undisturbed so that he could check his navigation and concentrate on trying to make the ship's homing-beacon work. He was unfamiliar with it, of course, and although it was very efficient, and could reduce our return flight by many minutes, they had no similar modern radio equipment in *Eagle*, and all the way out he had tried to tune in to it for a backbearing, without success. I was content to remain in silence; I needed time to simmer down, and snugly strapped in, in my warm cockpit, in bright moonlight, and with a horizon clearly defined by two different shades of darkness, there was no need to pay more than cursory attention to the night-flying instruments.

After the last thirty minutes of bloodcurdling flying, over a man-made volcano, we both needed a breathing-space to regain our sense of proportion. About an hour had elapsed before I had to hail Grieve on the voice-pipe again; I was uneasy.

'I'm a bit worried,' I said. 'We may be the only survivors. I shall be very surprised if we are not. I doubt whether any of the torpedo or bombing pilots got away with that, and I saw nothing of Kiggell's aircraft after he had dropped that last flare on the far side of the harbour. The Eyeties may have cottoned on to the delay action of the flares and tried shooting ahead of them. They would have been very dumb if they hadn't; and if he was hit I doubt whether we would have seen it happen, amongst all those other explosions'.

'I'm afraid you are right,' said Grieve. 'But we can't do anything about it now.'

'No, but we should be thinking about what we are going to say. All the top brass will want to know exactly what happened and whether the attack was a success, and how many hits were scored, and so on, and if we are the only survivors they will expect us to know. Frankly, I saw nothing, apart from the flak, which covered the whole harbour. I couldn't see beyond it. Did you see whether Neil Kemp and company got any hits?'

'You were throwing the aircraft about like a madman, half the time, and every time I tried to look over the side, the slipstream nearly whipped off my goggles! The harbour was blanked out by ack-ack and I had to check with the compass to see which way we were facing!'

It must have been a very uncomfortable half-hour for him, crouched behind a thin canvas fuselage with all those shells whistling past. On the way back from these parties I always breathed a small prayer of thanks that I was not an observer. Their responsibilities ended at the target until it was time to go home again, and then they had to be very cool-headed and accurate, and do difficult sums. While the excitement was at its height all they could do was sit tight and pray.

We droned on for quite a time before I saw the destroyer screen in the moon's path on the sea. They stood out very clearly, although about five or six miles away; tiny little pointed silhouettes, black against the sparkling dazzle of the moon's reflection, like small corks dotted across the band of shimmering water. It was a splendid piece of navigation by Grieve without a beacon to help him. When I hailed him on the voice-pipe there was no answer and it was obvious that he had unplugged, so I waggled my wings. It was the accepted signal to an observer to plug in again.

'What is it now?' he asked, rather testily.

'Got your recognition cartridge in the pistol?' I asked, and when he said: 'Yes – what for?' I said: 'Well, pop one off now, will you please? You can go on if you like, but I'm going to land. There's the destroyer screen, down there, on the starboard side, ahead, in the path of the moon. We don't want them to start taking pot-shots at us. They may be better at it than the Eyeties!'

When the aircraft was struck down to the hangar on the lift, I wondered what we were going to say that would explain why the hangar was empty of all Swordfish except ours. When the lift reached the hangar deck, Burns and Brown leaped on to the stub-plane, as the aircraft was being pushed aft. Their faces were expressive with relief.

'When nearly all the other had got back without you, we began to think you had bought it!' Brown said, shaking his head reprovingly; then he jumped down to help push.

I craned my head round in astonishment to look aft. I saw that the hangar was stacked with aircraft, in neat rows, swarming with men, and I stood up on my parachute to stare in disbelief.

'Only three to come, sir,' said Burns cheerfully, and as he spoke we heard the thud of wheels landing on the flight-deck, and the scream of the arrester wires running through the blocks overhead. 'Belay that – only two to come!' he added happily. Grieve and I exchanged mystified glances; it was nothing short of a miracle.

'Bad news, I'm afraid, sir,' said Brown, looking up at me from the hangar deck uneasily. 'We've got to do a "major" on the aircraft during the day, to get her ready for tonight . . .'

'Tonight?' I said, my heart sinking. 'For Christ's sake, let's get some sleep before we start thinking about "tonight". You mean "tomorrow". What have we got to do tomorrow?'

'It's nearly three in the morning, sir, so I'm afraid it's "tonight", not "tomorrow". You've all got to go back to Taranto, and do it all over again.'

As we walked up the ladders to the briefing room we were both silent. Then I said: 'It looks as though we made a complete cock of it tonight, which is why we've got to go back again. But I don't see how it can be any better on a second attempt. Rather the opposite!' Grieve answered my words with a look of sickened dismay, and we went into the briefing room to face the intelligence officers and to make our report. All the others had been de-briefed and were down below in the ante-room, slaking their thirsts, and eventually we joined them. The stewards had painted a sign saying 'Welcome Home' which was hanging from the deckhead. The Paymaster-Commander thrust an enormous whisky and soda into my hands and said, 'What do you think of the welcome sign? It was done by the stewards without any prompting. All their own effort!'

I looked at him – rather bleakly, I suspect. 'I shall be more pleased to see it at this time tomorrow,' I said, and he smiled paternally.

'Drink that, and you'll feel better. Then have another. I've got a feeling in my water that none of you will be going back. Want to take a bet on it?'

That was one bet I was very relieved to lose. During the day the weather worsened and Lyster and Boyd made a signal to the C-in-C saying 'Weather conditions unsuitable for return. Taranto is your bird.'

I think most of us felt that Captain Boyd had sent up a little prayer for that storm. He was the most suitable person amongst us to do so, and the most likely to have his prayers answered.

At noon, when we had all slept, and bathed, and dressed, the news began to come through; the RAF Glenn Martins had done a good job at first light, and had taken some startling photographs, from which they deduced that one *Cavour* class battleship had been sunk, the huge *Littorio* had been hit by three torpedoes and would be out of action for many months to come, and a battleship of the *Duilio* class had been beached to prevent her sinking. Three cruisers and one destroyer had been badly damaged, and both harbours were a mass of black floating oil.

In the past, for security reasons, all our Swordfish attacks had been ascribed to the RAF. Although I am sure that the Italians knew that the attacking aircraft were from an aircraft carrier, and that our attacks were not by shore-based aircraft, it was considered wise to refrain from saying so because the fleet's speed of departure was limited; at the most we could only be thirty miles away one hour afterwards, and three hundred miles ten hours later, and it would have been a complete giveaway of the whole Fleet's position to say that any of our attacks had been done by naval aircraft. But Taranto was too big a success for this treatment, and the ship's name was household news all over the world for the next few days. Hitler ordered Goering to send his most efficient squadrons of Stuka dive-bombers to Sicily, to sink *Illustrious* at all costs, and at long last the German forces entered the war in the Mediterranean.

The rest of the Italian fleet was moved to Naples, and, as the Captain said, in a talk to the ship's company: 'We have achieved our aim.' He went on to say that in one night the ship's aircraft had achieved a greater amount of damage to the enemy than Nelson achieved in the Battle of Trafalgar, and nearly twice the amount that the entire British fleet achieved at the Battle of Jutland in the First World War. But what was more important, it was the first good news to reach the bomb-weary British since the war began. 'It will cheer the entire free world,' he said.

16
Liaison

The change in the situation in the Mediterranean after Taranto became very marked indeed, and it was immediately evident that the battle had been a turning-point in the war. Supplies to Malta, from Egypt and from Great Britain, no longer presented the same problem; arms and ammunition could be taken to Greece, with only sporadic opposition from Italian bomber pilots, who were fully occupied in Greece, trying to bolster the pathetic efforts of their hapless army. With the supplies brought from Britain the little Hellenic army was more than holding its own. In November, to the huge delight of the Albanians, who had been under Italian domination since being invaded by their bullying neighbour on the Good Friday of 1939, the Greeks managed to force the Italians back into the Albanian mountains, and on 22 November captured the Albanian town of Koritza.

Another advantage to accrue from Taranto was the new-found ability of the Fleet to bring arms and ammunition, and other vast supplies including thousands of men, to the British Army of the Middle East in Egypt. During November large forces of Australians and New Zealanders were also landed in Alexandria, en route for the desert. On 11 December Wavell captured Graziani's stronghold at Sidi Barrani, and began the wholesale destruction of the Italian legions in Libya which culminated in the capture of Benghazi two months later.

Throughout this campaign some of the seventeen Swordfish from *Eagle* flew with the Army in the Egyptian and Libyan deserts. The practice of using Swordfish in the desert had become fashionable in August, when three of *Eagle*'s Stringbags were disembarked at Dekheila while the ship was undergoing repairs from the July bombing. An RAF Blenheim crew had reported the presence of an enemy submarine and a destroyer, and two other vessels, in a little creek near Tobruk, called Bomba Bay. Armed with torpedoes and led by Captain Oliver Patch, Royal Marines, who had been flying with the Fleet Air Arm since 1937, and who later was one of *Eagle*'s bomber pilots at Taranto, the three aircraft were flown to Sidi Barrani for onward briefing. Then, flying on to Bomba Bay, Patch led the other two pilots through the mouth of the creek, after a low run-in from the sea. The submarine was at anchor inside the mouth of the creek and her crew opened fire with machine guns; so 'Ollie' Patch put a torpedo into her from a range of three hundred yards, sinking her at once. The other two pilots, Lieutenants Cheeseman and Wellham, flew on, and sank a depot ship at anchor.

Later, the desert Swordfish were used for dive-bombing attacks on enemy tanks, and were successful at this too. They were armed with special anti-tank bombs which had a very long nose-fuse, so that they exploded on the surface on immediate contact, and not after burying themselves in the sand.

A Swordfish back from the desert became easily recognizable because few managed to retain their tail-wheels, which were liable to be wrenched off when landing in soft sand. In its place a form of desert tail-skid was improvised, entailing some rather heavy strengthening of the tail-bay; but this additional weight was compensated for by the removal of the arrester hook assembly, which was only needed when the aircraft was required for use in carriers.

Airframe spares for Swordfish were virtually unobtainable from Britain at this time, because the main Fleet Air Arm stores depot had been based in Coventry, and on 14 November that great city had been heavily bombed and the stores depot completely destroyed. The effects of this were felt by Swordfish squadrons all over the world.

After the loss of Williamson, Neil Kemp assumed temporary command of the squadron until Lieutenant-Commander John de F. Jago arrived on board to take over from Neil. Like Williamson he had been away from flying, too, and we spent all our evenings at Dekheila doing night formations until he was in practice again, instead of going ashore.

During one of those night formations over Dekheila, Jackie Jago gave me permission to take up a Polish colonel whom I had met in Alexandria. After an earlier trip in daylight the Pole was keen to repeat the experience in the dark. It seems a weird wish to cherish but the Poles are a strange race of people.

Before we took off, Ken Griffiths, the telegraphist air gunner, showed the Pole how to clip the observer-type parachute pack to the front of his harness, in case of emergency, and how to pull the ripcord. This is ordinary, everyday drill for any passenger who is unfamiliar with Swordfish. Somehow we managed to get it across to him that the pack is only buttoned on when a state of emergency actually exists: no observer or passenger could sit in comfort in the rear cockpit with that cumbersome object under his chin. The Pole's English was not very good, but he grinned and nodded his head to show that he understood.

When formating on another aircraft in the dark it is impossible for the pilot to know where he is in relation to the ground, or to take more than an occasional glance at his aircraft instruments. His eyes must remain glued to the leader, and to stay in position it is necessary to adjust the throttle settings constantly. At about five thousand feet in V formation I was on Jackie's immediate righthand side and had been tucked in quite happily for about half an hour when there was a series of explosions and my engine disintegrated. Pieces of red-hot cylinder kept shooting past my head in the most alarming way, and I gather that from the ground the engine looked like a Catherine Wheel.

Alexandria was blacked out, of course, though I could see the dimmed lights of traffic below me, right ahead, but at first I was not sure whether I was over the land or the sea. Fortunately the explosion had been seen and heard, not only at Dekheila but by most of the ship's officers in the harbour, and the flare-path lights came on almost at once. I was relieved to find that I was right over the harbour itself, and within easy gliding distance of the airfield.

I hailed the TAG on the voice-pipe. 'Clip the parachute pack to the Pole's harness,' I said. 'There's a chance that the other cylinders will break up too – they are all red hot – and we might catch fire. Put your own on, too.'

Without an engine I had to concentrate on making an accurate glide approach without undershooting, and after that brief conversation the aircraft went through a short period of turbulence, which I assumed was the hot air rising from the ship's funnels below. For a few moments 'Q' for 'Queenie' bounced about, and shuddered violently, and I had quite a struggle to keep control; but then it passed, and we settled down again, and with plenty of height to play with, it was quite a simple forced landing to make. At the end of my landing run I undid my straps and stood up on my parachute to apologize to the Pole and to explain that we would have to sit there and wait to be towed in, but to my amazement he was not there. The air gunner was alone in the cockpit.

'Where's the Pole?' I asked.

'He baled out,' said Ken Griffiths, phlegmatically. 'I tried to stop him, but the minute I clipped on his parachute he was off! We fought like mad for a few minutes – I thought you would have felt it going on – but I couldn't restrain him, and I was afraid that he was making it difficult for you, so I let him go. We had told him that parachutes were only worn in a state of emergency, and with all those bits of red-hot iron whizzing past his ears, he reckoned that it was time to go!'

That accounted for the period of turbulence; it was the TAG struggling with the Pole.

'He must have come down in the sea,' I said. 'We'd better get a boat and go after him, before he drowns!'

'I don't think you need worry,' said Ken. 'His parachute opened up all right, and it was floodlit by the flames from the engine for a bit. He went down looking like an exhibition at an air display, lit up by searchlights. The whole of Alexandria must have seen it – and heard it. I bet all those Gyppoes have rushed to the nearest air raid shelter, thinking there was a raid on!'

In fact his dramatic descent had been seen by a very large audience, and there was nearly a nasty collision between all the ships' boats which rushed to his rescue.

The Poles are a very demonstrative race. I expected him to be angry with me for exposing him to so much danger; but afterwards, whenever I met him by chance, in the streets of Alexandria, he embarrassed me enormously by insisting on kissing me on both cheeks. I dislike being kissed by my own sex at all times, but Polish colonels in three-cornered hats are difficult to stop when they bear down on one in public thoroughfares. It is less likely to arouse public interest if one submits gracefully.

One of the most interesting officers on board *Illustrious* was Arthur Sowman, the Paymaster Lieutenant-Commander in charge of ship's stores. He had attacked me about the missing Irvine Flying Jackets when we first embarked at Plymouth, but when I had told him the whole story he became a staunch ally, and was very good at writing fobbing-off letters.

'There will be a day of reckoning,' he warned me, 'but perhaps you will have been bumped off, or taken prisoner by then, in which case we can write them off as a bad debt.'

He had a long bent nose, which had been battered in many rugby scrums and in boxing rings, ever since his Dartmouth days; and he was a quiet retiring sort of chap with a devastating sense of humour lurking in the background. He had been Captain Boyd's secretary at Vernon, but when a new Captain's secretary was appointed for the *Illustrious* commission, he opted for the job of 'nuts and bolts' in order to stay with Denis Boyd, knowing that if and when Boyd was promoted to Rear-Admiral, once again he would become his secretary.

Towards the end of December he asked me quite casually how much of the squadron's stores I had disembarked to Dekheila. 'I take it you have a "ready use" store there, for your use when the squadron is disembarked?'

'Yes,' I said, 'but I keep the minimum there. We can always come back to the ship if we want anything sizeable, like a spare engine or an airscrew.'

'I think you should work it the other way round,' he said. 'Keep on board only the day-to-day things you require, like cleaning gear and that sort of thing.'

'Why?' I asked. 'Do you think the ship is going to be sunk or something?'

He shook his head. 'No, but the war is shifting about the Med, in the desert, and Greece, and so on. The squadrons might be required to disembark – to join *Eagle*'s boys in the desert for example – and if you had to fly off from the middle of the Mediterranean you would have to leave behind all the heavy things you will need most, like trolley-acks, and torpedo trolleys, and sheer-legs. If you like I will get my supply assistants to make a list of what they think you should keep on board, and you can disembark the rest. They will help with the offloading. We'll do it tomorrow morning while we remember.'

It made good sense to me, and the next morning, when I was busy hoisting out heavy crates of gear into lighters, I saw that the other squadrons were doing the same. The stores were ferried ashore and taken in trucks to the store-rooms at Dekheila, where they were kept under the watchful eye of Paymaster-Commander

'Lucy' Waters, an enormous red-faced ex-hooker from the Navy scrum. He and the ship's Master-at-Arms, Mr Luddington, had done battle for the Navy at Twickenham for many years, as front-row forwards. Luddington had been capped for England thirteen times and was the managing director of a famous firm of brewers in Portsmouth, where he employed many retired naval officers, including – according to rumour – one retired admiral. In 1939 he had been called up from the reserve and sent as the 'Jaunty' of *Illustrious*: but his deportment on board was immaculate, and he gave no sign of this interesting and superior background – except perhaps at the Captain's Table, when he couldn't bear to hear a defaulter giving what was obviously very false evidence. On those occasions he was inclined to lean over the table in front of the Captain and say: 'You bloody liar!' which always brought a sharp reproof from Captain Boyd.

It was thoughtful of Arthur Sowman to persuade us to land so much equipment. Being close to the Captain he sensed trouble ahead and had a pretty shrewd idea of the odds the ship was about to face; but it was clever of him to organize this massive offloading without alarming any of us. By taking his advice we saved most of our equipment and were able to keep going for the next few months on our own in some very outlandish areas, where spares and tools, and heavy equipment, would have been unobtainable. Without his guidance a number of us might not have survived, through lack of spares, and essential supplies, and consequent aircraft unserviceability.

Within a fortnight of this prudent thinking by Sowman nearly half the ship's company were killed, including Mr Luddington, when German bombers began the process of tearing the ship apart. It began on 10 January and during that fearsome day, and the two terrible weeks which followed when *Illustrious* was alongside in Malta's Grand Harbour under constant attack, day and night, Arthur Sowman saved many lives. He remained cool and imperturbably cheerful, in circumstances which no human being could have anticipated, and which I sincerely hope no man will ever have to face again.

17
The Fearful Day

On 10 January 1941, in company with the entire Fleet, *Illustrious* was to escort a big convoy through the Skerki Channel bound for Malta and Greece. From the flying programme I saw that I was to do the inner anti-submarine patrol in the morning, when we were due to meet the convoy in bomb alley, taking off at 0830 and landing at 1230 when the next patrol was to be flown off.

Because I had to search five-mile stretches of sea in front of the destroyer screen, and would be in sight of the Fleet and the ship, I was not being provided with an observer. Ken Griffiths would man the radio and the Lewis gun, and it was known that I liked to use the Aldis lamp myself in the front cockpit.

From the programme I saw that the Fulmars of 806 Squadron had a big day ahead, too; and that Lieutenant Michael ('Tiffy') Torrens-Spence, the Senior Pilot in 819 Squadron, would be doing the outer Swordfish patrol, out of sight of the Fleet, with a full crew.

I strolled out on to the quarter-deck for my after-breakfast cigarette, which is always the best moment of the day for me. Standing right aft, under the overhang of the deck above, bathed in warm early morning Mediterranean sunshine, I was looking over the ship's burbling wake piling up astern in great frothy waves. HMS *Gallant* was astern about three miles away, a destroyer which had been stationed on our port quarter since we left Alexandria. She was much too far astern and was trying to catch up. Her bow-wave was a fine sight, cleaving through that serene blue sea, throwing a continuous white spume into the air.

Torrens-Spence joined me and we stood admiring the destroyer.

'She has probably been doing a stern-chase during the night,' he said, 'and is trying to get back on station. She is doing well over thirty knots.'

As we stood looking at the destroyer she broke into two pieces and the fo'c'sle sank at once, leaving the bulk of the ship wallowing on the surface like an open-ended tin box. A second or two later we heard the dull thud of the explosion. Immediately, the *Illustrious* began a slow turn to starboard to allow some of the destroyers to race to the aid of the damaged ship and yet remain ahead of the carrier.

'God! What a horrid sight,' I said. Tiffy agreed, but was already analysing what had happened.

'She was going too fast to have been torpedoed, so it must have been a mine. But the channel should have been swept before the convoy comes through. Perhaps that was "the one that got away!" I hope there aren't many more scudding about, because it's going to be difficult enough, today, without the additional hazard of mines.'

I glanced up at him – he is very tall – and asked him what he meant. 'Do you think that the Eyeties are going to put up much opposition? They've been pretty quiet since the eleventh of November.'

'Its not the Italians I'm worried about, it's the bloody Germans,' he said morosely. 'They are going to steal the show today, didn't you know?'

'I didn't even know that they were taking part in the war out here,' I said dumbly. 'When did this happen?'

Being the Senior Pilot of his squadron, and a Flight-Commander, he would be shown signals which never came my way.

He laughed, but his laughter contained no merriment.

'As a result of all that publicity over Taranto, Mussolini has asked Hitler to come to his aid. They want to sink *Illustrious*. The convoy is important too; now that Germany is moving forces to the Med this is probably our last chance to get supplies through to Malta and Greece. The Hun now has a complete Fliegerkorps based in Sicily, and we are going to see them in action today, and we shall be their target.' He looked down at me and I saw that he was a very worried man. 'There are well over three hundred aircraft in a Fliegerkorps, and most of them are Stuka dive-bombers. The maddening thing is that we are their prime target and there is no need for us to be here at all . . .'

'But we have got to escort the convoy through bomb alley, surely?'

'Yes, but we could do it quite comfortably with the ship out of range of the German aircraft . . .'

'Then why don't we?'

'Boyd and Lyster made a signal to the C-in-C pointing out that there was no need for *Illustrious* to be brought into range of the Stukas and that 806 Squadron is down to only half a dozen or so serviceable fighters. They have had a rough passage lately.'

'What was the C-in-C's reaction to that?'

'He said that the morale of the Fleet is always so high when *Illustrious* is in sight that he could not answer for the consequences if we were not, and that we were to remain on station.'

'But the sailors would see the aircraft operating and would know that the ship was still around somewhere. Their captains could tell them what was going on?'

'Precisely,' said Tiffy. 'But what they don't understand is that the ship is only a floating platform from which we operate, and if that platform is damaged or sunk they will lose not only their immediate protection from the air, but all air cover throughout the Med. It's pretty basic, really.' He shook his head incredulously. 'What the C-in-C's reply really meant was "Shut up – stick to your orders – don't argue – get on with the job".'

'It seems very strange,' I murmured, doubtfully.

'Well,' said Tiffy, 'perhaps you can see why the mining we have just seen is only the beginning. This is a day you will never forget. You can thank your lucky stars that you are flying this morning, and not sitting in the hangar at action stations.'

I must have been exceptionally dull that morning, because I can remember running up my engine and taking off with a comparatively easy mind, even though Tiffy Spence was one of the most intelligent people on board and not given to making wild statements. After I had climbed to my station ahead of the Fleet I began my submarine hunt without thinking about Tiffy's conversation for more than a few seconds at a time, when I glanced upwards apprehensively; but the cloudless sky was quite clear. Time passed slowly, in silence, for the first half-hour. The TAG and I seldom spoke. He was a man of few words and was always busy, and I had no observer to bother about – I thought – until an educated voice came through the Gosport Tubes and startled me out of my wits.

'I think you should fly on a more north-easterly course to keep parallel with the destroyer screen, sir,' said the voice. 'In my opinion we are a little too close to the Fleet.'

'Who the hell are you?' I asked.

'Midshipman Wallington, sir,' he said primly, as though I was a half-wit to ask such a stupid question.

In the front cockpit I conjured up a face – thin features, and a rather anxious expression. A nice young man from the other squadron.

'I'm sorry to have to tell you – you are not only in the wrong aircraft, but you're in the wrong squadron!' I said.

'This is "Q" for "Queenie", isn't it?'

'Yes, but it's 815's, not 819's. If you are the observer of 819's "Q" for "Queenie" you should be flying behind Denman Whatley.'

There was a pause and the boy said, 'Well, who are you, sir?' and I told him, and there was another prolonged silence. Then he apologized and said: 'I must have climbed into the wrong aircraft by mistake. Can you take me back to the ship?'

'I'm afraid not,' I said. 'I've got to remain on patrol until landing at 12.30, when the next lot take-off. The *Illustrious* wouldn't turn into wind just for one cab, unless it was an emergency landing.'

At 12.30 I was in the waiting position over the port quarter of *Illustrious*, watching her turn into wind. She flew off the Swordfish for the anti-submarine patrols, and a gaggle of Fulmars. 'Haggis' Russell, the Deck Landing Control Officer, was in his accustomed position by the 4.5-gun turrets on the port side of the flight-deck, waving his yellow bats and I started my approach. I had jettisoned my bombs in accordance with orders – we were never allowed to land-on with live bombs, in case the jerk of the arrester-hook catching a wire caused them to drop from the bomb-racks and explode on the flight-deck – and the TAG had set the depth-charge to 'safe'. This was carried between the undercarriage legs, like a bird carrying an egg, and was quite safe unless one landed in the sea, when, although it was set to 'safe', it would blow up at a certain depth. As I turned gently to port with my arrester-hook down, Haggis suddenly disappeared from sight in a great burst of smoke from all the 4.5-guns under his feet; but even then I was not aware that anything was wrong. We often took off and landed with all the ship's guns firing.

Banking a little more to port I straightened up to approach the round-down of the flight-deck, on my up-wind leg, and saw that the after-lift was down. It would be up by the time I got there, or Haggis would wave me round again. Then a strange aircraft came into view, flying from port to starboard, right in front of me, across the flight-deck. Its huge swastika was painted red on the starboard side of the grey fuselage. As I pressed the trigger of my Vickers gun, the Stuka was right ahead in my sights, but it dipped as though in salute and dropped an enormous great bomb right down the after-lift well, which was still gaping. The bomb looked like a GPO pillar-box, painted black. By the flames which shot out of the hole in the deck I realized that it had exploded in the hangar. Then the lift itself burst out of the deck and shot a few feet into the air and sank back into the lift-well on its side, like a great wedge-shaped hunk of cheese.

The first Stuka was followed by another, flying right through the barrage, dipping down low over the flight-deck, and then soaring past the funnel; and with my right thumb pressed on the trigger of the gun I opened the throttle wide and jinked to starboard and went round again.

It all happened so fast that I had reacted instinctively, and had no time to think 'we are being attacked' until right in the middle of it, which was probably a good thing.

The next short period of time might have been ten minutes or twenty, or even sixty – I have no idea how long we battled for survival. When every second is packed with feverish activity, time has no meaning. Ten seconds can seem like an hour and a minute can be a lifetime. From the moment I opened the throttle and climbed to starboard I was amongst the Stukas – without the option – and although they were travelling at lightning speed, the spectacle of a sitting duck, spitting fire from both ends, was too provoking for the Germans, and some of them paused for a pot-shot before speeding back to Sicily; a quick climbing turn, a half-roll and a short dive – and they expected to find me sitting in their sights waiting to be shot down. Staggering along at about a hundred feet above the sea, but well out to starboard of the ship, to avoid them I had to spin the aircraft like a top, in tight little circles at the point of stall, so that the fuselage and wings were hanging sideways from the propeller. In heaven-sent intervals between attacks, only by easing the stick forward and kicking on opposite rudder did I manage to stay in the air. The throttle was at maximum setting all the time, and I had my thumb pressed on the firing button almost continuously, yet after the fourth attack I found that I was only a few hundred yards ahead of the ship's position, though about a mile away to starboard. Our progress over the water had been minimal, and the Stukas must have thought that they were attacking some weird sort of hovering flying bedstead which could spin round within its own wing-span.

There was no time to speak to either of the two in the rear cockpit, but through the back of my head I could feel them firing the Lewis gun and was surprised that they weren't blacking-out in those ghastly tight turns. It was essential to get away from the ship, because I was receiving more punishment than I was dishing out; sprays of bullet-holes and great gashes in the wings were appearing everywhere, and one line of bullets, which had started at the trailing edge of my starboard lower mainplane, had ended by shooting away the red handle of the locking-pin which kept the wings from folding, and at any moment I expected the starboard wings to fold; but it must have been only the handle that was shot away. The wings remained locked in the spread position – thank God.

In a lull between those desperate turns I managed a quick look upwards to see where all the Stukas were coming from, and saw several clusters in tight formation, circling very high in the sky, like wasps awaiting their turn to dive on a pot of jam. I saw them peeling off, one by one; tiny objects, their wings glinting in the sun. They rolled away from the formation slowly – almost casually – as though they were taking part in some air display, and had all the time in the world. As each silvery dot sped downwards, it grew bigger with every fraction of a second, and its dive became more steep until it was a huge blob of an aeroplane with a swastika on its side, diving vertically through the ship's barrage. Their flying was very skilled, and they pressed home their attacks with no thought for their own safety. The difference between the Germans' methods and those of the Italians could never have been demonstrated more clearly. They had only one bomb per aircraft, so they had to come right down to deliver it personally. Since it was enormous – it weighed 500 kg – their determination not to waste their one big egg was understandable. They began their pull-out at about five thousand feet, when they had built up their speed to the maximum, from a ten-thousand-foot start, and they released their bomb while still diving, at about five hundred feet, so that it followed after them with sickening accuracy. The Stuka was an ugly aircraft to look at, but it was damn good at its job.

Because the first bomb had been neatly planted down the after-lift and had exploded inside the hangar, the blast effect was upwards and outwards, under the flight-deck. It was sufficiently powerful to bend all three hundred tons of the forward-lift into a parabola and all the armoured properties of the flight-deck, which had been the Navy's pride, and the pride of Vickers-Armstrong's yard, were destroyed at once. Thereafter, in addition to many near-misses which damaged the ship's steering machinery and bent her keel, three more armour-piercing bombs went through the three-inch Czechslovakian steel flight-deck as though it wasn't there – or was made of cardboard. Being fully armour-piercing, some of them penetrated the deck of the hangar too, before exploding below it, in the wardroom. One RAF officer who had come with us as an interested spectator was unable to take any further interest: sitting in the ante-room, with all that hullabaloo going on outside, he must have thought himself reasonably secure from danger. Later, he was found sitting in a scorched arm-chair, headless, but still clutching an open copy of *The Times* in both hands.

The wardroom stanchions of tubular steel, about as thick as the average lamp-post, were twisted into spirals like ornamental candles; yet the wardroom clock was still ticking away, keeping accurate time. The effect of blast is always incalculable. It can kill a man yet only rustle the flowers in a vase.

Worse things were happening in the hangar – some of them indescribable. Men lying with their brains spilling on to the deck were commonplace. From my cockpit, ahead of the ship, I thought that I could imagine what it must have been like; but nobody could visualize that horror unless they had listened to first-hand descriptions as I had to do, weeks afterwards, ad nauseam, to let the poor devils get it off their chests. I had often tried to visualize it in advance, when sitting inside the hangar with Dick Janvrin. Whenever the alarm for action stations was sounded-off, all air departments officers who were unlucky enough not to be flying had to close-up in the hangar until the party was over – why, I shall never know, because it was the one place where certain death awaited everyone if a bomb exploded within the confines of that metal casket. As well as housing all the inflammable aircraft, containing hundreds of gallons of high-octane fuel, and thousands of rounds of live ammunition, the sides were stacked with 'ready-use' torpedoes and other objects like depth-charges, on which we sat, trying to read a book, because there was no duty to perform until the worst occurred, when we were supposed to be able to put out fires. Dick and I always searched for a space on the deck which was not immediately underneath a heavy crate in the overhead stowages, containing a spare engine or airscrew, because we agreed that we would rather be blown up by the torpedo on which we were sitting than be crushed under some heavy crate. We had to sit inside, unable to see what was happening, listening to the barrel-organ music of the six multiple pom-poms grinding out their barrage; and the continuous bark of the sixteen 4.5s, not to mention the chatter of the twenty-nine close-range guns, all doing their best to drown the voice of the Reverend Henry Lloyd saying '. . . a bomb is falling and I think it is going to miss our port quarter – yes – (BOOM!) it has!' It seemed so silly, to close us up in the centre of an inflammable drum, with nothing to do except wait for the inevitable.

For once, fact was much worse than fantasy. When the first bomb exploded after bouncing off the lift, all the metal fire-screen curtains were down, dividing the hangar into three separate 'fire-proof' compartments. When subjected to a blast which was capable of bending a three hundred-ton lift they were useless and disintegrated at once, bursting apart in masses of red-hot steel splinters about three or four feet long, which tore through every obstruction, setting all the aircraft on fire which weren't already burning as a result of the explosion itself, and decapitating anyone standing in the way. Poor Neil Kemp was killed by one of them immediately. He had been standing in the centre of the hangar talking to Jackie Jago when the first sudden explosion occurred. Jackie found himself facing a headless body, which was all that was left of a fine chap who would have made a wonderful admiral had he lived. Even in death Neil refused to lie down, until Jackie gave his grim remains a little push.

The people in the hangar threw themselves on their faces on the steel deck to let everything pass over them. The bullets from the burning aircraft were whizzing round and round the hangar like hundreds of rubber balls being fired into an enclosed squash court, and nobody could stay in the hangar and live. The heat was quite unsupportable, and noxious fumes were escaping from exploding oxygen chambers, and from the burning acid of batteries. The unfortunate men inside seized the first opportunity to rush out of the hangar through the airtight doors to the comparative safety of the battery-space outside; but after the first bomb there were very few left alive to do so.

After that day new ships were fitted with 'Fearnought' fire-retardant curtains.

After the first attack, few of the ship's decks were recognizable, and below the flight-deck there was just a gaping shell with dead bodies plastered against the bulkheads wherever one looked. Surgeon-Commander Keevil was indefatigable. Apparently his nerves were on holiday, because he was as calm and collected as though he was dealing out medicines from his dispensary at an ordinary sick-parade. For the next fortnight, in Malta, when the attacks on the ship were almost continuous, according to one eyewitness he ate snatched meals and slept for a few moments when he could, and never ceased to tend the wounded and the dying, the maimed and the burned, for which he was awarded the DSO. Many of those who owed their lives to him felt that he deserved the VC.

Another DSO which was greeted with shouts of delight by the surviving sailors was awarded to the Reverend Henry Lloyd, whose cheerful voice between explosions kept insanity at bay; and any number of people have told me how they were encouraged by Arthur Sowman, who appeared like some genie from a magician's bottle wherever a bomb exploded, saying: 'Come on chaps, man the hoses, let's put this fire out . . .' as calmly as if he were encouraging a rugby team from the touch-line. For his efforts he was awarded a Mention in Despatches, which is often referred to as 'the poor man's VC'.

Mr Luddington, the Master-at-Arms, knew that the hangar was a raging inferno where men were dying in droves, and because he was a very big, tough chap, he must have thought that perhaps he could haul someone to safety. Whatever his reasons, his body was found in the hangar, where I doubt if he had ever set foot before. He had been asphyxiated by the fumes and very badly burned.

All this happened within the first few minutes. Flying around the fore-end of the flight-deck, feeling immeasurably sad at the sight of the running battle, I saw dozens of men rushing about the flight-deck with hoses. Around them the 753-foot length and the 93-foot breadth of iron deck was a mass of steam; the heat from the hangar below immediately turned water into vapour as soon as it touched the hot steel beneath their scorched feet. But all the ship's guns were blazing away, and I was in danger of being shot down by them, and in any case I was probably in their way. I felt as though I were deserting my home and the people I loved when they were in peril, but there was nothing to be gained by staying, so I turned to the north-east in the vague direction of Malta and concentrated on trying to keep the aircraft stable. The inboard end of the starboard lower mainplane had parted from the fuselage and was hanging by its struts and flying wires, suspended from the top mainplane, and the aircraft had become heavy to handle and needed a lot of opposite aileron. But she was still airworthy, and I yelled down the tube to my impromptu observer, 'Give me a course for Malta, will you, please?'

'I can't,' he said, almost in a whisper. 'The Bigsworth Board is floating about in petrol.'

'Petrol? In the rear cockpit? What are you talking about?'

'It's true,' he said. 'I'm up to my knees in it. So is the air gunner.'

I was about to say, 'Why the hell didn't you tell me before?' but acknowledged to myself that there hadn't been very much time for conversation. The poor devils in the back must have been feeling very sick, with petrol splashing into their faces. I peered at the fuel indicator, which in a Swordfish is buried away over the engine a long way from the cockpit and can only be seen through a hole in the dashboard, put there for that purpose. It should have been reading about 80 gallons, but, as I looked, I saw the figure 48 change to 47, and then 46, and knew that we would have to ditch in the sea quickly. Under normal conditions the indicator revolved very slowly, but now the petrol was pouring out, and there was real danger that we might explode in a sheet of flame at any second – if the engine didn't cut first. Our main tank must have been hit, perhaps by a piece of shrapnel from the Fleet's gunnery, or perhaps from the cannon-fire of the Stukas, or both. It was going to be difficult to find a clear patch of sea to land on because its entire surface – wherever I looked – was a forest of splashes – everywhere – little spurts of water about eight or ten feet high which looked like watery Christmas trees. Every gun in the Fleet was firing into the heavens directly overhead, and all the shell splinters were falling back into the sea from ten thousand feet – thousands upon thousands of them. It was an amazing sight, as though under the surface a battle of sea monsters was taking place, and the Mediterranean had gone mad.

'Pass me the Aldis lamp,' I shouted to the Midshipman, and when he had thrust it over my shoulder I flashed at a destroyer which was on our port bow. When she answered I made: 'Am ditching. Please recover,' and to my delight I was given the letter 'R', meaning 'Message received', and I saw her turning into wind and the hands running down the deck to man the falls and lower a boat. I did a gentle turn to port – it was unsafe to turn the other way with only one out of two wings serviceable – and saw that another Swordfish was formating on my port quarter. I wondered how long it had been there. Then I saw its letter, marked on the tail 'Q' for 'Queenie', and despite the helmet and goggles recognized Denman Whatley's grinning features.

'Wallington,' I yelled, 'how long has Whatley been there?'

'He's just arrived. I think he is hoping that we will guide him to Malta as he hasn't got an observer.'

I looked across again, and Whatley shook his fist in a humorous way, pointing to his observer in my rear cockpit. I waved him away but he just sat there grinning. Being on my port side he was unable to see that my starboard wing was about to drop off. Nor could he know that the pair in the rear cockpit were standing knee-deep in petrol.

'Wave him away,' I shouted in the voice-pipe. 'Both of you. We are about to ditch. Point at the sea and give him the thumbs-down sign – do anything – but get rid of him. Point in the direction of Malta – if he follows us down he will end up in the sea himself.'

I had never ditched an aircraft before. With a fixed under-carriage we would somersault on to our backs if the wheels touched first. But with all that petrol in the rear cockpit we were tail-heavy, which was a help. The starboard wing was now only hanging by a spider's web and would break away altogether at any moment. I prayed that it would stay with me for a few more seconds. We were flying on our port ailerons only, with a little help from the starboard top wing, and the aircraft was very heavy to handle. I did a wide shallow turn to port, astern of the destroyer – their whaler was just touching the water, I was glad to see – and came in as low as I dared so that if the wing did drop off we hadn't far to fall. Straightening up, I began the up-wind approach and throttled back gently and eased the nose up, and up, and up, and then closed the throttle altogether so that we were gliding and the sea was rushing past very near, and it was time to ease the nose up a little more to keep the wheels in the air. In her last few moments of life 'Q' for 'Queenie' gave a little sigh as she stalled and did a perfect belly-flop, and we slid through the water for a second and the wheels sank in deep and the tail came up-and-up-and up – and then my face was in the sea and it felt as though we had hit a brick wall.

The last few seconds were rather violent because the heavy engine went straight down until she was floating by the wings. Just before the sea poured into the cockpit I caught a fleeting glimpse of

Whatley's wheels just missing the water, and heard him open the throttle wide and climb away just in time. Over my head before being swamped I saw two pairs of legs and feet, and two shapeless forms, catapulting in a neat parabola through the air, and two simultaneous splashes about twenty yards ahead. 'That'll teach them to do up their jock-straps in future!' I thought.

I undid my straps, clinging to the sides of the cockpit, which were pointing downwards, and climbed out, standing on the trailing edge of the port lower mainplane. All Swordfish have a life-raft tucked into the port wing which should inflate automatically when immersed in water. An oxygen cylinder is there for that purpose. Ours had only half inflated, but while the air gunner and the Midshipman swam back to the aircraft I hauled the rest of the rubber dinghy out of the wing and was relieved to see that it inflated as I pulled. 'Good old Brown,' I thought, 'he will be glad to hear that his gear worked, right up the last ditch!' Then I pushed the dinghy into the sea and climbed in.

The destroyer was drifting off to port but her whaler was approaching slowly – her crew were rowing very badly – their oars were dipping in and out in any old fashion, and some of the men were 'catching crabs' and rolling back on their thwarts with shouts of laughter. I realized that they were all slightly hysterical after being bombed for the last hour. The aircraft was sinking fairly fast and I saw that the dinghy was attached to the port wing by a thin cord. My two swimmers rolled into the little craft and lay gasping; I tore the cord away and gave the wing a push and we slid across the sea's surface for a few feet, and it was at the precise moment that I remembered the depth-charge – with a sickening feeling of dismay. Although set to 'safe' it would explode at a certain depth – I had no idea how deep – or how much time we had. I looked round at the destroyer and saw the Captain's head on the bridge, watching the proceedings through his binoculars. The big chrome letters of the ship's name – HMS *Juno* – were gleaming in the bright sun, and I thought, 'He's not going to be very pleased in a minute, when his whaler and crew are blown sky-high because of the stupidity of the crew they have come to rescue!'

We grabbed the sides of the boat and rolled in, and the rubber dinghy slid away under our feet. The coxswain of the whaler was keen to recover it, but I said, 'No – let it go – come on, get going . . .' and I took over from the surprised man and stood up in the stern-sheets and said: 'Come on, row, you silly buggers – pull

together – in – out – in – out – in – out – one – two – pull together –
in – out . . .' and I kept it up, all the way back, until we were under
the scrambling net dangling over the ship's side.

The Midshipman and the air gunner were looking at me with
expressions of marked disapproval. I could not say why I was in
such a hurry or the men might have panicked and their rowing
would have been even worse. The temptation to grab that rope net
and scramble to safety was almost overwhelming, but because I
had led them into danger, and was the only man amongst them
who knew that danger existed, I had to be the last out of the boat,
and I yelled at them to hurry. When they were all out and
scrambling up the ship's side I leaped on to it, breathing heavily.
Never have I been so glad to get out of a boat, before or since. Now
poor old 'Q' for 'Queenie' could blow up whenever she liked.

The gallant old aircraft had held on for as long as she could, but
her final death-throes erupted as I climbed up the net. I felt the
ship heel over with the shock, and the ear-splitting cacophony
behind me pushed me flat against the steel hull. Over my shoulder
I saw a huge mountain of water cascading into the air, much too
close for comfort. But while turning my head to look I caught a
glimpse of something even more astounding; while heaving myself
up the net I had been looking at one of *Juno*'s ratings, standing on
the upper deck peering down at me. He was not wearing a cap and
as the sea erupted behind me I saw every hair on his head stand on
end! It might have been the blast from the explosion but I don't
think that it was. I firmly believe that I have actually seen a man's
hair rise from his scalp with fright, before flopping down again,
and it is a sight I shall always remember.

Perhaps as a delayed form of relief, the spectacle of the man's
hair standing on end sent me into a fit of hysterical giggles. I was
still trying vainly not to laugh when I arrived on the bridge to face
the Captain. Lieutenant-Commander Sir St John R. J. Tyrwhitt,
Bart, Royal Navy, was a typical destroyer man, with lean, clear-
cut features, which were showing no signs of amusement what-
sover. The explosion must have startled him too.

'I wish you Fleet Air Arm people would remember your depth-
charges before you ditch an aircraft, instead of frightening the lives
out of the ship's companies who are good enough to come to your
rescue!' he said, tartly. 'If you paid more attention to your own
affairs instead of behaving in an officious manner in their boat, it
would be much more seamanlike and much better manners!'

I was choking in my attempts to stop laughing and couldn't answer for a second or two.

'What do you find so amusing?' I was asked, very coldly.

'I'm terribly sorry, sir,' I said. 'You see, it was because I remembered the depth-charge that I felt it necessary to take over your boat's crew. But – I have just seen one of your ratings' hair stand on end – when the depth-charge blew up his hair went straight up too . . .'

'I'm not surprised,' said St John Tyrwhitt. 'If you'd been up here with me you would have seen mine do the same, I expect.'

At the time he was not in the least amused; but I managed to persuade him to laugh about it later.

18
The Aftermath

The next two weeks were most interesting, but rather confused. HMS *Juno* was scheduled to accompany the convoy all the way to Athens, but after steaming two hundred miles to the east, as one of a powerful escort for several big merchant ships, an SOS was broadcast by the cruiser *Southampton*, off Malta, and *Juno* was detached to go to her aid.

Although *Illustrious* had been the Stuka's main target, on 11 January they had managed to strike at almost every ship in the Fleet, and the *Southampton* had been set on fire. For six hours her crew wrestled with the flames, but without assistance they were fighting a losing battle. We raced back at top speed, but we heard that her officers and men had been taken off, and the cruiser had been sunk by gunfire from our own ships. So, *Juno* turned about, and sailed eastwards again, to Crete, anchoring in Suda Bay a day later.

While we had been with the convoy we had been closed-up at action stations almost continuously. Wave after wave of enemy aircraft bombed the cargo ships and it was obvious that future convoys were going to be horribly vulnerable without the aircraft from a carrier to defend them. Anti-aircraft fire from surface vessels was a poor defence against a determined enemy, attacking from the air. The German bombers selected only those which contained fighter aircraft for Greece: none of the other merchantmen were attacked. Either the enemy's intelligence was very good indeed, or there had been some very careless talk at home when the ships were loaded.

At anchor in the shelter of the high snow-capped hills at Suda Bay, for the first time for some weeks the *Juno*'s officers and men were able to relax, and the Captain came down to the wardroom for lunch. It was my first opportunity to thank him properly for rescuing us, and I apologized again for nearly blowing up his ship. He told me that before *Illustrious* disappeared in a cloud of smoke in the direction of Malta he had managed to flash a message to her saying 'Swordfish crew of three recovered'.

'They were fully occupied with their own problems and I didn't waste time passing names,' he said.

Thinking about this I was only mildly anxious. When the ship was blazing from end to end, stacked with ammunition, and with tanks carrying thousands of gallons of high-octane petrol ready to explode in flames at any moment, I doubted whether anyone on board *Illustrious* would have had time to worry about which aircrew had been saved and which lost. From *Juno*'s decks that afternoon I had watched the great ship, listing heavily to port in a cloud of smoke and flame, and flying the signals warning all other ships that she was out of control; her steering-gear had been damaged and she was wallowing in wide circles in a desperate attempt to reach Malta before nightfall. Miraculously, her main engines were undamaged. With all that smoke and flame, and with the ship's guns firing at the Stukas, she was a target the enemy could see for many miles; and they did their utmost to sink her before she reached the protection of the harbour defences. At such a time my survival was insignificant, when 83 men had been killed and 100 injured.

'I'm surprised that they had time to take your message, sir,' I said, 'but I think the fact that you said "Three" may have puzzled them, if they have been able to think about it since then.' I explained about Wallington's mistake. 'Nobody on board will know that he was flying in my aircraft. They thought that I was accompanied only by the air gunner, and had no observer. But – as you say – they had more important things to think about.'

Neither Lieutenant-Commander Sir St John Tyrwhitt, Bart, nor I had the slightest inkling of the horrid consequences which had already resulted from the Midshipman's mistake. The day following the first attack, when alongside in Malta, 'Streamline' Robertson tried to work out which aircrew had been lost so that he could reply to an immediate signal from the Admiralty; *Juno*'s message that she had recovered a Swordfish crew of three ruled out any possibility that the aircraft which had ditched by *Juno* was mine. His task was extremely difficult because some of the pilots and observers in the hangar had been blown into unrecognizable pieces and no trace of them was ever seen again; and every single aircraft on board was completely gutted.

In his signal to the Admiralty, Commander Robertson included the TAG and me amongst those who were listed as 'missing'.

When Denman Whatley landed at Hal Far it did not occur to him to report the fate of his absent observer because he had seen us being picked up by *Juno* and knew that we were safe. He hesitated to go on board *Illustrious* when she was alongside in French Creek and under constant attack; he had no wish to bother a head of department with unimportant details when the whole ship's company was struggling for survival.

On 12 January, when *Illustrious* was headline news in all the papers at home, and when hourly broadcasts about her epic battle in Malta harbour were being made by the BBC, my poor wife received her first telegram telling her that I was 'missing'. It was a most unwelcome background to the BBC's terrifying news bulletins. Naturally, I had no knowledge of this until I arrived in Alexandria a fortnight later, by which time poor Jo had assumed that I was amongst those who were referred to as 'the many unknown dead'.

For the whole fourteen days in Malta the ship's Fulmar pilots fought an hourly battle with the Stukas and it was at this stage that Sub-Lieutenant Sparke became a figher pilot and left 815 Squadron. Charles Evans had had his eye on him, as an exceptional pilot, for some time; and in Malta, when he was desperately short of pilots, Sparke was a ready volunteer. From then onwards he was under the command of Charles Evans until losing his life four months later, flying from HMS *Formidable*. At the time of his death Sparke had acquired two bars to his DOO.

While in Malta, *Illustrious* was hit by two more bombs, but they were 1100 pounders, and three near-misses lifted her out of the water and hurled her against the Parlatario Wharf, doing more damage to her steel hull; but the steel in the hearts and minds of the men who fought to save her was no less tough. 'Pincher' Martin, the ship's Senior Engineer, toiled day and night with his men to repair the steering machinery. Until they could succeed the ship was totally helpless, and they worked on, through every moment of each day and night, the men in watches but Lieutenant-Commander Martin nonstop, pausing only during the attacks to avoid being killed – until he was able to report that the ship was 'ready for sea'.

Martin's successful efforts earned him a DSC. The task had taken him fourteen days and nights of murderous toil in disgusting conditions of filth and squalor in that befouled water; but he had saved the ship, and on 24 January, under cover of darkness, Denis Boyd was able to stand on his crippled bridge and take the ship out to sea. She sailed under her own power at 26 knots and arrived at Alexandria on 26 January, when she was given a hero's welcome.

After she had gone, the inhabitants of Malta held special thanksgiving services; although glad that their ordeal was over they had slaved around the clock to help her recover from what might otherwise have been mortal wounds, and her name will always be part of that little island's history.

A German Tailpiece
by
Lieutenant-Colonel Paul-Werner Hozzel
German Luftwaffe

I met Lieutenant-Colonel Hozzell after the war and persuaded him to write his story of the attack for me, and have produced it here exactly as he wrote it, without any editing or alterations. He was a swarthy, loose-limbed, good-looking chap, with unwavering eyes.

German Supreme Command ordered first days January 1941, Stuka-Geschwader 3 from France to Sicily, Italian air station Trapani, situated at the North West corner of the island. This 'Geschwader' was composed of two 'Grappen' [wings], one 1 Stuka 1, and two 1 Stuka 2, each of them consisting of three squadrons, the whole 'Geschwader' altogether having about 100 dive bomber aircrafts.

This move was ordered for the aim of a surprising raid against the British convoys from Gibraltar, Malta, and Alexandria and vice versa.

I was at that time Commander of the one 1 Stuka 1 peace-station, Iusterburg, East Prussia. The Commodore (Lt. Col. Edert) ordered me to organize the moving of the ground crew by train, and after that, come down to Trapani with those aircrafts left over, being not cleared at the beginning of the move. So I did, and landed Trapani on 13th January, with about 15 aircrafts.

Immediately after landing I was told by my friend, Major Enneccerus, Commander II 1 Stuka 2, that the Geschwader made an attack with about 80 machines against a big convoy, having been on the way from Gibraltar to Alexandria, protected by the aircarrier *Illustrious*, cruiser *Exeter* (or this class) and a flotilla of destroyers. Major Enneccerus, who had to lead this raid, was ordered to attack three main targets only: *Illustrious*, the cruiser, and the biggest transporter.

It was 10 January, blue sky, without any clouds, about lunch time when Geschwader started, armament 500 kilo bomb each. So far as I remember they got the convoys a few miles west of the isle of Pantellaria, operational height about 16 000 feet, distribution of targets: gros on *Illustrious*, one squadron on cruiser, one squadron on biggest transporter. Attack started, fighter cover none, bomb release point 700 m max. 1500 mm (2300/1600 feet). As observed during attack *Illustrious* got four bombs, the cruiser two and transporter two bombs. *Illustrious* got lop-sided and seemed to be unremovable. Cruiser and transporter sunk. An intended second attack could not be started for, as I remember, bombs were failing, [in supply] and bad weather came up from the west. Last reconnaissance report mentioned *Illustrious* lop-sided unremoveable, protected by four destroyers.

Bad weather lasted for several days, air reconnaissance and attacks not possible. On 13 January, recce was possible again, reported *Illustrious* and parts of convoy at La Valetta, AA of all calibre, about 92 batteries [that may be exaggerated], about 40 Hurricanes on two or three emergency airfields upon the island.

This was the situation, when Supreme Commander of the Luftwaffe, [Field-Marshal Goering] ordered us to make sink *Illustrious* at the quays of La Valetta. So began the heavy missions against La Valetta. We had no losses during the attacks at sea. We now lost our best crews in the following attacks. When I rose in the morning I knew with certainty that by sinking sun, some five or six crews would have gone. One day, after the last mission, the leader of my 2nd squadron, who was a very hard chap, could not report to me for tears: he was the last of his squadron, all his old chaps he lost.

Meantime we got fighter-cover from Catania by a ME 109 Wing, led by Flight Lieutenant Muucheberg, who was a very brave fighter, soon decorated with the 'oak leaf' to the 'Knight's Cross'. Nevertheless, in all attacks up till now *Illustrious* was not further hurted severely. But now we got new strict orders to do our best to make this ship sink. So we went to Catania air station and there loaded 1000 kg bombs. [2500 lb]. With these bombs under the belly we needed about 1½ hours to reach an altitude of 3000 m [about 10 000 feet]. Four of these bombs we succeeded in dropping on the deck of *Illustrious*, but she did not sink for our bombs were not able to penetrate the armoured decks below and because of numerous bulk-heads.

On the afternoon of the day that HMS *Juno* anchored in Crete's Suda Bay I was guilty of a tactical error. After an alcoholic lunchtime session in the wardroom, I was persuaded to go ashore with the ship's doctor, a bearded Surgeon-Lieutenant RNVR, who was also the wardroom's 'Wine Officer'. He insisted that he would be glad of my help in selecting some suitable Greek and Cypriot wines and liqueurs for the wardroom wine store, and he hoped to find something tasteful amongst the local wines for dinner on board that evening.

As a mere passenger in the ship I was delighted to be asked to do something useful for a change. It was naïve of me, but I was under the impression that doctors were trustworthy and sober represent-atives of the professional classes. In his company I visited any number of cave-like grottoes, and sampled all manner of liquids which he assured me were intended for human consumption. In every cavern we were joined by enthusiastic and colourful gentlemen of the locality, with rubicund complexions and leathery skins, whose hands and moustaches were as vast as their prodigious thirsts. They spoke no English but were alarmingly friendly, and to have declined their hospitality might have had serious consequences.

Worse was to come: after many arduous weeks at sea, in wartime the officers in a Fleet destroyer usually ask the Captain down to the wardroom on their first night in harbour for what is known as a 'hooley', which is by no means an abstemious way of passing an evening. All would have been well, and my behaviour in-conspicuous, had it not been for the unexpected arrival of HMS *Eagle* at 11 p.m. when the hooley was in full swing. The moment her anchor-cable had stopped rattling through the hawsepipe *Eagle*'s signal-lamps began to flash and the destroyer's Captain was instructed to transfer the 'Swordfish crew of three' forthwith, and the Commander of *Eagle* sent a boat across to avoid delay. All the officers in *Eagle*, from the Captain downwards, were determined to hear what had happened to *Illustrious* from first-hand witnesses.

When climbing into *Eagle*'s boat, inadvertently I trod on someone's face in the dark, and from the unnatural silence which followed can only assume that it was poor Midshipman Wallington's, because Ken Griffiths would have protested at once. I was escorted from *Eagle*'s quarter-deck by an Officer of the Watch who was disgustingly sober. In the ante-room I found a reception committee of all the ship's officers awaiting me, standing in solemn silence, and gazing at me with expressions of distaste which reminded me of my reverend father's expression when reading my headmaster's end-of-term report. I searched the blank caverns of my mind for something to say and had to fall back on the catch-phrase sometimes used by aviators when exaggerating a parlous situation.

'Gentlemen,' I said, 'there I was, at ten grand, upside down, and with nothing on the clock . . .' but at that point a kindly Commander Keighley-Peach escorted me to his day cabin, aft, for a good night's sleep. When away from Alexandria he slept in his sea cabin on the bridge.

The next morning I was able to describe the *Illustrious*'s battle in a coherent manner.

Flying from *Eagle* for the next week was an interesting experience and my admiration for everyone on board increased daily. The flight-deck was so thin that it wobbled underfoot if one was misguided enough to jump up and down. I could not understand how they had managed to survive seven months of continuous bombing without mental breakdown. One direct hit would have blown the old girl sky-high, and I was not surprised to discover that the 'action station' for *Eagle*'s non-flying aviators was the bar of the ante-room. It seemed the most sensible place to be, since one might as well die with a glass in one's hand. On 23 January I was unashamedly relieved when she returned to Alexandria.

The next day, *Illustrious*'s remaining Swordfish arrived at Dekheila after a long formation flight from Malta via Crete and Libya. Jackie Jago was astounded to see me, and it was then that I learned that I had been 'missing' for a fortnight, and I sent Jo a reassuring cable straight away.

Jago told me that 815 was being re-formed from the survivors of both squadrons, and that as soon as we were ready we were going out into the desert. History was repeating itself. 815 had started from the survivors of the two Swordfish squadrons in *Courageous*, and now we were to do it all over again from the survivors of the two squadrons from *Illustrious*. 819 Squadron was to be disbanded altogether.

The ratings arrived at Alexandria in the *Illustrious* on 26 January. There were just enough of them left to form one squadron. The ship sailed into the harbour to the accompaniment of a cacophony of tremendous noise. Every ship sounded a 'greeting' on their sirens, and she dropped her anchor to a background of ringing cheers from every officer and man in the Fleet. I rushed on board to be greeted by Burns and Brown, standing on deck at the brow, with asinine grins spread all over their ugly faces; and as soon as we could, we slipped ashore to the Fleet Club to drink to the immortal memory of 'Q' for 'Queenie'. Before we left the ship I had a good look round and the sight which met my eyes was a hundred per cent worse than anything I had imagined. She had been such a beautiful ship inside, with quiet passages and neat cabins, nicely furnished. The hangar had always been the show-piece of the ship and the squadrons had vied with each other to keep it spotless. Now it was no longer there. There was no trace of its deck – just a gaping void surrounded by grey tangled metal, and the ship's sides visible to a height of some fifty or sixty feet. Wherever one looked there were the signs of violent death in an open space of twisted disorder. I took one fearful look and fled.

Most of the decks below the hangar had been flooded because of fire, but I found my cabin, eventually, after a nightmare search which still features in my dreams when I have a bad night. It had been completely filled with oily water, right up to the deck-head, and nothing remained. What was left of my clothing was unrecognizable, but I found my little portable typewriter. Its keyboard was grinning at me with an obscene grimace; some trick of blast had folded it in two, like a sandwich, as though it had been squashed in some giant vice of destruction. The smells which rose from the deck were too reminiscent of the *Courageous* just before she sank, and I hurried away wondering how she could have sailed the eight hundred miles from Malta to Alexandria without foundering. It had been a triumph of mind over matter, inspired by the calm, pipe-smoking Denis Boyd, whose grim smile was always available to cheer the hearts of those who faltered.

Back on deck I found an atmosphere of hilarity. People were

rushing about shaking hands with each other and skipping with excitement. A signal had just been received from Admiralty promoting Captain Denis Boyd to Rear-Admiral; Gerald Tuck, the Commander, had been made a Captain, and was to relieve Boyd in command of the ship and take her through the Suez Canal to the United States to be rebuilt by the neutral Americans. Arthur Sowman and 'Pincher' Martin and 'Ginger' Hale were now Commanders . . . Admiral Lyster was to be flown home, to become the Fifth Sea Lord, and Denis Boyd was to take his place as our Admiral in the Mediterranean.

'Come on, sir,' grinned Brown. 'Old Burns is thirsty.'

A few days later I was sent for by the new Admiral. He had set up offices in Ras-el-tin, in Alexandria. When I arrived at his pleasantly cool building I was greeted by the Admiral's new secretary, Paymaster-Commander Arthur Sowman, who viewed me across his desk with great solemnity.

'I'm afraid I've got some bad news for you,' he began.

'What's the matter?' I smelt a leg-pull at once. 'The Admiral isn't going to send me home at last, is he?'

Sowman waved the suggestion aside as though the reason for my visit was unimportant compared with his bad news.

'No. You can go in and see him in a minute – he's got another odd job for you. But I wanted to sympathize with you over your sad loss. I'm sorry to have to tell you that all those Irvine Flying Jackets on your charge were destroyed during the bombing. I've had to take the necessary stores procedure to write them off your slate. I hope you will be able to manage without them?'

The *Illustrious* was not seen again until spring 1942 at Madagascar when she was the flagship of Rear-Admiral Boyd, who was Rear-Admiral Aircraft Carriers, Eastern Fleet. But a lot of things happened in the interval.

PART IV

Picnic Ashore

19
The Rebirth of a Squadron

Denis Boyd's new appointment as our Admiral in the Mediterranean coincided with the final phase of General Wavell's defeat of the Italians in North Africa; and as soon as we were ready he sent us out into the Libyan desert to assist the Army until the Italians surrendered. Our task was to bomb their shipping in Benghazi every night, to speed their surrender.

Our desert campaign was planned as a temporary phase: as soon as Benghazi was captured by the Allies we were scheduled to fly to Crete and then to Greece to assist the Greeks in their struggle against Italy. On 29 January, the day we took off from Dekheila to fly out into the Libyan desert, we heard that the Greek leader, General Metaxas, had died, and from his death-bed had appealed to Britain to send immediate aid to Greece. His last, heartrending words were: 'The women of Greece shall not dance again until this war is won.'

Plans to move 30 000 troops from North Africa to Greece were set in train at once, by the Commanders-in-Chief of both land and sea forces. Our task was to be the protection of these troops as their ships passed through the Kithera Channel north of Crete, on their way to Piraeus, and constructional engineers were already preparing a new airstrip for us at Máleme, in Crete. In the meantime we had a desert campaign to fight.

During the last week of January, 815 Squadron had reformed at Dekheila, the naval airfield near Alexandria in Egypt, using the surviving Swordfish of both 815 and 819 Squadrons from *Illustrious*, plus a consignment of new aircraft which had been flown out from England by newcomers to the Squadron. It was pleasant to be joining forces with 819, but I was glad that we had retained the identity of 815, since it had started life from the survivors of the two Swordfish squadrons which had been sunk in *Courageous*. After the bombing of *Illustrious* history had repeated itself in less than two years of the squadron's existence.

As squadron stores officer I had to sign for twenty-two aircraft, and although there were plenty of pilots there were only about a dozen observers, which worried Caldecott-Smith, who was now the Senior Observer. We reassured him that 'a looker' in the back seat is an unnecessary luxury when flying over the land, but we made that foolish boast before we had gained experience of flying over the desert, where accurate navigation is just as important as it is over the sea.

Just as the desert campaign was becoming interesting I was summoned back to Alexandria by the Staff Officer Operations to Denis Boyd. Commander Charles Thompson was a terse individual. He told me to load all the squadron stores into the hold of a small steamer lying alongside in Alex harbour. Anything left over was to be put on board the battleship *Barham*.

'Try and get as much as you can into the cargo ship,' he said, 'because Captain Cooke, of *Barham*, is already complaining that there isn't room to spare. You will have to be tactful because there are two heavy lorries to go across on her quarter-deck. Your squadron ratings are taking passage in her and she already has a load of your bombs, torpedoes and depth-charges.'

He showed me to the door and told me that I was to report to him when everything had been done and not before. 'I don't want to see you again until both ships are fully loaded. If you have any problems, sort them out yourself and don't come running to me.'

An Engineer Captain named Jones was sharing the office with him and he followed me out.

'Give me a ring if you want any help,' he said, with a mischievous grin. 'I've never got enough to do, unlike the rest of the staff who are overworked.' He then told me his name and added that he was the Fleet Air Arm Technical Officer. 'Short title "FATO" – to rhyme with heart!'

I wondered how we were going to get our little run-about van across to Crete. I had come by it illegally some weeks before. I saw it in the dockyard with a load of new gear addressed to a new naval establishment near Port Said, which had not even finished building. All I had to do was to paint '815 Squadron, Dekheila' over its intended address. I was very pleased when it was delivered to us a few days later.

Without it in Crete we would be unable to visit the Grottoes for a drink, or do any shopping. Obviously the battleship wouldn't be keen on having a third vehicle, and I was going to have a struggle to persuade them to park the two lorries on their quarter-deck. I decided that I would stow it on top of the little steamer's hatch when the ship was fully loaded. This meant more painting, because the lifting capacity marked on the ship's only derrick was 5 tons, and the van had the figures '7.5 tons' clearly marked on the driver's door. By removing all four wheels to lighten it and painting '815, Máleme' over the figures on the door, all was well, though I was very relieved when it was safely stowed on the hatch. I had always suspected that the weight limits on ship's derricks concealed a wide safety margin.

While I was loading the ship the squadron pilots were whooping it up in Benghazi. When the Italians conceded defeat, they rode into the town they had been bombing every night, with the conquering Australians, who were hell-bent and thirsty. The traffic was still being conducted by courteous Italian police, and polite Italian barmen served the squadron officers as though they were pleased to see them, which I think they were because their hearts had not been in Mussolini's desert battle from the beginning. All over Libya tens of thousands of Italian troops were surrendering gladly – often two or three thousand men to one British or Commonwealth officer. They did so with obvious relief that the battle was over.

Although the squadron's first desert campaign had lasted only nine days, when they arrived back at Dekheila they all looked weary and were covered in dust and sand. The aircraft were all choked with it, and it took us a couple of days to clear the engine filters. Every day they had moved their base further west, and for that crowded nine days they had hammered at the shipping and the harbour defences in Benghazi. Spencer Lea and his air gunner had to be sent to hospital for a few days to recover, and sitting at their bedside I listened to a story that might have come from the Arabian nights.

Lea had come to 815 from 819, in the amalgamation. In his teens he had been a makee-learn sheep-farmer in Australia's outback, and he was a tough, sandy-haired warrior who had been one of 819's torpedo pilots at Taranto. On one of the Benghazi raids his engine was hit by flak, and he suffered a severe oil leak. Because of the shortage of observers, and the near-impossibility of finding an isolated spot in the desert's wastes in the dark, all return flights were to be around the coast, turning in over the land at a fixed point and then flying on a pre-determined course for a specific time. With a severe oil leak Lea decided to fly back direct, but in the end he had to force-land to repair the leak. He managed to do it by the light of the moon, which was no mean feat; but he was then unable to restart his engine. He was not aware that a Bristol Pegasus engine will seldom restart when it is hot, and he and Bob Boddy, the air gunner, took it in turns to wind on the inertia handle until they were cross-eyed with fatigue. In the end they gave up, and in desperation, before running out of energy altogether, and before the sun rose to roast them alive, Lea decided to walk towards the British lines to summon aid. He thought that there was an Australian camp about twenty miles to the east. Before setting out he told the air gunner to stay with the aircraft until help arrived.

For some reason Lea was always called the 'Sprog', which implies youthful innocence. He was neither young nor innocent, but by the end of this adventure he was an even older and wiser man. After walking through the rest of the night and most of the following day, without food or water, he climbed a sand dune, and gazed eastward. From his hospital bed he described the view with the language of an Australian sheep-farmer.

'Miles and bloody miles of sweet fanny adams,' he said wryly. 'Not an effing thing in sight, just effing desert, miles and effing miles of it!'

Although he was almost out on his feet, which had acquired sores the size of small saucers, and was crazy with thirst, he had no alternative but to retrace his steps. Without water he might have perished, but the Sprog was always an incredibly lucky man and by some miracle he stumbled on a well. The water was many feet below ground level and out of his reach, but with typical ingenuity he took off all his clothes and tied them end-to-end, until he managed to dangle a sock into the water. Hoisting it out he squeezed the water through parched lips, repeating the process until his thirst was assuaged.

This was probably a trick he had learned in Australia's outback. Long association with sheep had undoubtedly dulled his sense of taste because he described the flavour of the water strained through his socks as nectar from the gods.

By another miracle he found his way back to the abandoned

aircraft. There was no sign of the air gunner, but pinned to the windscreen of the front cockpit was a note from him: 'Can't stand the solitude for another minute. Sorry! Am poking-off too . . .'

With strength derived from utter desperation, and inspired by an all-consuming thirst, the Sprog summoned up his last reserves of adrenalin and wound on the starter handle. Of course by then the engine was quite cool, and when he pulled the inertia starter toggle, to his amazement it started up at once. Scarcely believing his luck he plunged into the cockpit and took off. After a fruitless square-search for his air gunner he flew eastward to the Australian camp he had been seeking on foot.

'How far was it, from where you force-landed?' I asked.

He grinned at me weakly. 'About eighty bloody miles!' he said sadly. 'It's just as well I turned back!'

The Australians had to lift him out of the cockpit. When he had drunk his fill and had tried to eat something ('my lips were so swollen I couldn't swallow to start with,' he told me), they put him to bed. Before passing out he appealed to them to go in search of Bob Boddy, the air gunner.

Several hours later he awoke to the shrill clamour of Arab voices, and peering through the tent flap he saw a party of Bedouin leading their camels into the encampment. On the back of one of them was the recumbent figure of the air gunner.

They both survived this remarkable adventure to fly with us to Crete on 14 February. The day before I had succeeded in loading everything left over on board HMS *Barham*, including the two lorries which were lashed down on the battleship's quarter-deck where they looked entirely out of place. The Officer of the Watch clearly disapproved.

'When you have quite finished,' he said coldly, 'I have instructions to take you down to the Captain.'

Captain Cooke took me to the cuddy to meet Vice-Admiral Pridham-Wippell.

'This is the young man who has turned our quarter-deck into a car park,' was his introduction. The Admiral gave me a sherry.

'I'm glad we can help,' he said, 'but I must confess I have never seen lorries parked on a battleship's quarter-deck before!'

'I think that Nelson must be turning in his grave, sir,' said Captain Cooke with a laugh.

The were both very charming officers, and the Captain took me on a tour of the ship's mess decks so that I could see where the squadron ratings were bedded down. When I returned to the quarter-deck the Officer of the Watch was still appalled. 'You Fleet Air Arm people have no sense of tradition,' he said. 'It is sacrilege to load trucks on to a quarter-deck!'

'Never mind,' I said soothingly. 'Perhaps you will sink on the way over.'

In fact HMS *Barham* remained afloat for a further valuable nine months and took a prominent part in the Battle of Matapan. But on 25 November that year, she was torpedoed by a U-boat and blew up with very few survivors. Captain Cooke was not amongst them, I was sorry to see, but Admiral Pridham-Wippell was pulled out of the sea unharmed.

The action took place off the Bay of Sollum, in North Africa. The battleship *Valiant* was immediately astern and Captain C. E. Morgan, in command of HMS *Valiant*, reported that four minutes and thirty-five seconds after the explosion all trace of the mighty *Barham* had disappeared for ever.

Prior to the desert campaign the incidence of engine failure with our Swordfish had been negligible. Pilots had been able to rely on their Pegasus engines as surely as they could rely on their bank managers to write 'Dear Sir – Unless' letters the moment they overdrew their accounts. Except when damaged by the enemy the oil pressure gauges remained at a constant 60 lb per square inch and never wavered. Whenever they did, an immediate forced landing was essential.

Until the *Illustrious* was bombed the squadron aircraft had been serviced regularly, in accordance with strict maintenance schedules; but on 10 January the engine and airframe log books and the ratings' tool kits had all been destroyed when the hangar was gutted. Since then they had flown the 880 miles from Malta to Alexandria, via Crete, and had been exposed to the sandy plains of Egypt and Libya, almost without any servicing at all. They all needed a thorough inspection such as a 'major', but without proper tools and with very little time available, the men hesitated to dismantle them when they would almost certainly be required at short notice. Daily inspections were all that could safely be managed.

There had been a number of forced landings while we were helping to chase the Italians out of Libya, particularly in the desert sandstorms, often called siroccos. These have to be experienced to be believed because no description can depict them adequately. Whirling particles of grit as densely concentrated as the heaviest rainstorm form an impenetrable yellow fog which obscures the light, blots out the sun, and makes breathing difficult. No aircraft engine can continue to function in them for long and the only safe action, when caught in a sirocco, is to fly out of it in the shortest direction or land at once. But visibility becomes so bad that it is difficult to see land in a smothering blanket of swirling sand. In one of these devastating storms I had managed to land near a tented camp somewhere near Tobruk. I had lost all sense of direction while trying to fly by instruments when the sun was suddenly obscured, and had no idea where I was, and was grateful when a dim figure appeared out of the gale and seized my port wing-tip. By making frantic signs he guided me past boulders and ditches and then gave me the signal to cut my engine by drawing his fingers across his throat. I switched off the engine and wondered whether the Italians used the same signal, and hoped that my guide was not one of the enemy. When I had groped my way towards him I was astonished to see that he was a Captain RN, wearing khaki battledress. I stood gaping at his four gold stripes on black shoulder straps. His naval cap with gold braid around the peak looked incongruous above his rough khaki jacket and trousers.

He grabbed my elbow and led me down some steps out of the wind. I found myself in a comfortable tent, lined with sacking, where the sand had been dug away to give more head-room. My guide told me his name was Poland.

When I had recovered my breath I said: 'You're a long way from the sea, sir! What in God's name is a naval Captain doing out here?'

Captain Poland grinned cheerfully and poured me out a gin, topping it up with water from the corked tin bottle wrapped in cloth which was slung from his shoulder.

'Liaising with the pongoes,' he said, and I had to be content with that. 'As soon as this storm abates a little you must take off at the double, because you have just landed in no-man's land. I think I guided you in far enough but your aircraft is outside our defences.'

He was a most entertaining host and I was sorry to go without finding out what he was doing out in the desert. I never did discover his secret.

On 10 February Jago and Caldecott-Smith led half the squadron to Heraklion in Crete where they were to be our advance party until Máleme was ready. They flew down the Egyptian coast to Mersa Matruh before turning north over the sea, and told us to use the same route when we joined them. Alexandria to Crete, direct, is entirely over the sea, and a distance of 395 miles. Flying via Mersa Matruh reduced the distance over the sea by 95 miles. There were no air-sea rescue organizations of any kind in the Mediterranean at that time, so flights over the sea were made as short as possible, especially now that our engines were not as reliable as they had been. When flying from the *Illustrious* no air-sea rescue organization had existed either, but our engines were then properly serviced, and we had the cold comfort of the knowledge that a screening destroyer *might* come to our rescue if we had to ditch, provided we were not too far away at the time. From 10 January onwards we were strictly on our own.

The same lack of aid had applied to flights over the desert, and although a man can only walk in the desert sun for a limited time before perishing either of thirst or sunstroke, at least he can step away from the crashed aircraft on to terra firma. Most engine failures over the sea were irrevocable, and pilots and observers were seldom rescued. Drifting in a rubber dinghy at the whim of the wind, praying for a miracle which is unlikely to occur, would not be my favourite method of ending my days.

With the superb backing of Burns and Brown I felt secure in the knowledge that if any of the squadron engines were to falter it was unlikely to be mine.

By 14 February Máleme airfield was ready and we were given orders to fly to Crete to join Jago and the advance party, who had been flying from Heraklion. After crossing the flat Egyptian coast at Mersa Matruh, for nearly three hours we droned along peacefully in open formation, flying to the north-west at 3000 feet. For the last hour over the blue Mediterranean the misty heat of the horizon nursed a low bank of cumulus cloud which grew larger as we approached, and gradually solidified into the snowy peaks of the Cretan mountains. The southern coast of Crete looks most forbidding to a pilot approaching to land for the first time; flying towards the mountain range the plateau stretches from east to west for 130 miles, which is farther than the eye can see on a hot misty day, even at 3000 feet. The peaks seemed to grow taller as we drew close and then rose to meet us until they were right ahead at the same height and we had to climb to pass over them. Looking down I thrilled at the sight of the granite face of the mountains below me, dropping sheer into the sea, a series of shadowy clefts between sunlit crags of grey and brown, topped with white snow; forbidding, yet strangely pleasing to the eye after three hours with nothing ahead but the azure water concealing the depths of over a thouand fathoms.

Once over the mountain range, Torrens-Spence throttled back and led us down towards Suda Bay and the flat plains which form the north face of the island. Crete is only twenty-five miles wide and in a few moments we were rumbling over the roofs of Canea, the capital, little squares of white amongst the greenery, lit by the sun. Continuing his turn to the west, for the first time we saw the red earth of Máleme airfield, dead ahead, surrounded by little green hills of unending olive groves. Our tents were nestling amongst the dark green foliage and the wiry tree-trunks, and after the desert it all looked beguilingly attractive.

20
The Greek Campaign

One month after the German seizure of Czechoslovakia in March 1939, the British Government guaranteed the independence and integrity of Greece. Less than two years later, in January 1941, when the dying Greek leader appealed to Britain for help, that guarantee had to be upheld. 30 000 men were shipped across the Mediterranean on a forlorn mission, and the unsuccessful campaign which followed was undertaken as an honourable obligation to a brave ally facing overwhelming odds.

The campaign was not expected to be entirely unsuccessful, but when it proved expensive in men and material many armchair critics have since questioned the wisdom of denuding North Africa of men for a cause which was bound to fail. To them I would point out that history has often proved that failure can sometimes be as glorious – and as productive – as victory.

While the full strength of the Royal Navy was engaged in the eastern Mediterranean convoying troops to Greece, it was inevitable that the naval effort elsewhere had to be relaxed. Admiral Cunningham had no choice but to concentrate his resources on the successful launching of the Greek campaign. Later, while our troops were spread across the Greek frontiers in the mountains of Albania, the Germans pushed into Libya with a force more powerful than the Allied units which had been sent to Greece. They seized this opportunity to land Rommel and his Panzer divisions in Tripolitania, and his rapid reconquest of the whole North African front was brought about because we had withdrawn our troops from the African scene. But this was the price we had to pay for keeping our word. Ultimately, by forcing the Germans to fight over a very wide front, too wide even for their resources, we were able to exact a terrible price from them too; and in retrospect it is clear that the short two and a half months of the ill-fated Greek campaign, though unsuccessful at the time, were a valuable contribution to ultimate victory.

From the very beginning of the war, after the ignominy of being sunk in HMS *Courageous*, with the exception of the Taranto attack, 815 Squadron's history was a constant repetition of involvement in campaigns which ended in German victory; but all these were the groundwork which provided the essential base on which victory could be built. Our minelaying off the German coast and our attempts to check the German advance in Holland, and our flying over Dunkirk, had all been forlorn attempts to help stem the tide of Nazi triumphs which were inevitable at that stage in the war. All these struggles, including our success at Taranto, had taken place when Britain stood entirely alone and, like the Greeks in the spring of 1941, at a time when we faced overwhelming odds. In the North African desert Wavell's victory had been made more certain because of the presence of New Zealand and Australian divisions, who were also a substantial percentage of the 30 000 men to pour into Greece on a forlorn errand of mercy; but their initial landing in North Africa and their successful arrival in Greece would not have been possible while an Italian fleet, nearly double the size of the British fleet, was monopolizing the tactical picture in Taranto harbour. We were encouraged that our successful attack had had such far-reaching consequences, and had contributed in a significant way to Wavell's victory and to Cunningham's ability to send these convoys to Greece. The part played in Greece by the same Swordfish aircrews was scarcely noticed, or recorded in the history of that campaign, because their efforts were concentrated against shipping in the Adriatic from a secret base in the Albanian mountains, which was well out of everyone's sight. But as always their participation went far beyond the concept of what was expected of them. That they were there at all is scarcely known, even in naval circles, and I write about them now with pride that I was of their company.

The stream which gurgled through the olive grove where our tents were pitched was pure melted snow and ice, from the mountains. We bathed in it daily and boiled it in tin cans over camp fires for shaving and tea-making. For twenty-two days we lived an idyllic existence, interrupted by occasional air raids when a huge bell, suspended from a gallows mounted outside our marquee overlooking the airfield, would clang a doleful alarm, warning us to take immediate cover. In the air, daylight anti-submarine patrols ahead of the convoys were enlivened by the occasional attack by German and Italian aircraft operating from their bases in the Dodecanese islands, which were only about sixty to eighty miles to the north-east. The enemy aircraft were the responsibility of Lieutenant-Commander Alan Black, and his Brewsters and Fulmars, also operating from Máleme, and the RAF Hurricanes from Heraklion, and during the attack we had to drop down to sea level to avoid being seen.

The Germans were not at war with the Greeks, but the war at sea, and in the air, was open to all comers, and Máleme airfield was a daily target. Puffs of smoke, exploding noisily over the snow-topped mountains in the clear blue sky, fired by the ack-ack gunners of the Black Watch who were defending the airfield, were constant reminders that we were not on holiday; but the local inhabitants were so friendly, and the atmosphere in the olive groves so relaxed, that the sight and sound of these occasional bursts and the sharp tolling of the bell always came as a shock.

While we were in Crete we knew that we were only marking time. When all the ships had negotiated the Kithera Channel and reached Piraeus, our usefulness would be over and we would move on to Greece. Our torpedoes and bombs, and the heavy equipment, such as torpedo trolleys, needed for stowing and loading them, had been taken by the fleet direct to Piraeus to await us at Eleusis, the big airfield ten miles to the north-west of Athens on the banks of the Gulf, opposite Salamis Island. The only weapons we needed in Crete were anti-submarine bombs and depth-charges, but in Greece once again we would be on the offensive. With the arrival of Allied troops in Greece, German intervention was inevitable, and it was only a matter of time before we would be needed to help stem a German invasion from the sea, across the Straits of Otranto at the bottom of the Adriatic.

Sixteen days after our arrival in Crete, without warning, Germany invaded Bulgaria. It was Sunday, 2 March, when I was happily engaged in refereeing a boxing match in the main square of Canea. The Army had erected the ring in the sunlit piazza, and a huge crowd had gathered to watch this friendly inter-service match between the mad English. Suddenly we were deafened by the roar of scores of strange Junkers aircraft, flying low over our heads, with their wheels and flaps down, obviously intent on landing at Máleme. Since there had been no air raid warning, and no guns had been fired, and it was evident that they were not attacking the island, I signed to the boxers to box on. Later in the programme the spectators were joined by a milling throng of swarthy airmen in Oxford blue uniforms of unfamiliar design, bearing strange stripes and insignia. They were Bulgarian airmen who had fled before the invading Hun that afternoon, and had just landed en route for Egypt. They were in a highly excited frame of mind and were not content to watch: after some puzzling negotiations with the army officials in charge of the boxing arrangements, they explained that they had the welter-weight champion of the Bulgarian air force amongst them, who challenged all comers at his weight of 64 kilos. Eventually, to preserve the peace, the army produced a much-tattooed British corporal with a broken nose and a pushed-in face, who appeared to relish the forthcoming battle; and for three rounds my referee's platform was surrounded by throngs of sinister and rather hostile uniformed foreigners, eyeing me in a threatening manner between the rounds. In amateur boxing during the war the referee sat outside the ring on a dais, and the two judges were surrounded by the Bulgarians too, and grinned at me sheepishly; it was abundantly clear that if the British corporal won on points the decision would be most unpopular and might start an international incident. Certainly our safety would be in jeopardy. Fortunately, towards the end of the third round the corporal knocked out his Bulgarian opponent who had to be carried out of the ring. Unpleasantness was avoided, and *entente cordiale* maintained. I was very grateful to the corporal, and bought him a drink afterwards.

Eight days later our holiday in Crete was over and the observers had to squat over the camp fire and smoke their pieces of glass. In strong sunlight, the Swordfish were very vulnerable to fighter attack from the direction of the sun, and the only way to spot them when they dived from the pilot's blind side was for the observer or airgunner to sit staring into the sun through smoked glass. Like our single Vickers gun, forward, and the Lewis gun, aft, smoked glass had proved very effective in the First World War, but unlike the guns we found that it was not to be despised in the Second World War.

At Eleusis, the Athens airport, we were greeted by a crowd of the squadron maintenance ratings and armourers who had been ferried to Greece in a destroyer a few days earlier. Burns and Brown looked sunburned but disgruntled. When I asked them what was wrong they told me that the atmosphere in Athens was tense.

'It's a nice place, sir,' said Burns, rather sourly, 'and the Greeks seem very pleased to see us, but because Germany is not at war with them, some of the German bastards are walking about the streets in uniform! They're swaggering about in the pubs and cafés, and in the shops, as cool as you like. Apparently they are attached to the German Embassy and have diplomatic immunity or something, whatever that may mean.'

'It means we can't clock them on the flipping nose without being arrested,' said Brown, ruefully. Then his expression brightened. 'There have been a few lovely scenes, though! Some of the lads got into trouble on their first run ashore. They'd had a few, of course – and it's lovely beer here , sir, as smooth as silk – and when they saw a German in uniform walking towards them they pushed the bastard through a shop-front window!'

'What happened then?' I asked apprehensively. 'They're not under arrest, are they?'

'No. The Greek police handed them over to the naval patrol because they couldn't make the lads understand what they were trying to say. The patrol ticked them off and let them go. But we had a visit from some senior officer from the Greek navy – a captain I think – the next day, who explained that we had to put up with it because Germany isn't at war with Greece.'

'They soon will be!' grunted Burns. 'It's all very well, sir,' he grumbled, 'but they're bloody well at war with us, and it sticks in my gullet to have to share the cafés and pubs with the bastards when they've been bombing us, and our wives and kids, for the last year and a half. There's going to be a right set-to shortly, which won't just be a punch-up!'

Clearly, trouble as brewing. It certainly was the most impossible situation. I wondered how Jago would cope if he had to deal with a defaulter on a charge of 'assaulting the enemy'!

Shortly after we landed, J. Jago, Caldecott-Smith, Torrens-Spence, and Sutton were whisked away in a chauffeur-driven car to meet Air Vice-Marshal John D'Albiac, the Commander of all the British forces in Greece. While we waited in the hangar to hear what was being cooked up for our immediate future we sorted out our camping kits. The camp beds were wonderfully compact when stowed, and very comfortable to sleep in. We checked that there was plenty of corned beef and gin and other essential supplies in

The Deck Landing Control Officer (the 'Batsman') signals the Swordfish pilot to cut his engine prior to touch-down

The arrester hook below the fuselage scrapes along the deck until it engages the arrester wire

I happened to be the last pilot to land on the deck of *Courageous* a few minutes before she was torpedoed; photographed from the stern of *Impulsive*

The first H.M. ship to be sunk in World War Two: survivors escaping down the sides of *Courageous* on 17 September 1939

A Swordfish being pushed aft into the hangar. The wings had to be folded on deck

Typical deck-park on a small carrier

Wedding-day: Charlton All Saints, Wiltshire, 20 September 1939, three days after the sinking of *Courageous*

Survivors from *Courageous* being entertained by the Lord Mayor of Cardiff in February 1940. *Back row: third from left*, Launce Kiggell; *second from right*, Julian Sparke. *Front row: second from left*, Neil Kemp; I am second from the right

Illustrious seen from beneath the guns of *Mauritius*

Using the 'safety barrier', we always tried to land-on at 10-second intervals. The first to land did so without lowering his arrester hook to save precious seconds

Captain Ian 'Streamline' Robertson and Vice-Admiral Sir Lumley Lyster.
As a Rear-Admiral Sir Lumley flew his flag in *Illustrious* in 1940 for the
attack on the Italian Fleet at Taranto, which he had planned when
Captain of *Glorious* at the time of Munich. 'Streamline' Robertson was the
first Commander Flying in *Illustrious* in 1940

Illustrious seen from above. Both aircraft lifts are in the down position in
the hangar. The landing area is abaft the bridge structure known as the
Island.

Vice-Admiral Sir Denis
Boyd, the first Captain of
Illustrious, when he was
Fifth Sea Lord in 1943

Ken Dickens Griffiths, the
Telegraphist Airgunner who
was flying with me when our
engine disintegrated over
Alexandria harbour in 1940,
and in January 1941, when we
were shot down. He was killed
after I had been taken prisoner

The morning after the Swordfish attack on Taranto, 11 November 1940: two 10,000-ton cruisers with oil spreading from them, and other damaged ships

An Italian battleship of the *Duilio* class photographed by an Italian airman on the morning after the Swordfish attack

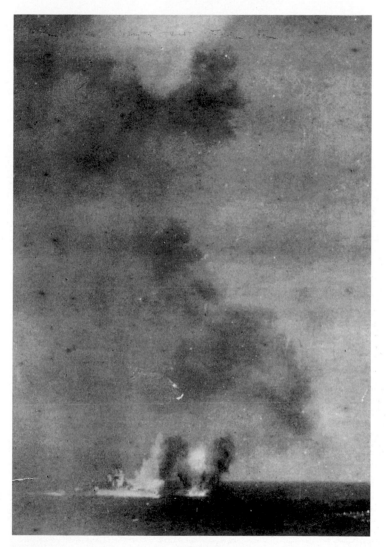

Flak and shrapnel flying through the air during the first Stuka attack on
Valiant on 10 January 1941

The flight-deck of *Illustrious* as I saw it a few minutes before being shot down. The ship had already been hit by three armour-piercing bombs. The aircraft lift can be seen aft, blown out of the deck, which is steaming with the heat of the burning hangar below

Stuka attack on *Illustrious* in Malta Harbour. The flight-deck can be seen between the biggest pall of smoke and the crane. While the ship's company repaired the damaged steering gear the attacks were continuous, but two weeks later Captain Boyd took the ship to Egypt under her own steam at 26 knots

My Swordfish standing on its nose in the mud of the salt lake near Sousse, North Africa. Taken by the observer, John Malcolm Robertson, on the ill-fated morning of 17 September 1941

Standing on a parachute pack up to my knees in mud in the salt lake; also taken by Robertson before we set off for firm ground – and fourteen months in prison

The barbed-wire fence round
the prison camp at Laghouat,
in the Sahara

Machine-gun post and sentry
immediately above my
quarters in Laghouat

The boxing-ring in Laghouat prison

With three Sub-Lieutenants (A), R.N.V.R., on return from Laghouat in
January 1943

H.M. King George VI at Rosyth inspecting my Flight-Deck Division in
Implacable on return from the Arctic before sailing for the Pacific war in
1945

Implacable entering Sydney harbour after the Japanese surrender, showing some of the ship's 82 aircraft, and the ship's company lining the flight-deck.

'Taranto Dinner', 12 November 1954, on board *Illustrious* before the ship was broken up. To celebrate the victory at Taranto these dinners are held annually throughout the Fleet Air Arm, when the surviving Taranto aircrew are honoured guests

the back of each aircraft, and we were sure that we would be taking off in a hurry at any moment. When Jago and the others returned the whole squadron mustered behind closed doors in one of the hangar offices. It was Monday, 10 March 1941.

Jago told us that we were to fly to our forward base in the mountains two days later, on Wednesday, 12 March, for an attack on enemy shipping in Valona harbour the following night. Then he outlined the various aspects of the move, which were fascinating.

'I'm afraid that we shall have to leave most of the ratings here,' he said, 'because our base is right up in the mountains, well into Albania, on enemy territory. It can't be got at by road, so it's inaccessible except by air, and when we fly up there we shall have full crews, and the aircraft will all be carrying a torpedo, so not only will there be no room for you in the back, but the aircraft would be overweight if we tried to take you too. We may be able to take one or two of you up there later.

'There are two RAF squadrons already there, a Blenheim squadron and a Wimpey squadron. They have been bombing inland enemy positions for some weeks, and the Italians are trying hard to find out where they are based so that they can return the compliment. It is vital to keep the whereabouts of the base a secret, particularly until the Germans invade Greece, which is certain to happen soon. Although the Italians have tried very hard, and have searched the mountains daily with reconnaissance aircraft, they haven't yet been able to find it, and from the directions we have just been given on how to get there I'm not in the least surprised! It's going to be difficult enough to find even though we have been told where it is.'

He described our route, which was simple in the early stages. We had to fly up the Gulf of Corinth, and then out to sea through the Gulf of Patras, and up the west coast of Greece to the island of Corfu.

'From the southernmost tip of Corfu we set course due east, and fly to the Albanian coast, a distance of only ten or so miles. *But*' – he accentuated the word – 'if we are sighted by fighters we are to turn back at once. In no circumstances are we to lead them to the base, which is called the "Valley of Paramythia". The AVM was very forthright on that point; he said that it would be better to lose the entire Swordfish squadron than give away the position of the RAF's secret airfield.

'When we fly towards Albania from Corfu we should be able to see a huge range of mountains on our starboard hand. The whole country is a mass of mountains, so it is important to take an accurate departure from Corfu on the first occasion, to make sure that we arrive with the correct mountain range on our right. But we have a good landmark to help us: the tallest of the mountains, just over seven thousand feet high, is in the range we want.' He looked at us with a grin. 'It's the third on the right as we fly into Albania! When we get closer to it we should be able to see a wide dry river-bed at its foot. This points to the north and all we have to do is to follow it all the way to Paramythia. Apparently it is clearly visible from the air, but it curves like a snake so don't be surprised if we keep altering course. It ends in the valley just before the RAF camp, so it takes us all the way, and leads us through a gap in the mountains surrounding the valley. The gap is wide enough for the Blenheim squadron so it must be wide enough for us, but just in case one of you isn't looking where he's going we'll get into line astern when we cross the Albanian coast.

'The valley of Paramythia is ten miles long, and three thousand feet deep, surrounded by mountains all the way round it, which are six thousand feet high. Since the valley is three thousand feet above sea level, when we take off to do the attack we shall have to climb at least another three thousand feet before we can set course for Valona. With torpedoes, our speed when climbing will be reduced to about 70 knots, so it will take some time to clear the mountains. On taking off we shall have to circle, inside the valley, before we are clear, and that's what is worrying the Air Marshal. It's pretty grim territory for flying, and because of the danger of hitting the mountains the Blenheims and the Wimpeys won't fly at night. They argue that in any case they would never be able to find the river-bed in the dark. I have explained that we are a night-attack squadron and that we would rather take the chance of hitting the mountains than attack Valona in daylight. The AVM was very doubtful and took some persuading. However, we pointed out that we can time our attacks so that we approach the valley at dawn, when the river-bed should be visible. As a compromise he insists that we only fly from Paramythia when there is a moon, and I agree with that. It might be a bit dicey on a pitch-dark night, without a moon.'

Jackie explained that he was taking us up to the mountains a day early so that we could have a good look at the surroundings, and do a practice night take-off in formation, without torpedoes.

'The new moon is due tomorrow, so we are going to have a busy fortnight. After each sortie we return to Paramythia for a meal and a rest, but only to top up with enough fuel to fly back to Eleusis. There is only limited fuel available at Paramythia, which was taken there in big drums by a squadron of Bostons. But it is for the Blenheims and Wimpeys, not for us. The Bostons can take more up there, but only when absolutely necessary, because the less air traffic in and out of the valley the less likely the enemy are to find it. In any case we have to fly back to Athens to rearm with torpedoes, so all we need at Paramythia is a quick top-up. We can refuel fully when we arrive back here.'

Somebody asked why we couldn't have a store of torpedoes in the forward base and Jackie explained that they would have had to be flown there, plus heavy torpedo-trolleys for loading them, and it wasn't possible.

'After the first attack, when we all know the way in and out of Valona and Paramythia, it will be necessary to split the squadron into two flights, or possibly three, so that there is always one flight of Swordfish armed with torpedoes, ready to attack, up in the mountains, while the others are rearming in Athens.'

He told us about Valona harbour and its strategic importance to the Italians. All Italian troops, and their arms and ammunition, had to be landed there becaue it was the nearest Albanian port to the Greek frontier.

'Italy is only fifty miles from Valona, across the Straits of Otranto, but there is only one road leading to the south from Valona, which is easily bombed in daylight, so the Italians have to cross the mountainous territory on foot. It isn't possible to move large forces of men and machinery about in Albania in the dark, even by the only road, so they have no alternative but to travel over the mountains in daylight. The only other port which they can use is Durazzo, which is a further sixty miles to the north, and the same applies: there is only one road connecting the two ports along the coast, and if the Italians had to disembark their troops at Durazzo they would have to travel overland in daylight. The distance from Valona to the Greek frontier is nearly a hundred miles, but the distance from Durazzo overland would be about a hundred and eighty miles – of terrible country. So our aim is to make it impossible for the Italians to go on using Valona; then they will have to use the longer route from Durazzo.

'They won't be expecting night torpedo attacks from the air – at first, anyway – so for a while we shall have the advantage of surprise. I see no reason why we shouldn't sink a lot of shipping in

Valona, and then Durazzo, and later perhaps, out in the Adriatic.'

There were a great many things to do in the next twenty-four hours before taking off. Jago had asked the AVM if there was anything in particular we could take with us for the two RAF squadrons, and he had suggested canned beer. As the squadron stores officer I had to sign for thirty-six cases from the NAAFI.

The flight to Paramythia was across 220 miles of the loveliest scenery I have ever seen. In open formation we had to concentrate on flying and could only gain a fleeting impression of the quiet serenity of the deep blue waters of the Gulf of Corinth, and the little villages nestling amongst the vines and the olive groves on the sides of mountains which slipped under our wings very slowly in the bright sun. Each aircraft had a crew of three, plus a torpedo, two crates of beer, and other essentials such as gin and corned beef, and anything else we had been able to cram into the limited space in the rear cockpit. By the time we had reached the Gulf of Patras, and flown up the Greek coast to Corfu and then to Albania and the river-bed, we had been airborne for two and a half hours. The observers and air gunners had to sit with their eyes glued to their pieces of smoked glass all the way. The need to spot enemy fighters was of even greater importance on our way to Paramythia, because the survival of two RAF squadrons and their base were also at risk. We were all very hot and stiff when we climbed out on to the grassy field at Paramythia.

Standing on the stubplane I lifted my parachute out of the cockpit and slung it over my shoulder and climbed down on to the grass, breathing in the pure mountain air with delight. Then I glanced around me, and upwards at the overpowering mountains, and experienced one of those magic moments which remain in one's memory for all of life. I was quite overcome by the incredible beauty of it all. It had been very aptly named by generations of Albanians, centuries before: in their own tongue they called it 'The Valley of Fairy Tales'. The AVM had told Jackie Jago and he had pulled our legs about it, saying that no doubt some of us would feel doubly at home there.

Ten miles of fairyland, high in the mountains, a picturesque haven of changing beauty. I warmed to the thought that I could spend many hours studying it in the next few weeks. It had been inaccessible since the days of Adam and Eve and I wondered how many other such remote spots exist which can only be reached by air in the pressing needs of war.

That night, when the moon appeared above the mountains,

filling the valley with deep shadows. I realized that it had been shining down on that same scenery, completely undisturbed, for four hundred and ninety million years, and would go on doing so, presumably, until Doomsday.

The thought made our own affairs seem completely unimportant, and our presence there ridiculous. The two RAF squadrons at Paramythia were delighted to see us and were so pleased with the beer that we lived on their food, free of charge, all the time we were there. Normally there would have been a small mess bill for each officer, because officers of all three services are expected to feed themselves at their own expense no matter where they are – on board ship, in barracks, in the desert – even in the mountains of Albania. A grateful Government pays for the food eaten by ratings and other ranks, but not for officers, who are considered a privileged class and, apart from a daily ration allowance of a shilling or two, must fend for themselves.

Food presented no problem in the mountains, and there were times when we had too much. The local Albanians came down from the mountains into the camp several times a week, bearing huge carcasses slung from a pole between their shoulders. Conversation was impossible, but their friendly smiles, and the pleasure they showed when drinking our beer and gin and when smoking our cigarettes, made words unnecessary. In cheerful silence, declining all aid, they would build a fire and set up a barbecue, and then roast the meat for us, squatting on their heels, their dark faces glistening in the light from the fire, and with broad grins and much handshaking when we handed them drinks. When the meat was cooked they would stand up, and indicate that it was ready, by making a graceful gesture with the back of their hands, like royalty acknowledging the cheers of the crowd; and then disappear into the night, refusing all payment.

When I was next in Athens, I did some research to find out why they were so friendly. After all, they were allies of the Italians and not the Greeks, and we were on enemy territory. I learned that they had disliked being under the domination of the Italians ever since Mussolini had caused his armies to descend on them on Good Friday in 1939. When Italy invaded Greece in October 1940, they had gone out of their way to make things easy for the Greeks; and although the Italians had an initial success, and reached a position in Greece well to the south of Paramythia, with Albanian aid the Greeks had driven them back, out of Greece. A passive non-assistance to their conquerors, and a silent co-operation with the Greeks, had made all the difference; and the Italians might have been driven out of Albania altogether had it not been for the worst winter in living memory, when driving snow stopped all movement in any direction.

When we arrived at Paramythia the land fighting was well to the south of us and, officially, we were on enemy territory; but it was obvious from the reaction of the people living in that valley that we had nothing to fear from them. There was no danger that the Italians would ever learn of the existence of a British airfield behind their lines from such a reluctant ally.

Flying from that extraordinary mountain stronghold was made more difficult because there was no means of discovering the local barometric pressure, either in Paramythia, or, of course, in Valona. We knew that the field was three thousand feet above sea level, yet when I landed, my altimeter was reading less than two thousand feet. When taking off from Greece we had set the pressure for Eleusis, which is right down at sea level, on the banks of the Gulf of Athens. But of course, barometric pressure varies with height, temperature, and weather conditions; and in places of high altitude and strange wind conditions it can change hourly, either up or down. One millibar equals 32.8 feet of height and so an error if five millibars could show a wrong altitude by a minimum of one hundred and fifty feet. Every airstrip, particularly at high altitudes, has local errors peculiar to itself, and the barometric pressure can be either high or low by as much as twenty degrees or more, changing from day to day and from hour to hour. Nowadays the pressure is passed to pilots by radio as they fly from area to area so that they can adjust their altimeters and apply what are known as 'regional settings'. By turning a little milled knob on the altimeter to reset the pressure, the instrument can be adjusted to show the pilot his exact height above sea level in the area in which he is flying at the time.

All we could do was to set the altimeter at three thousand feet when we took off from Paramythia. But it was bound to be different in Valona harbour, when accurate height was of vital importance – *and* when we returned to land; and it was necessary to fly by eye, in the dark, and make visual adjustments whenever we could check our height against some known landmark.

Like Paramythia, Valona harbour is ten miles long and five miles wide, and it is surrounded by mountains and hills to seaward and to the south, which vary between nearly 3000 feet and 1000.

One mountain to the south-west is called St Vasilio, and is 2750 feet high. Our system of approach was to climb over the sea in the vicinity of Corfu, to a height of about 10 000 feet, which took all of half an hour with a torpedo, and then descend in the dark at half-throttle, entering the harbour through a gap to the south-west between St Vasilio and its neighbouring hill. From the chart we knew that this gap was exactly 1250 feet high, and when descending through it, a quick adjustment to the altimeter, adding one's own height above the gap, should have enabled us to fly across the harbour so that the aircraft arrived at the anchorage sixty feet above the sea, ready to fire its torpedo.

In theory this was the answer to our problem, but in practice it wasn't quite so easy, as I discovered on our first attack. At 3 a.m. that night – 13 March – we had discussed the plan in great detail in the marquee at Paramythia. Just before we were due to take off I was alarmed by John Caldecott-Smith's manner. He is a quiet individual who normally showed very little emotion, and like all of us had no inhibitions about discussing his nervousness and tension, but that night he had a strong sense of foreboding. He was looking unnaturally pale and his mouth was set in a straight line and I asked him if he was feeling ill. He looked at me glumly and said, 'I don't like it. I don't know why, but tonight I've got the shakes.'

I tried to cheer him up. 'At least we've got the shelter of the hills when we have dropped our fish – and against that dark background we should be up and over them before they know what's hit them!' We knew from a previous reconnaissance by one of the Wimpey pilots who had flown over Valona that afternoon that the anchorage was ripe with fat pickings. There were at least half a dozen big ships lying at anchor in deep water, and our torpedoes were fitted with Duplex Pistols. A torpedo attack from the air was the last thing they were expecting, and with the lights of the town behind the ships, we couldn't miss.

I tried to convey this to John. 'When their shipping starts to blow up they won't be able to see us, to seaward. They will be blinded by the explosions in the ships.'

'I know,' he said bleakly, looking even more glum. 'But I've got a feeling in my water that this is it, for Jackie and me, anyway.'

An hour later, at about 4 a.m., I followed Jackie and Caldecott-Smith and Pat Beagley, the TAG, down through the gap, and reset my altimeter to thirteen hundred feet as we passed through. It wasn't possible to do it accurately, because I had to concentrate on the blue formation light of Jackie's aircraft very close ahead, and the gap between the black shadows of the hills was not very wide. A few seconds later, when we were gliding across the inside of the harbour, with the throttles almost closed, steadily losing height, the flaming onions streaked past us on either side and Jackie's light disappeared. I guessed that he had been hit and had dropped into the water, because there was no explosion; perhaps they had hit his propeller or engine and stopped him in his tracks. One second he was there and the next he had gone. From that moment I was leading, and I thought that I had plenty of height to reach the shipping at anchor right ahead, which was almost within range, when my wheels struck the water with a dreadful lurch, and my throat constricted in the awful spasm which people have in mind when they say 'my heart leapt into my mouth'. Instinctively I held the aircraft steady in case it somersaulted, and opened the throttle wide and pressed the release button, because the water would have activated the Duplex Pistol on the nose of the torpedo and started the propeller. The sudden deceleration only lasted for about two seconds, when we were airborne again, but they were the longest two seconds I have ever known. Fortunately we were within fifteen hundred yards of a big ship, right ahead, her hulk a black shape against a searchlight wavering about from the town behind her, so my fish wasn't wasted. But after that experience I set my altimeter with very great care when coming through that gap, and insisted on the aircraft entering the harbour in very open formation, so that there was time to do so.

It says a great deal for the sturdy construction of the Swordfish undercarriage that it could be dipped into the sea at a speed of 90 knots or more, and held there for a few seconds, without being torn off; and for the power of the Bristol engine and the stability of the aircraft as a whole, that the ailerons and wings were sufficiently strong to keep it steady with such a sudden deceleration, and force it through the water into the air again without any damage whatever. On the night of our attack at Taranto, when Torrens-Spence remarked afterwards that he had touched the sea with his wheels as he flew through the harbour entrance, he had to put up with some leg-pulling, because it seemed unlikely that any aircraft could do such a thing without somersaulting. He had explained how he held it steady before easing back on the control column, to avoid that very thing, and I must have made a mental note at the time because I had followed his example instinctively. The immediate reaction would be to yank the control back, to lift the nose, and I am sure that I would have done so, had it not been for Tiffy, a qualified test pilot and one of the Navy's most expert aviators. When we were back at Paramythia at dawn I thanked him for having shown me the way to survival.

All the way back I wondered if we still had an undercarriage and asked Ken Sims, the air gunner, to peer over the side to check. He was one of our experienced TAGs and did his best, but owing to slipstream and the dark it was impossible to see anything which convinced us both that the undercarriage had been ripped off and we would have to do a belly landing. But at Paramythia the wheels were still there and we ran to the end of a normal landing without a sign of trouble and breathed again.

The next day, listening to the Italian radio, we heard that 'a dastardly sneak attack by the British' had been made on the Italian shipping at Valona harbour, but that very little damage had been sustained, and that three aircraft had been shot down and their pilots taken prisoner. We had lost the CO's aircraft only, with its crew of three, and from this report we knew that all three, pilot, observer and air gunner, had been picked up. The statement that they had shot down three was about as reliable as their claim that we had achieved no hits. We knew that both statements were untrue because our departure from the harbour had been made easier by the lights from the fires in at least three burning ships.

Back in Athens I sent a cable to John's wife, saying that he and Jackie and Pat Beagley, the air gunner, had been taken prisoner. I knew that this was breaking every rule in the book, but I wanted all three wives to be spared an agonizing wait while officialdom checked and double-checked, and there was no doubt whatever that my information was correct. I found myself in some very hot water indeed for sending that cable, but it was worth it.

After the loss of Jago and Caldecott-Smith, Torrens-Spence took over as CO of 815, and A. W. F. Sutton, known as Alfie, became the Senior Observer. The squadron was divided in half so that one half could be in the mountains ready to attack when the other was rearming at Athens. Because our successes became more extensive in the following four days, the captains of the ships were reluctant to remain at anchor in harbour at night, and by the end of the first week they took to mooring outside, along the coast, which made our task of finding them more difficult. So each half was divided again; one flight could search the coast up to and including Durazzo while the other went into Valona.

The defences of that harbour sharpened up considerably; they quickly realized that we were entering by the St Vasilio gap and moored a belligerent little flak ship on that side of the harbour, just where we came in; and others were dotted about on the line of our approach to Valona itself. On the first occasion that I led my flight of six through the gap we were all startled when flaming onions appeared from an unexpected quarter. When the other ships opened up we were even more startled, because by the time we reached them we had lost height and were closing in for our drops, and the violent noise of the guns made us jump. Normally, when flying under fire, the pilot can only see the flames from the gun and the shells streaking into the air; because of the noise of the engine, and his flying helmet, the noise of the guns is drowned. The crack was most alarming at close range.

That night there were no ships at anchor inside the harbour other than the flak ships, and so on our way out we did a circuit of the bay to the south to avoid the flak ships in the centre, which brought us round on the blind side of the belligerent little ship waiting to catch us on our way out. He was expecting us on his other side and it was a simple matter to put a torpedo into him from the south. He was only the size of a fishing vessel and it was really rather a waste of a torpedo which was designed to sink a ship ten times his size, and I felt rather a bully, but he was a menace to us all on that mooring, and it must have been a quick end for them all. I doubt whether anyone on board ever knew what had hit them.

Another ingenious method of defence, used in the Italians' efforts to continue to use Valona, nearly put paid to us all. Our success depended on being able to approach the shipping unseen; and a spidery biplane, scooting across the harbour in the dark, with plenty of forward speed after a dive approach and using very little throttle, was a difficult target for them to see or hear. One night we were horrified to find what looked like an illuminated buoy in the centre of the harbour, as big as the Albert Hall. It was so brilliantly lit that it had no discernible shape, and no matter from which direction we approached Valona, we were bound to be silhouetted against it for one or other of the groups of guns on the banks. Realizing the immediate need to extinguish that revealing glare, the 'tail-end Charlie' Swordfish pilot – the last in the queue – seeing that the five aircraft ahead of him were in trouble because of it, very rightly put his torpedo into the middle of it, and all the lights went out almost at once. Afterwards on their radio the

Italians claimed that we had sunk a hospital ship which had been 'fully illuminated'. They made great play on this theme, saying that Mussolini's daughter, the Countess Ciano, was 'the last to leave this sinking vessel'.

These things happen in wartime, and although we doubted the veracity of the Italian broadcast, it might have been true; though there were no red crosses, and the ship (if ship it was) was certainly being put to military use. Those of us who got back to Egypt were asked some very searching questions by Admiral Boyd before he was satisfied that we had not committed an international crime intentionally.

After a successful attack on shipping in Durazzo, when next in Athens I was sent for by Air Marshal D'Albiac, who required a full report from me in person. Afterwards he took me to lunch in the Grande Bretagne Hotel in the centre of Athens, with some of his staff. We had been seated for quite a few minutes when the German Ambassador and his staff, from the German embassy, were shown to the next table, well within earshot. From the expressions on the back of their necks it was obvious that they were listening to every word we said, and eventually the AVM turned to his senior air staff officer, a fair-headed Group Captain, and in a very clear voice he asked him a question. 'Sasso,' he said, 'have you given any thought to the problem of what we might do with Germany after the war?'

For a second the Group Captain looked a bit startled, and the necks of our neighbours turned a brighter red while everyone waited for his reply. Then, in an equally clear voice, tinged perhaps with a touch of boredom, the Group Captain said: 'I haven't had time to give the matter much thought, sir, but it might be a good idea if we gave it to the Poles!'

A few minutes later our Germanic neighbours moved to another table.

One consequence of that luncheon was that I missed the formation flight back to Paramythia with my half of the squadron, and had to fly back on my own. I had told the others not to wait, because I knew they wanted to get their heads down, in the peace and quiet of the Valley of Fairy Tales, before the night attack in the small hours. Afterwards, my companions accused me of adding to those fairy tales, but what happened was verified by the young Sub-Lieutenant observer who was with me, and by other indisputable evidence.

The Sub-Lieutenant was a volunteer to fly back with me because he had a luncheon date with a girl-friend in Athens. By then I knew the way well, but needed someone to sit in the back and keep a lookout through his smoked glass for fighters. This was a firm rule in case someone flying on his own unwittingly led a tailing shadower to Paramythia. It was just as well that he was there, because at about five thousand feet over Corfu he shouted: 'Fighters astern – on both sides!' A hasty glance over my shoulder revealed two Italian CR22s – little biplane fighers fitted with a Fiat engine capable of 240 m.p.h., and twin machine-guns firing 12.7 mm shells. I saw them clearly in the blinding glare of the sun, two little black squares, tearing downwards towards my stern, but fortunately a thousand feet higher. With the sun astern I was presenting an ideal target.

I jettisoned my torpedo immediately and hoped that I was over the sea, I learned later that it blew a sizeable hole in the south-west corner of Corfu. Then the routine I had learned in Bermuda came to my rescue, and as the Fiats opened fire I stood the Swordfish on its tail and their bullets missed ahead, and they spun over on to their backs and nearly collided. I hoped that the Sub-Lieutenant was firmly strapped in, because I had to get down to sea level in double-quick time, and then pull out of the dive in a violent manoeuvre which might toss him out of the aircraft; but there was no time to speak. I have never dived a Swordfish so close to the vertical before, nor pulled out so close to the sea. In the dive I kept the throttle almost fully open, and the engine screamed in protest. When I banged the throttle into the closed position and hauled the aircraft out of the dive, I was doing nearly 200 knots, and would not have been surprised if the wings had folded or come off completely. I only just missed the sea and had to do a steep climbing turn to avoid it, which blacked-out the observer completely for a few seconds.

The Fiats then made a fatal error: they had recovered from their inverted spin and had climbed to attack again, and they came in together, in unison, almost side by side. Had they attacked separately, one after the other, they would have shot me out of the sky as easily as snuffing a candle. I had enough time to dive down to water level again, to build up speed in order to climb vertically with the throttle closed, so that the aircraft stalled. This time I let it go slightly over the vertical, in a tightly stalled upward half of a loop, and then had to jam the throttle wide open and roll sideways into a completely stalled turn, and for once only just avoided an immediate spin; but the engine pulled her round, though for a split second I am sure that the whole weight of the Swordfish was hanging from the propeller. At the commencement of that turn I was just in time to see two big splashes as both Italians spun into the sea.

The distance from Corfu to Paramythia was only about twenty or so miles, and I made one or two attempts to get the Sub-Lieutenant to answer, but beyond murmuring that he had not been hit when I asked, he maintained an uncomfortable silence. I hoped that all was well with him and as soon as I had landed I stood up and looked into the rear cockpit. He had been violently sick and was in tears. I felt very sympathetic, but I suspect that he was desperately unhappy that I had seen him in such a mess. It was embarrassing in his eyes, but not in mine.

When Burns and Brown heard about this incident with the fighters, they pulled my leg. 'If only you'd fired your front gun, sir,' said Brown. 'Just one little bullet, that's all. Then you could claim two enemy fighters!'

There hadn't been time to press the trigger. Until I landed I thought that it had been a straightforward battle of airmanship and that bullets hadn't really been involved at all. But when I lifted my parachute out of the bucket seat in the front cockpit and went to sling it over my shoulder in the normal way, it fell to pieces, spilling an unexploded Italian bullet on to the empty metal seat with a clang and a rattle. There was a big jagged hole in the seat. Why it had failed to explode I shall never know. Perhaps my guardian angel had waved her wand? The shell had come through the underbelly of the aircraft and, presumably, had been cushioned by the soft silk of the parachute after penetrating the metal of the seat. It must have been less than a foot from my most sensitive anatomy, and thereafter I flew with a heavy sheet of armour plating between my parachute and the aircraft seat, on the principle that prevention is better than cure.

What worried me about that bullet, in retrospect, was the clear indication it gave that I had turned over the vertical to an inverted position much too early in that second attack. In their first attempt the Italian's bullets were nowhere near me, and in the second, they had no opportunity to fire upwards, because when they screamed past they were both upside down themselves, and on their way to a watery grave. So I must have presented my underbelly to them as they were diving, which was poor timing on my part. But when I found that unexploded bullet I knew that I was going to survive the war.

21
The Changing Scene

By Sunday, 23 March, when the moon had begun to wane, the squadron had sunk an acknowledged score of five ships of over ten thousand tons or more. Our losses, in aircraft more than men, fortunately, had been heavy, and the rising incidence of engine failure was beginning to be very worrying. After a forced landing by Spencer Lea on the previous Wednesday, the problem had to be solved quickly.

When the Sprog and his observer failed to return from a raid, and were missing for three days, although we were all anxious on their behalf I felt sure that they would reappear. As he had proved in the desert, there was something indestructible about Sprog Lea, and when he and his observer walked into the marquee on the Saturday evening I suspect that I was less surprised than anyone else.

For a few aggravating moments he just grinned happily and resisted our questioning, but when he did speak he shocked us all.

'My prop fell off,' he said calmly, as though it was an everyday occurrence like a puncture. 'You'll be surprised to learn that you can't fly without a prop.' He helped himself to a large whisky and gave another to the observer. Downing it in one gulp, he poured out two more.

We bombarded him with questions, and I said: 'Props don't just fall off, Sprog! You must have been hit by flak or something, surely?'

He shook his head. 'Nope. There was no flak on Wednesday night. I didn't see a shot fired in anger. The ships were anchored under the cliffs outside Durazzo, remember?'

He was quite right. There had been very little opposition because we caught them with their pants down, and everyone on board the ship asleep, including the watchkeepers – if any.

'I was over the river-bed at the foot of that bloody great mountain at the time,' he said. 'The engine started to race like mad and when I throttled back it was no better. Not surprising, when the flipping prop had just dropped off! Ever heard a car's engine when the throttle cable breaks? Just like that, only much worse. It was screaming like a woman being raped by the soldiers. I thought it was going to burst into flames at any moment so I switched off the ignition. Sure enough – no prop! There wasn't enough height to bale out and no time to make a decent forced-landing so I crash-landed on the flipping river-bed. Unfortunately I landed on a slope and the cab rolled over and ended up upside down. It was a total write-off so we set fire to it.'

We asked him how he had got back to Paramythia and he laughed.

'Walked, of course. How do you think I got back? In a taxi? There aren't any flipping roads in this neck of the woods, so we walked along the bloody river-bed. Pretty rugged going as a matter of fact. Mostly forests.' He shook his head grimly. 'Walking seems to be my forte in this outfit! I'm beginning to feel like Felix the flipping cat!'

As the crow flies, Paramythia was about fifteen miles from the foot of the tall mountain, but the river-bed wound through at least thirty miles of hilly forests which looked most forbidding from the air. No wonder they had taken three days. It must have been very tough going.

The next day Torrens-Spence dispatched me to Egypt to persuade Admiral Boyd to let us have some replacement aircraft before the moon rose again on 10 April. I arrived at Ras el Tin on Tuesday, 25 March, and explained to the Admiral why I was there.

I learned that six Swordfish, earmarked for 815 Squadron, were on board the *Formidable*. She had been held up at Suez for weeks, waiting for the Suez Canal to be cleared of mines, and had only just arrived in the Med. The Admiral told me that she was with the fleet at sea and was not due in Alexandria for about ten days. I explained about Paramythia, and the Air Marshal's insistence that we flew only when there was a moon.

'It's due to rise again on the tenth of April, sir, and I must be back well before then.'

'Take a stand-easy at Dekheila for a few days,' he said. 'Come back to this office on Thursday, the third of April, when I should have news of the *Formidable* and your aircraft. That will give you a week to get them across to Athens.' He thought carefully for a second or two and then answered my unspoken question. 'There is now a pool of spare pilots at Dekheila awaiting the *Formidable*. You can take five of them as far as Crete in the other Swordfish. I will arrange for them to be flown back from Crete, and will make sure that Torrens-Spence is at Máleme with enough chaps to take the replacement aircraft back to Greece.'

I thanked him and left. My week's 'stand-easy' in Alexandria was a welcome respite, but, in the days which followed, so much happened all over the Mediterranean that the tactical scene became most confused. World-shattering events piled up, one after the other. On the day that I called on the Admiral, the Premier of Jugoslavia signed a pact with the Axis powers in Vienna, against the wishes of the people, and this was going to have a terrible effect on the survival of Greece. The Greek people were relying on Jugoslavia to defend their Bulgarian border in the event of a German invasion. Now, they could be overrun from the north, through Serbia. But the very next day the men who had signed the pact were thrown out of office by an angry public and placed under arrest, and the young King Peter assumed the direction of Jugoslavian affairs.

On the day that the Jugoslavs rose in wrath against their betrayers, the Italian fleet was ordered to sea to attack Greece, on Hitler's insistence, to provide a diversion while the Germans landed Rommel and his Panzer division at Tripoli. The German Afrika Korps, which they succeeded in landing in North Africa, was even stronger than the force we had landed in Greece, and for the next seven days I listened to the news with mounting alarm. By the time I had to return to the Admiral's office, Rommel had recaptured Benghazi and was hacking his way into Libya.

To make matters even more confusing, when the news seeped through that what was left of the Italian navy had actually sailed and was advancing towards Crete, Cunningham raced to the attack and Alexandria harbour was suddenly empty. Three days later, when they returned, the Battle of Matapan had become naval history.

On 28 March, the *Formidable* launched her Albacores against the *Vittorio Veneto*, hitting the Italian battleship with several torpedoes. In Malta, to keep all the Italian and German aircraft on the ground which might otherwise have bombed Cunningham's fleet,

830 Swordfish Squadron, and some RAF Blenheims, were ordered to bomb the airfield at Lecce, in southern Italy. The Swordfish and the Blenheims kept up their attacks on Lecce; and at Máleme airfield in Crete, Torrens-Spence, who was already there awaiting the new Swordfish, took off with a torpedo and did a daylight attack on the Italian cruiser, *Pola*, scoring a direct hit on her engine-room which destroyed all her electrics so that she was unable to fire her guns. When she began to sink, the destroyer *Jervis* went alongside and took off her captain and crew, and as he stepped on board the *Jervis* the Italian captain said: 'Either that pilot was mad or he is the bravest man in the world.'

Tiffy Spence is a highly strung person but by no means mad. Because of his innate nervousness he always forced himself to press home his attacks to a suicidal degree and the Italian's assessment was no exaggeration.

Admiral Pridham-Wippell was the first to sight the enemy fleet, from the cruiser *Orion*. In company with *Ajax, Perth* and *Gloucester* he lured them into range of Cunningham's big guns. He reported that 'during the chase a number of 15-inch shells fell close to us, but like all the other ships we escaped without chipping our paint.'

The *Vittorio Veneto* had to turn for home after being hit by *Formidable*'s Albacores, and although she escaped the battle, the three Italian cruisers were sunk by the big guns of the battleships *Warspite, Barham* and *Valiant*, and from then onwards the Italian fleet ceased to exist as a fighting force. The loss of three cruisers and the damage to one battleship would not in itself constitute a *coup de grâce*, but when added to the damage inflicted at Taranto all sting had been taken from the Italians' naval tail.

When the British fleet returned to Alexandria I met some of the officers ashore and congratulated them on a great naval victory. One lieutenant-commander who was a physical training officer (a specialization which is now extinct) whom I had met in the boxing fraternity, remarked that what was so nice about the Battle of Matapan was the fact that no aircraft were involved. Notwithstanding my knowledge that 'Springers' – as PT officers were known – were distinguished by an excess of brawn rather than brain, I could not let this pass unnoticed, since he meant it quite seriously. The Albacores from *Formidable* had been backed by RAF bombers flying from Malta who also scored many hits on the Italian battleship, and I felt that this should at least be acknowledged, even by a Springer. However, I contented myself by saying that I hoped that nobody would make the mistake of giving voice to such nonsense in the hearing of Lieutenant-Commander Stead's widow.

'Who is Lieutenant-Commander Stead?' I was asked.

'He was the only British casualty of the whole battle,' I said. 'He was shot down when attacking the *Vittorio Veneto* in a Swordfish.'

The immediate award of many DSOS and scores of DSCS after the Battle of Matapan reflected Cunningham's pleasure at the success of this engagement. At the time, only two DSOS and four DSCS had been awarded for the Battle of Taranto, and however hard one tried, it was a comparison that one could not avoid making. Hale and Williamson had each received immediate DSOS, and four DSCS had been awarded to two observers and one pilot from *Eagle*, and one observer, 'Blood' Scarlett, from *Illustrious*. The entire ship's company of *Illustrious* protested about this. The ratings were most indignant because not one single pilot from their ship, which mounted the attack, was honoured, apart from the two squadron COs.

After the Matapan awards were announced Denis Boyd persuaded a Member of Parliament to ask a question in the House of Commons about the Taranto honours list and, as a result, eight months after the attack, in May 1941, two more DSOS and fourteen DSCS were added to the original list. The other eighteen officers who took part (which included me) received Mentions in Despatches. These belated marks of recognition were made when twenty of the forty men who had flown into Taranto had been killed.

Throughout all those stirring events in Alexandria I was having a wonderfully relaxing time, swimming, and playing golf, and drinking far too much *crème de menthe* in the evenings, around Alexandria's fascinating *estaminets*. On my last night I remembered that Kiggell had given me a message for the barman of one of Alexandria's famous nightclubs called the Faliron. It was known as the Flat Iron in the Fleet. The barman was the exact double of a famous pre-war Hollywood star named Wallace Beery – a 'toughie' with a heart of gold, a face like a battered chimpanzee with delirium tremens, and a voice which rumbled from his throat. When I had delivered the message the barman croaked a question. ' 'Ow ees Meestair Keeggell?' At the time I was wondering rather gloomily whether he was still alive, and how many of the aircraft had come down in the sea since I had flown to Egypt, and without thinking I replied: 'He is probably dead by now.' A few moments later there was a roll on the drums and the stage manager walked on to the dancefloor and called for silence.

'I 'ave terribull news. Ladees and Gentlemen . . . Meestair Keeggell . . . 'e is dead!' He pronounced this in heart-rending tones, and there was an immediate chorus of wails from scores of feminine throats. The manager then called for two minutes' silence in memory of 'Meestair Keeggell', and this solemn ceremony was prefaced – and brought to a merciful end – by more dramatic rolls on the drums. It was too late to intercede and I left quickly before being asked any more questions, but not before I had gazed in astonishment at all the lovely creatures who were standing with their heads bowed and with tears streaming down their cheeks.

My opinion of Lance Kiggell rose one hundred per cent that evening, and the next day, when I rejoined him, I told him that a national holiday would probably be declared all over Alexandria when he returned, and they discovered that he was still alive.

'Tripe!' said the Sprog. 'They were only crying because he probaby owes them a lot of money!'

On Sunday, 6 April, my six aircraft were ready for the flight to Crete. Just before we took off we heard that Germany had invaded Greece that morning. Piraeus had been bombed and I was sorry to hear that one of my old ships in the Clan Line, the *Clan Fraser*, had been sunk in the harbour. At the same time, probably in revenge for the uprising against their unsuccessful plot to annex Jugoslavia, that country was invaded too. Both invasions were on an unprecedented scale and without warning. The attack on Greece was made across the Bulgarian frontier, without opposition from the Jugoslavian army which had been destroyed while it was on its way by road from the north to defend that very border. The army was without air defence as it marched down the single road, and by nightfall it had been strafed and blasted to smithereens.

The attack on Jugoslavia was launched by tanks, paratroopers, and bombers, from Austria, Hungary, and Bulgaria. As the brave little army lay dying on the roadside, Belgrade became a smoking ruin.

By Wednesday, 9 April, 815 Squadron was back at Paramythia with the added capability of six new Swordfish. The moon was due to rise the next day.

The curtain fell on Paramythia on Thursday, 17 April, by which time we had sunk another two ships.

During April the Swordfish had become 'the last of the Mohicans'. All the Blenheims had been destroyed in their daylight raids on the Germans, and there was only one Wellington left, but it was without a crew. All the Wellington pilots had been killed. It was sitting on the grass under the lee of the mountain at the end of the valley, looking forlorn and neglected, and I planned to fly it out myself, having flown twins before the war. But my plans were overtaken by events and what remains of the lonely Wellington may still be sitting up there, shielded from the weather by the mountains.

On that ill-fated Thursday I was in Athens with my flight, and Tiffy and Kiggell were up in the mountains with theirs, so I missed the final act and the fall of the curtain. We were still doing the day-on-day-off routine, and on most days the two halves of the squadron passed each other over the Gulf of Corinth, flying in opposite directions. During the second week in April the Germans had advanced to Yanina, a big central town and marshalling point which had been used by the Allied forces as a main focal point. It was only about thirty-five miles to our south-west, and when it fell to the enemy we were surrounded by Germans, though in our hidey-hole we saw nothing of them, and we made quite sure that they saw nothing of us – during the day. They still had no idea that we were there, right in their midst, because we operated at night under cover of darkness when there was little chance of discovery. By day it was becoming rather tricky; the last stages of our approach from Athens had to be right down on the water, and we crept into the valley in line astern at dusk, at tree-top height, keeping well below the mountains. We all knew that it was only a matter of days before this stage of the squadron's history was over.

On Thursday, 17 April, after their supper of corned beef and gin, Tiffy and his aircrew were sitting on the grass outside the marquee enjoying the scenery, which was always superb in the dying evening sun. They were about to turn in for a few hours' sleep before taking off when a twin-engined aircraft appeared in the gap between the mountains, obviously approaching to land. Its wheels and flaps were down, and it was losing height on a slow run-in, up the valley. At first, everyone watched it with idle curiosity, until someone yelled: 'It's a Junkers 88!' when they scrambled to their feet in alarm.

Our makeshift airfield had no defences of any kind. We assumed that we would never be discovered, and if we were, that there would be no point in shooting it out. The effort of transporting anti-aircraft guns over those mountains, and the logistics of bringing shells to Paramythia, would have been very time-wasting, and in the event of an attack we planned to leap into our aircraft and get the hell out of it as best we could. This was another reason why it was not feasible to have the squadron ratings with us in the mountains, which was a statement I had to repeat to a disgruntled Burns and Brown every time I returned to Eleusis.

In a scurrying mass the squadron raced across the grass, with their revolvers in hand, to arrest the interloper. Tiffy had the longest legs and got there first. He ran on an interception course, to arrive at the end of the Junkers' landing run before the pilot could turn out of wind. The rest of the pilots and observers were panting along behind him. When the aircraft stopped, Tiffy leaped at the door and wrenched it open, thrusting his revolver inside.

There were three passengers sitting in the long compartment, facing aft. One of them was a handsome young man who stood up and introduced himself.

'I am King Peter of Jugoslavia,' he said and, pointing at one of the other passengers, 'and that gentleman is my Prime Minister.'

'And I'm Father Christmas!' said Tiffy. 'Now come on, get out . . .'

Tiffy's prisoner was indeed the young monarch. He had been snatched out of Jugoslavia from under the noses of the occupying Germans by the pilot and crew of that aircraft, who were Greeks, or Bulgarians, or Jugoslavians, we never discovered which. They had been given instructions to land at Paramythia, to refuel on their way to Athens. I believe that the third passenger was a VIP German who had been used as a hostage while the King was snatched. The German was certainly their prisoner all the time he was at Paramythia. By this dramatic action the pilot had anticipated present-day methods of hijacking by some thirty-five years.

Kiggell told me the full story the next day when we were sitting in the hangar at Eleusis, during an air raid on Athens. The squadron was together for the first time since 6 April, because after King Peter's flight we had to abandon Paramythia for good.

'As soon as he got out of the aircraft we recognized the young King,' said Kiggell. 'We took them all across to the marquee for refreshments while the crew refuelled the Junkers. They were in rather a hurry and only had time for a quickie or two. We offered them some corned beef, which they refused, and some gin, which they accepted. The Prime Minister didn't speak English, but young Peter was educated at Oundle or somewhere, and spoke it perfectly, so we assumed that the Prime Minister did too. Macaulay was pouring out the gin, and he said to the Minister, "say when", and when the chap didn't respond Mac went on pouring. Afterwards, when Tiffy ticked him off, he said that he had heard that the Jugoslavs were in the habit of drinking vodka like beer, and he assumed that the same applied to gin. Anyway, he gave the wretched man half a pint of gin, and then stood in open-mouthed admiration when the Prime Minister sank it in two gulps. So – he refilled his glass with another half pint, and said, "Encore, Monsieur", and "Bravo!" and that sort of malarkey. You know what Macaulay's like!'

I nodded, and waited, but Kiggell was looking into the distance, obviously savouring the memory.

'Come on!' I said impatiently. 'What happened then?'

Kiggell laughed. 'Well, we carried the Prime Minister out to his aircraft and they all took off.'

At Athens they were to be picked up by an RAF Sunderland and flown to Jerusalem, and everything worked according to plan. Presumably the Prime Minister recovered from his hangover while enjoying the hospitality of Coastal Command in the flying-boat. But the King's aircraft had been shadowed into Paramythia and the enemy had discovered our mountain base at long last.

As expected, shortly after the young monarch had gone, a squadron of Heinkels flew around the valley like wasps in a jar of honey, and dropped bombs all over the place.

'They couldn't get at us without flying into the mountains,' said Kiggell, with a grin. 'So they did very little damage. But they succeeded in frightening the lives out of us, and it was obvious that this wasn't going to last. They were bound to clobber us in time. All they had to do was a quick run just over the tops of the mountains from the south, dropping their bombs on us at the end of their run, and they couldn't miss. So we got out at the double, and here we are!'

22
Evacuation

On 14 April, three days before the squadron left Paramythia, Piraeus was heavily bombarded and the Gulf of Athens mined. Many ships were sunk, including the *Clan Cumming* which struck a mine and sank at once. Five days later, on the 19th, the Germans made their heaviest raid of all. It was a devastating attack which was almost undefended in the air, through no fault of the RAF. The shortage of fighters throughout the Greek campaign had proved our undoing; ships carrying Hurricanes to Greece were always the ones selected for attack, and initially, what fighters there were had to operate from the forward air bases which were very conspicuous and where dispersal was impossible owing to the mountainous terrain surrounding the airstrips. Because of this the fighter squadrons had been very vulnerable to air-to-ground attacks and their losses had been heavy.

In the last few days most of the RAF squadrons had to be withdrawn from Greece altogether, and the situation facing the last of our fighter pilots was quite impossible.

The effect of that attack on the 19th was so overwhelming that the Greek Government made up its mind that Greece could not continue to resist the Germans, and they asked all remaining British and Commonwealth forces to withdraw from Greece by the 21st. This was impossible, of course, but we did our best.

The 19th was a Saturday, and on that day the ack-ack gunners defending Eleusis airfield succeeded in shooting down three Stuka dive-bombers. The pilot of one was captured by the Australians defending the airfield, who turned him over to us for safe-keeping until an escort arrived to take him away. They thrust him through a doorway into the hangar, very forcibly.

'Look after this bastard, will you, until a guard turns up?' they shouted, propelling him towards us with a shove that sent him hurtling across the hangar-deck.

The German straightened up and stood looking at us. He was a dishevelled and unhappy figure who had obviously been roughly treated since being forced to bale out of his Stuka. He was a pleasant-looking chap with fair hair and a nice face, which was expressing surprise at finding himself in the company of a group of naval officers standing about with glasses in their hands about to have lunch. The corned beef was spread on bread, and plates of it were in a neat circle on crates. It was not what he expected to find, in a hangar, during an air raid.

He could not be expected to know that the hangar had been our home for some days. While Athens was under constant attack all movement was impossible, and we had lived and slept in it since arriving from Paramythia.

Macaulay handed the German pilot a glass of gin and said: 'Have a drink.' At this unexpected gesture his expression of surprise changed to incredulity, but he accepted the drink with a polite 'Thank you' and gave Macaulay a little bow.

'The British navy are gentlemen,' he said, pronouncing each syllable separately, his face rigid with emotion. 'But the Australians are not gentlemen.'

We asked him what was troubling him and he murmured that they had kicked his behind, torn off his buttons and ribbons, and stolen his Iron Cross.

We asked him in what battle he had won his Iron Cross and he said: 'For bombing the air-carrier *Illustrious* off Malta in January.'

At this we all shouted with laughter, and he looked puzzled and offended, so we explained that most of us had been on board the ship at the time.

'Impossible!' he cried. 'You could not have lived. After so many bombs she must be sunk!'

We assured him that the ship had sailed from Malta under her own steam at 26 knots, but it was clear that he thought that we were lying. The Germans would have lied in the same circumstances, of course, so there was no point in trying to convince him.

'Give him another gin,' said Tiffy, in a resigned voice. 'I reckon that he deserved his Iron Cross.'

When Macaulay recharged his glass he sniffed it suspiciously, and it was evident that he suspected our motives in being so hospitable. He probably doubted that even the mad British would offer drinks to a man who had bombed their own ship.

'It's not poisoned!' Macaulay laughed, and seized the opportunity to recharge his own. 'Look!' he said, swallowing the contents ostentatiously.

We asked him various questions about himself, and the attack on *Illustrious*, and he admitted that when bombing the ship in Malta they had suffered very heavy losses. Perhaps to ingratiate himself with us, he protested that he was not a German – he was an Austrian from the Tyrol – and he said that Goering had co-opted all his countrymen into the front-line regiments and air units, and that they were always given the most dangerous tasks. 'We are always the dirty dogs,' he said with a certain amount of resentment, which made me suspect that he was probably speaking the truth.

When the guard arrived he clicked his heels and was marched away. We wished him luck as he left, and at this he looked rather bewildered. It was clear that he had found the short meeting with us difficult to understand. He had expected abuse, not gin and good wishes, and this probably didn't tie up with what he had been told about the vile British.

During those raids two of our aircraft were destroyed, which was a bitter blow. We were doing our utmost to service the few remaining Swordfish for the 160-mile flight to Crete that day, with a gradually reducing complement of maintenance ratings, who were being evacuated by sea, direct to Egypt, at every opportunity. Every aircraft which was written-off meant yet another pilot and crew to be put on board some ship. But the time had come to go, or be captured. The Germans were out-flanking our forces with parachute troops, dropped as near as Corinth, and in those last days it was impossible to go into the town or to move beyond the precincts of the airfield. When we flew to Crete we could only muster ten aircraft and everyone else had to be scrambled on board ships, in the dark and confusion of a massed evacuation. Two destroyers, the *Diamond* and the *Wryneck*, were sunk in the Gulf when evacuating troops; but on the whole it was a success, and not as difficult as Dunkirk because the men being rescued were fully fit and not exhausted or injured.

The next two days back at Crete were hectic, and we lost another two aircraft doing anti-submarine patrols ahead of the evacuating ships, this time going south through the Kithera Channel, heading for Egypt. Lieutenant Denman Whatley and a young observer named Green had to force-land on the beaches of Antikithera when their engine failed. They were stuck there for a few days, awaiting a Walrus amphibian which was flown from a cruiser to pick them up, and while waiting were royally entertained by the king of the island, who was also its postman. Lieutenant Burnaby-Drayson was not so lucky. He had a full crew when his engine failed over the sea, and we searched for them for forty-eight hours when flying to and from our anti-submarine patrols. Unfortunately, out of the eight remaining aircraft only three were serviceable to fly, and we were working on them to prepare them for the long flight to Egypt and only one could be spared at a time. Burnaby-Drayson, his observer, and his air gunner, Freddie Faulkes, floated about in their dinghy almost within swimming distance of Máleme, and for two days and nights they could see us flying off to look for them, but could do nothing to attract our attention. On the third day, after the three serviceable Swordfish had flown back to Egypt, an offshore wind started to blow them farther away from the land and, ignoring the pleas of his companions, Burnaby-Drayson slipped out of his clothes and dived into the sea. The shore probably looked deceptively close after so long without food and water, but even for a strong swimmer in the peak of condition it was much too far away.

Wind and weather can play cruel tricks; an hour after the pilot had swum away on his suicidal attempt to summon aid it changed direction completely, and increased in strength, and for the first time blew the little rubber craft towards the island. There was a tiny little church on the seaward bank of Máleme airfield, and months before, we had given the Cretans permission to walk across the airfield for their church services, and on occasions we had joined them. During one of these services the dinghy floated within sight of the worshippers and they rushed out to tell the squadron.

The two men in the dinghy recovered, but the body of Burnaby-Drayson was washed ashore a few days later.

Perhaps it was the absence of his additional weight which enabled the dinghy to float in the wind to safety? It could have made just that little bit of difference. But the fact that he lost his life in a vain endeavour to save his companions should be recorded in the pages of Fleet Air Arm history.

In the last days of April and early in May the Germans were massing in Greece for an all-out attack on Crete, and their reconnaissance aircraft flew over the island daily, pin-pointing the gun emplacements. I shared an office with Alan Black, the CO of a handful of naval fighters at Máleme, and pointed out to him that at least the reconnaissance aircraft couldn't photograph our defences! Our office was the only brick building on the airfield, and in a rack against one wall we had twelve .303 rifles. With them we were expected to defend Máleme when the Germans descended from the skies in their parachutes.

Our remaining Swordfish were not really fit to fly. In an appeal for speedy help we managed to get a message through to Admiral Boyd, via a departing RAF pilot, and the Admiral flew over with his Engineer Captain, 'FATO' Jones, the very next day. They arrived in a Walrus amphibian and Captain Jones spent an entire morning examining all the engines of our eight surviving Swordfish, five of which needed complete engine changes. We were cannibalizing the five to service the three which were reasonable, but Captain Jones said that in his opinion none of them was fit to take to the air again. When Tiffy protested, and explained that we hoped to have the three airborne within twenty-four hours, Jones was dubious.

'Without any maintenance ratings?' he asked.

'There are one or two still here, sir, who didn't come to Greece. And Lieutenant-Commander Black has lent us some of his. In any case we can do a lot of the work ourselves.'

The ultimate decision was left to us, but in their present state they had been grounded – officially.

Before the Admiral and the Captain took off to return to Egypt, 'FATO' Jones turned to me. 'I suppose you realize that you might have to face a court martial if and when you get back to Egypt?'

'What for?' I asked, wondering which of my many sins had become public knowledge.

'Well, as squadron stores officer you have signed for twenty-two aircraft. I've got your signature in my office. Where the hell are they?'

The task of rebuilding three aircraft from five unserviceable machines would have been beyond most of us, but once again Torrens-Spence produced evidence of his genius. As the only qualified test pilot amongst us he did most of the work while we held his tools, and did as we were told. On the morning of 22 April we test-flew all three by doing one circuit and landing each. There was no time for more. Their engines were very rough and sounded terrible, but the alternative was to stay and perhaps be taken prisoner. Tiffy pointed out that there was a good chance that they would make the 300 miles to Mersa Matruh and be able to reach Dekheila overland, and the more people we got away the better. He and Alfie Sutton wanted to stay behind to assist the many thousands of soldiers to escape from the island. There were nearly 20 000 men to be evacuated, and somebody who understood the tricky seamanship problems of landing boats on that craggy coast, and of guiding non-seamen into them from a most hostile shore would be invaluable, and might save hundreds of lives. We disliked leaving Tiffy and the rest to face the Germans, but he was adamant.

Privately, I thought it was a moot point which was the more hazardous – to fly those old crates across 300 miles of open sea or to stay behind to face the Germans, and Ken Griffiths, my air gunner made that very point to me before we took off. But I knew that Torrens-Spence and Sutton would refuse to leave until they had helped every possible man to escape when the time came.

It was an epic flight which none of us will ever forget. We would have preferred to fly direct to Tobruk, which was only 210 miles across the sea, compared with the 300 to Mersa Matruh; but the German Afrika Korps had reached Sollum, which is well to the east of Tobruk, and Rommel was moving eastwards at such a fast pace that we would not have been surprised to find that the whole of Egypt had fallen by the time we reached Dekheila.

Kiggell was in the lead. The third pilot was Rudorf, a small, dynamic, jovial extrovert. We flew in open Vic formation, glancing up from our wavering oil pressure gauges from time to time, to grimace at each other. Mine was wavering between 50 and 60 lb per square inch the whole way, which would have been a good enough reason to make an emergency landing in normal circumstances, let alone undertake a trip of 300 miles out of sight of land. At about five thousand feet there was quite a lot of cumulus cloud, and we climbed through a gap, in formation, rather gingerly, levelling out above the clouds in the bright Mediterranean sunshine with some relief. For the next hour or so I did my best to avoid looking at the beastly pressure gauge. Its flickering needle was serving only as a constant reminder that a vast expanse of watery grave was waiting expectantly below the clouds. When we glimpsed part of an east-bound convoy, through a blue gap in our white carpet of cloud, the sight of those tiny ships down below, splashing along so slowly, was most welcome. To know that there were friendly ships in the vicinity was at least reassuring for a little of that long flight to freedom.

At the spectacle of that convoy Rudorf gave us a final thumbs-down sign, and pointed downwards with a resigned shrug. Before I had realized his intentions he had disappeared through the clouds, planning to ditch in the sea close to one of the ships while rescue was at hand. I rather envied him, but my engine was still functioning reasonably well. We flew on, hoping that he had been picked up, and Kiggell and I were very surprised when he landed at Dekheila an hour or two later. He explained that the convoy was being escorted by the old *Eagle*, which had been re-equipped with Fulmars, and new radar. To see whether we were friend or foe the ship's fighter pilots had been vectored towards us, and when Rudorf emerged from the clouds, right above the convoy, the Fulmars were climbing towards him in a most unfriendly manner. Wisely, he hurried back into the clouds, deciding that a faltering engine was less hostile than a Fulmar's .303 bullets, and offered a greater element of chance.

'When I came out of the clouds at six thousand feet I'd lost sight of the convoy, but the Fulmars had lost sight of me, so honours were even.' He went on to explain that by nursing his spluttering engine he managed to 'hiccup his way' to the Egyptian coast. He landed about half an hour after Kiggell. I had landed some forty minutes earlier, because unwittingly, Kiggell and I had become separated too.

That flight across the Mediterranean seemed to be the longest three and a half hours I had experienced. Then, to my intense relief, the blue horizon gradually changed to a yellowy blur, and the sea became sand. As we crossed the coastline I breathed a huge sigh of relief, and grinned across at Kiggell; but he shook his head doubtfully and held up a downward-pointing thumb.

His aircraft was behaving temperamentally, as though it had a mind of its own and was equally relieved to be over terra firma at last. Evidently it wanted to land without further procrastination, and it began to lose height; but when I throttled back to stay with him, Kiggell waved me on. We both knew that if one of us had to force-land on that desolate stretch of no-man's-land, unless the other arrived at our destination fairly smartly, to alert a Search and Rescue party, nobody would ever know that we had even been airborne, until our skeletons were discovered. Convinced that

Kiggell was attempting the remaining 140 miles on foot I flew along the Egyptian coast as fast as I dared, to send a party back to pick up him. Unbeknown to me he was following in my wake, many miles astern, and out of sight. When he had descended to a few hundred feet above the desert his aircraft appeared to take an immediate dislike to the un-ending vista of nothingness, and decided to pick up its skirts and forge ahead. Somehow he had managed to keep it going, which was more than I could boast. When I landed at Dekheila I had no engine at all, which was only partly my fault. It just fell to bits.

Nobody was expecting us at the airfield, and as I flew into the circuit I saw that Paymaster-Commander 'Lucy' Waters, and various other well-known 'boozeliers', were standing outside the wardroom, on the veranda, drinking the ghastly sherry someone had bought from Cyprus and which was sold to mess-members at half a piastre a glass. After the seventh it tasted quite reasonable. They were patently surprised to see a solitary Swordfish approaching from the west, and I couldn't resist the temptation to dive on their upturned faces. Perhaps I overdid it, at my joy to be back; but the dive was too much for my worn-out motor, which disintegrated as I climbed up again, shedding its cylinders in all directions. The last time this had happened had been in the dark, with Ken Griffiths in the back seat too, but now I was in the circuit in daylight and it presented no problem. Before landing, I had time to yell at Ken, 'You must be a Jonah!', but when we climbed out, and walked round to the front, it was a sad sight. Bits of pipe were sticking out here and there where the cylinders should have been.

'What a bloody shame!' said Ken with a big grin. 'After all that work we did at Máleme!'

We had gone into Greece from this airfield with twenty-two aircraft – only two and a half months ago – though it seemed like a lifetime. We had come back with three, and they all needed new engines, after flying over a path which had been traversed in many strange ways since the Minoans had traded with the Pharaohs, centuries before. I doubted whether that well-worn route had ever been covered in such a hazardous manner in its long history.

The Germans attacked Crete on 19 May. Their losses were 6000 killed and 11 000 wounded, but they captured the island after twelve days of fighting which was as bitter as anything which occurred in the Second World War. Tiffy and Alfie helped in the evacuation of over 16 000 officers and men, and when they got back to Egypt in the last boat to leave, Sutton had to go to hospital for a few days for repairs to his feet, which were like horse's hooves. He had worn out his shoes in the first forty-eight hours, clambering over the mountains and down the granite cliffs, to show the soldiers the way. As each boatload left, the occupants appealed to him to go with them, but neither he nor Tiffy would leave until they were satisfied that every man who could be got away had gone.

For his efforts in Crete, Sutton was awarded a bar to the DSC he had earned at Taranto, and in my opinion no gong was ever more richly deserved.

Another award was announced after the Battle of Crete, which gave the whole of 815 Squadron the most tremendous uplift. Tiffy Spence was awarded a Greek DFC, given to him by the Greek Government as a mark of appreciation to the whole Swordfish squadron. Nothing could have pleased us more.

During the twelve days of fighting in Crete, three cruisers and four destroyers were sunk, mainly because they had no defence from air attack. The first of these was HMS *Juno*, on 21 May. On the 25th, *Formidable* was bombed. The news took some time to filter through to me and when I heard I was very sorry indeed, particularly about the *Juno*; but there was little time for grief because as soon as I returned to Egypt Admiral Boyd sent me to Malta to do the biggest job I had yet been called upon to undertake, and throughout the Battle of Crete I was dodging bombs in that beleaguered island.

23
Malta

A few nights after flying back to Egypt I returned to Dekheila with Kiggell, Sprog Lea, Ian Swayne, and all the rest, after a splendid run around the halls in Alexandria. It was about two in the morning and I was startled to see a signal pinned to the notice-board with my name on it in great big red letters. The signal was unambiguous: I was to report to the Admiral, personally, at 0900 that morning.

Admiral Boyd's greeting did nothing to improve my hangover.

'Congratulations!' he said, his beaming smile a little less grim than usual. 'You are our first volunteer to go to Malta!'

At my expression of horror he said: 'You sail at once – as soon as you can get your bits and pieces together.'

While I stood in a daze trying to recover from the shock of this quite untrue statement – I had certainly not volunteered to go anywhere, least of all Malta – in fact we were all hoping to be sent home for a rest – he embarked on an outline of the tactical situation. Rommel's landing on 1 April had been far too successful. Somehow he had managed to sail past Malta with a vast armada of German shipping. 'He couldn't have landed several Panzer divisions armed with massive tanks without the prior knowledge of the Vichy-French. We know that German aircraft and submarines and MTBs are operating from Tripoli and Tunis so the Vichy-French have shown their hand. They have signed an armistice with the Italians and the Germans who are now in control and I understand that Tunisia and Algeria are now run by the Italian Armistice Commission, so to all intents and purposes the whole of North Africa, from Morocco to Rommel's present position at Sollum, is hostile.

'The capture of Greece has been a serious blow, and if our forces are defeated in Crete, which appears likely, the fall of Egypt and the evacuation of all British forces in the Mediteranean is a grim possibility. So we have got to stop Rommel at all costs, and the only way we can do this at present is to cut off his supplies from Italy.'

He explained that 830 Swordfish Squadron, based at Hal Far, in Malta, was the only night-striking force left in the whole Med with a capability of attacking ships at night with torpedoes from the air. 'Our submarines are out hunting, in force; and the RAF Blenheims and Wellingtons have been doing a magnificent job by day, and have bombed a lot of shipping; but as a result, the enemy avoids sailing within range of Malta in daylight. So, you can see that the Swordfish squadron at Hal Far must carry the major share of the responsibility, if Rommel's shipping gets through.'

He talked about the squadron, and admitted that they had been hard at it for ten long months and were probably exhausted.

'But they lose aircraft every time they take off,' he said. 'Their losses have been very high indeed; and too many ships have been getting through.'

He picked up an envelope from his desk and handed it to me.

'Read that,' he said grimly. I was surprised to see that the envelope, and the heading of the typewritten brief inside, were both addressed to me, and the brief was signed by the Admiral personally. I read it carefully and felt my face going red. It was dynamite, and only Denis Boyd could have taken such an unorthodox step. It contained a list of possible targets for the squadron in Sicily and Tripolitania, but it also contained a summary of past failures and achievements, the number of aircraft and aircrew lost per raid, and the number of ships sunk. It was a terrifying document, and although the Admiral was critical, on paper they seemed to have been flying very hard against over-whelming odds.

I had not been appointed in command, nor had I been given a named task, like senior pilot. At the bottom of the page, under the heading 'Action to be taken on arrival' were the three words, in capitals, in Denis Boyd's handwriting: SINK ROMMEL'S SHIPPING!

The Admiral was watching me steadily as I read it, and I was careful not to look surprised. When I had finished, I put it back in its envelope and then stowed it in the breast pocket of my white uniform tunic, and buttoned the pocket down.

'Go and find out what is wrong,' he said, 'and put it right. That paper is your authority from me to take whatever action you feel is necessary. Use it carefully, after you have been with them a few days, and try not to be intolerant. But' – and he paused, and the intensity of his last three words was quite vehement – 'SINK ROMMEL'S SHIPPING.'

With any other man I could have asked for a definite appointment, but I assumed that he had his own reasons for this oblique and unorthodox approach. One did not question Denis Boyd's motives.

'It was a choice between T-Spence, Kiggell and you,' he said. 'T-Spence is still in Crete, and as Kiggell is senior to you I want him to remain as a Flight Commander in 815 Squadron. Report to the Captain of HMS *Hero*, now, to make your number.'

He held out his hand and wished me luck, which I found most heartening.

Nearly two years passed before I saw Admiral Boyd again, but during all the trials and tribulations which followed I drew strength from the knowledge that he had sent me on that particular task and that I had his unqualified support.

My attempts to say good-bye to Burns and Brown and the rest of the squadron came to nothing. On board HMS *Hero* I was told that the plans had been changed. She was off in the opposite direction to do some operation or other, and I was to report, at once, to the Captain of HMS *Ilex*, another destroyer, because he was keen to sail as soon as I was ready. I had already made arrangements, by telephone, for my gear to be sent to *Hero*. I had to act swiftly to unscramble my last request, and it all took time. Then I had to discover the address of the laundry where my dhobi had been sent and collect it. By the time I had sorted myself out and embarked in the right ship it was too late to say good-bye to anyone at Dekheila, which was eight miles from the town.

If Burns and Brown are still alive and happen to read this perhaps they will now understand why I suddenly disappeared without so much as a 'Fare Thee Well' or a 'Thank you' to the two great guys who had kept me in the air, and alive and well, for so long. To be leaving them seemed like abandoning one's wife and family. 815 was more than just a squadron, it was a way of life. Only Kiggell and I had survived from the very beginning in *Courageous*, and it seemed strange just to go, as though their future was of no further interest to me. When the *Ilex* slipped quietly out of Alexandria harbour that evening, the lump in my throat was agonizing.

During the next few months I managed to follow the squadron's progress from reports by people passing through Malta from Egypt. Towards the end of May, after re-equipping with new Swordfish at Dekheila, and still under the command of Lieutenant Michael Torrens-Spence, they flew to Famagusta, in Cyprus, which was only 80 miles from the coast of Syria, where trouble was brewing.

Following the French armistice with Germany and Italy, that little country was ripe for Axis penetration. With Rommel deep inside Egypt, threatening Alexandria and Cairo, the German occupation of Syria would have closed the gap between the German Afrika Korps in the desert and the German forces in Greece and Crete, and the Suez Canal would have been closed to British and Allied shipping. The task of driving Rommel back into Libya would have been impossible and the whole of the Mediterranean, with the exception of Malta, would have been in German hands. So, on 8 June, taking an army of Free French with them to rub salt in the wound, the Allies crossed into Syria from Palestine, Transjordan, and Iraq. On the same day the fleet bombarded Syria from the sea and the destroyer *Havock* was amongst them. I mention this now because it has an important bearing on this story later.

From Cyprus, the pilots of 815 Squadron were kept very busy, attacking German, Italian and Vichy-French ships, trying to reach Syria. It was at this stage that Macaulay's flying became suicidal; not content with reporting that he had sunk a ship weighing so many thousands of tons, he insisted on reporting the ship by name. To do this he had to fly round its stern as it sank, reading the name and the port of registry by the light of an Aldis lamp, which he operated himself from the front cockpit.

This impudent act of folly must have infuriated the enemy on board the sinking vessel as much as it terrified the wretched observer crouched in the back of his Stringbag, and it was a clear indication that Macaulay had gone round the bend. Someone should have done something about it, but a few weeks later he dived his Swordfish too steeply during an attack and tore off its wings, and it was then too late.

In retrospect it is clear that Macaulay should have been grounded six months earlier when he had first started behaving strangely: but it is easy to be wise after the event. In any case, nobody in the squadron, myself included, was behaving normally, with the possible exception of Torrens-Spence; and even that great man was given to twirling his hair between long nervous fingers in the evenings, until we all felt like jumping on him. Nevertheless, Macaulay's death, and the death of his observer, Sub-Lieutenant Bailey, should not be forgotten, and will not have been in vain if the naval psychiatrists of the future take note of the circumstances which led up to it. I don't think that in 1941 our 'trick-cyclists' were aware that there are some people who are unable to crack when the strain becomes too great, but instead are driven by some irresistible internal urge to invite death by venturing where others do not dare, to the ultimate point when death must win. At the very first sign of mental imbalance they should be kept under careful scrutiny and grounded before they kill somebody of great value, like the late Sub-Lieutenant (A) Ronald Anthony Bailey, DSC, RN.

My place in the squadron was taken by a bearded Lieutenant named Clifford, who was shot down after he had torpedoed one of the ships in a Vichy-French convoy bound for Syria. When he dived into the sea from his Swordfish, he found himself swimming about with all the survivors of the ship which he had just sunk; and was picked out of the sea by the crew of another enemy ship in the convoy, which, in turn, was torpedoed and sunk by Sub-Lieutenants Macaulay and Bailey, a few moments after Clifford had clambered on board. Finding himself in the water for the second time in less than an hour, in company with the survivors of two ships, one of which he had sunk himself, when he was rescued by the crew of a third he could only pray that this time 815 Squadron would let the third ship stay afloat; because he then had reason to believe that he was far from popular with his Vichy-French captors.

The aftermath of this chapter of events was equally fascinating. The Vichy-French in Syria were quick to turn him over to the Italians before they surrendered to the Allies, because they knew that he would be freed when the Allies were victorious. Since the French were supposed to be neutral, and no state of war existed between France and England, this action was entirely contrary to the terms of the Geneva Convention concerning the treatment of internees and, in London, the Admiralty and the Foreign Office demanded his repatriation. The Italians would only agree to this on an exchange basis, and I was interested to learn the exchange rate for a Swordfish pilot of Lieutenant's rank in the Fleet Air Arm. No doubt the Italians thought that they had driven a hard bargain, but I suspect that the Admiralty considered the deal reasonable enough: Lieutenant Clifford was exchanged for two Italian majors and one Italian general – a fair swop!

Syria surrendered on 11 July, when 815 Squadron went back to the desert to fight Rommel. During that lengthy desert campaign it was common knowledge that one flight of Swordfish mistook some British tanks for German and attacked them with their special anti-tank bombs. There were several Swordfish squadrons in the desert at the time, and I have no idea which pilots made the mistake, but I doubt whether they were from 815. If they were, no doubt Tiffy Spence (DSO, DSC, AFC, and Greek DFC) made his apologies and explained that mistakes are bound to occur even in the best of squadrons – which is a fair description of 815. In my opinion it was the best squadron of them all, and Tiffy their finest leader.

24
The Task

A few weeks before HMS *Ilex* landed me at Kalafrana the air defence of Malta had been taken over by Air Vice-Marshal Lloyd. His predecessor had been Air Commodore Freddy Maynard who had held the fort since Italy first attacked the tiny island. Maynard's Personal Assistant was George Burges, who flew the famous Gladiators which had been found in crates at Kalafrana labelled 'HMS *Glorious*', long after that ship had left for the North Sea. In the first air battles over Malta they had been operated from Hal Far together with four Hurricanes which were the island's sole fighter defence. Between them they intercepted seventy-two enemy formations and shot down thirty-seven aircraft.

In July 1940, a consignment of twelve Hurricanes had been taken to the Mediterranean in the aircraft carrier HMS *Argus*, and flown off to Malta from her flight-deck. In the next seven months, during 141 raids, they intercepted every single one, and did battle with the entire Italian Regia Aeronautica, based in Sicily. It is not surprising that by March 1941 most of the Hurricanes had been destroyed.

George Burges was still in Malta when I arrived, much to my pleasure, as we were old friends; and Wing-Commander Darby Welland was in the island too. I had last met Burges when we did the nine-month navigation course together at Manston before the war; and Welland had been the Signals Officer when 815 Squadron was at Bircham Newton. During May, he had landed in Malta on his way to be the staff Signals Officer to the AOC, Middle East in Cairo. Because it was another non-flying job he pleaded with Hugh Pughe Lloyd to be allowed to stay in Malta, to fly with the Glen Martin reconnaissance squadron, and when I arrived he was well established as their commanding officer. It was a real delight to hear his Australian accent again, and to find his swarthy face leering at me over a glass. Five months later he was killed in the Libyan desert.

The three of us dined together in Valetta whenever we could, and during one of those jovial meals George Burges told me that he had flown in defence of the *Illustrious* when she had limped into Grand Harbour in January that year.

'How many of the ship's Fulmars managed to survive the battle at sea?' I asked. 'There were only five serviceable fighter aircraft on board that morning.'

'Three,' he said, 'and two of them were shot down over Malta during the attacks on the ship when she was alongside.'

'How many shore-based fighters were there, then?'

'Five Hurricanes,' was the astonishing reply. He had flown Faith, the last remaining Gladiator of that immortal trio, to help defend the ship. I told him about the Austrian Stuka pilot who was shot down over Athens, and remarked how surprised he would have been had he known that the heavy losses that he admitted the Stuka pilots had sustained over Malta had been inflicted by a mere handful of pilots.

On 3 April that year, a dozen Hurricanes had been brought to the Mediterranean in the *Ark Royal* and escorted to Malta by the ship's Skuas, which were two-seaters and carried an observer. It had ended in tragedy for the Skuas. The return flight would stretch their radius of action to the utmost, even in normal weather, but nobody had bargained for the sirocco which blew up during their return, and in that violent head-wind they all ran out of petrol and were lost. One crew floated in their rubber dinghy to the shores of Algeria, where they were taken prisoner by the Vichy-French.

In June 1941, the next consignment of Hurricanes landed at Hal Far, just after I joined 830 Squadron, Twenty-three of them were brought out to the Med on board HMS *Victorious*. During their passage the ship joined in the attack on the *Bismarck*, and in very rough weather one of her Swordfish pilots scored a hit on the *Bismarck*'s steering gear. When the Swordfish squadron landed again, the ship's flight-deck was rising and falling sixty feet every thirty seconds, but only one Swordfish was damaged: its tail-wheel collapsed.

At that time Malta was the only little piece of territory in the Mediterranean which was still coloured red on the map, indicating that it was in British hands. With the exception of Gibraltar at one end, and Alexandria and Cairo at the other , most of the main land masses were coloured black, indicating German occupation and control. When I studied the wall map in War Headquarters in Valetta, there was no doubt that the island was the key to Africa and to the entire Mediterranean theatre. One little pink blob in the middle of the sea, surrounded by sombre black, made a grim picture, and we all felt rather isolated.

On 25 May, HMS *Formidable* was hit by bombs off Crete, and after a few weeks in Dekheila to re-equip themselves, half a dozen pilots and observers from the *Formidable* were sent to 830 Squadron. One of them was a tough little lieutenant pilot who was only about five feet five inches tall, named George Myles Thomas Osborn. Ever since his Dartmouth days he had been known as 'Woozle', and the name suited him admirably. He was a tower of strength, and arrived in time to help me adjust the squadron and cope with its reorganization. Together we supervised the installation of the new instrument panels, cancelled all parades, did away with the senior officers' ante-room, and arranged daily transport for all the aircrew who flew each night down to the rocky bay at Kalafrana in the afternoons so that they could get some sleep, lying on the rocks in the sun after a swim, instead of huddling down air raid shelters. The suggestion was made to me by a splendid Chief Petty Officer who pointed out that the high incidence of twitch had been caused by lack of sleep.

'We've got a job to do, during the afternoons, sir, when the bombing permits, but we can sleep all night. You can't help us, so why don't you all go and get your heads down, in the sun? You do your stuff at night, and you've got to get some sleep sometime or other.'

At the end of each afternoon when we came back refreshed, ready for the night's flying, we found that the men had worked wonders during the afternoon repairing bomb damage and servicing the engines. During the raids they had to take cover, and the aircraft were all in dispersal bomb-pens, so our absence made no difference. If we turned in, in our beds, at Hal Far, we were unlikely to sleep because the three airfields, Luq, Takali, and Hal Far, were prime targets practically every single afternoon.

Almost before I was conscious of the change I found that I was with a squadron with which I could find no fault. And strangely enough, the serviceability rate improved, day by day. By the end of June we were able to muster twelve aircraft each night, and by July we were able to sink a monthly average of 50 000 tons of Rommel's shipping, and were guaranteeing seventy-five per cent hits.

During July, when we became the first squadron to be equipped with radar, our task was simplified. It was called Anti-Surface-Vessels – short title ASV, and it enabled us to see the enemy ships even on moonless nights. When the Germans and Italians realized that in some miraculous way we were able to see them in the dark, at first they appeared to assume that it had something to do with the wake of their ships and the tight convoy formation they adopted. When they heard us approaching they opened up their formation as far as they could and then stopped their engines. This was most obliging because it gave us a no-deflection shot, and it was then a case of picking them off from the radar screen, one by one.

In August we sank 100 000 tons. To be fair, the last of the ships to be sunk was sent to the bottom at ten minutes past midnight on 31 August, and it was therefore a September score; but as that month went past there were fewer and fewer ships to attack, which puzzled us, because Rommel's supplies must have been in great demand after all the sinkings of the two previous months. The reason became clear to me after the war when Count Ciano published his famous diary: on 9 November 1941, he made the following entry.

'Since September 19th we had given up trying to get convoys through to Libya; every attempt had been very costly, and the losses suffered by our merchant marine had reached such proportions as to discourage any further experiments. Tonight we tried it again; Libya needs materials, arms, fuel, more and more every day. And a convoy of seven ships left, accompanied by two ten-thousand-ton cruisers and ten destroyers, because it was known that at Malta the British had two battleships intended to act as wolves among the sheep. An engagement occurred, the results of which are inexplicable. All, I mean *all*, our ships were sunk, and one or maybe two or three destroyers. The British returned to their ports after having slaughtered us. Naturally, today our various headquarters are pulling out their usual inevitable and imaginary sinking of a British cruiser by a torpedo plane; nobody believes it. This morning Mussolini was depressed and indignant. This will undoubtedly have profound repercussions in Italy, Germany, and above all, in Libya.'

The presence of two British battleships in Malta was a figment of Italian imagination too, because Admiral Cunningham had abandoned Grand Harbour, Malta, as an anchorage for our capital ships ever since *Illustrious* had been forced to take refuge there in January and had been given such a hammering.

The events which led up to this started in August, when a tanker ran aground off Tripoli. Being a sitting duck, the AVM rang suggesting I torpedo it on my own, if I could get there before it was refloated. As a precaution I was accompanied by Lieutenant Robert Edgar Bibby, RNVR, loaded with bombs in case I missed. When we reached Tripoli the tanker had been refloated and was surrounded with anti-torpedo nets, so Bibby had to sink it with his bombs. While I was watching this I was fired at by a destroyer, also at anchor in the moonlight, and without torpedo nets; so that night two Swordfish accounted for two ships, which was most satisfactory.

Afterwards I asked the AVM how it was that he always knew about these enemy shipping movements so quickly and accurately, but he would not say. After an attack on 2nd September I was to discover the answer the hard way, by becoming the AVM's odd-job man. He rang me to say that he had sent a car for me and I was to report to him in his office.

I was about to enter the realm of cloak-and-dagger, and my life has never been quite the same since. It was a great mistake on my part, in some ways, but an odd-job man has little choice when he is sent to do a job of work, no matter what it is.

25
A Flight to Freedom

When I was shown into the Air Vice-Marshal's office he was standing beside a French civilian with dark, closely cropped hair. He looked very tired and strained, as though he had been without sleep for a long while, and when I was introduced he stared at me with bright, burning eyes as black as his hair. After shaking hands I endured his searching gaze for an embarrassing moment or two, and then to my surprise the Frenchman reached for my hand and shook it a second time, in a very emotional way. His eyes filled with tears and he shot out of the room as though overcome.

'What was all that about, sir?' I asked. The AVM waved me to a chair with his cigarette-holder.

'You asked me how I knew about that tanker running aground so soon after it happened. Well, that information, and all the information which has made it possible for your squadron to sink so much shipping, is provided by an organization of very brave civilians. The man you have just met is their leader.'

He gave me a broad outline of the organization, composed mainly of Free French and French Resistance workers, and what it achieved, and, in his brisk, even voice, told me of a way of life which I had never envisaged, peopled by men who risked their lives in an even more dangerous way than we did in our Swordfish, and who achieved a great deal more.

'He is upset because two of his best men are on the run in Algiers. They have twenty-four hours to escape from North Africa or die. It sounds melodramatic but I'm afraid that it's true. They have been doing some particularly valuable work but have been bowled out, and are now being watched, and there is little hope that they can escape without outside help. That is what we are going to provide.

'We were in touch with them by radio last night and they are contacting us again at six this evening for the last time; they then have to bury their transmitters. Later tonight they are catching a train from Algiers to Tripoli. When it arrives there, they would be met by an armed posse and shot.

'Naturally, they have no intention of staying on the train. In their *cri de coeur*, last night, they outlined a plan which is quite feasible.'

He offered me a cigarette and inserted a fresh one in his holder.

'At four in the morning, tomorrow, their train arrives at a little town called Enfidaville, on the Tunisian coast in the Gulf of Hammamet. Enfidaville is only about four miles inland, and its railway station is on the inland side of the main road from Tunis, and next to a big field which is on this side – the seaward side – of the road. It is a big enough field for an aircraft and they have appealed to us to have one there, ready to take off when the train arrives. They seem quite certain that they can escape from that little station in the dark, at that time in the morning; but the whole thing will have to be planned with great precision and the timing will have to be perfect, as you can imagine. They may be pursued, and they want the pilot to be sitting with his hand on the throttle, as it were, facing into wind, so that they can dive into the aircraft and be off the ground before the pursuers can catch up with them.

'I would like you to do this trip if possible, but, if not, I can probably find someone else.'

'Thanks for the compliment, sir,' I said, 'but what's to prevent my doing it? I mean, you've made up your mind haven't you? The Swordfish would be an ideal aircraft for this type of venture.'

'I wish it were,' he said dourly. 'Unfortunately it's too far for a Swordfish. Enfidaville to Malta is two hundred miles.'

'Tripoli is one hundred and ninety, sir, and we go there and back often enough.'

'Yes, but on your own admission, and of some of the other Swordfish pilots, after your Tripoli runs you have come back with your fuel indicator showing an empty tank, and this trip includes flying inland, finding a field in the dark, landing, perhaps waiting with your engine running, taking off again, and so on.' He shook his head doubtfully. 'You haven't had time to study the problem, but I have been up most of the night examining it from all angles. There are many other factors: after landing and taxiing down-wind you may have to wait for a long while. I've studied the large-scale map of the area and it's going to take those poor devils quite a time to escape from that station, cross the road, climb the hedge into the field, and then find the aircraft. If the Vichy-French are searching for them, or they are being followed, they may have to lie low and conceal themselves on their way to the aeroplane. There are two other factors which make the shortage of fuel critical: on the return flight there will be three people in the back, because you will need a very competent navigator, and there are two of these agents to be picked up; and the flight back will be in daylight, and you will have to fly between Pantellaria and Lampedusa.'

'The fighter patrols!' I exclaimed. 'I had forgotten them.'

'Precisely. The Italians operate those patrols continuously, from dawn to dusk. If you had to skirt round to the south of Lampedusa it would add another fifty miles to the return trip at least.'

'If a Swordfish flew back at sea level I doubt whether the Italians would see it,' I said, and the AVM agreed.

'But you would then be burning petrol at the most uneconomic rate possible.' It was clear that the Air Marshal had gone into the problem very thoroughly, with a Swordfish in mind. 'No,' he said, shaking his head again, 'even with an underslung petrol tank, you would still be short of about fifty gallons. You wouldn't be able to take one of those big tanks in the rear cockpit because we need every inch of space to cram in the passengers.'

His arguments were incontrovertible.

'How can I help, sir?'

'My knowledge of light aircraft is a bit out-of-date. If you will come with me and meet the Colonel who runs our intelligence section, and get all the detailed information from him, I would like you to work out what sort of aircraft is needed. Then I shall telephone Air Ministry and have it flown out here this afternoon or this evening. Our deadline for getting it to Enfidaville by dawn gives us until about midnight to get it out here. If you can think of an aircraft with the necessary short landing-run which also has the range, which you can fly, all the better. But if it has to be one you haven't flown, I can ask for a suitable pilot to be sent out with the aircraft when I ring.'

'How much space is there, in this field, sir?' I was thinking about the landing more than the take-off. 'At four in the morning there will be a heavy dew and the brakes won't be much good.'

'It's a typical Tunisian field of sandy stubble – there won't be any dew – but the Colonel will give you the exact dimensions. I think you've got about a thousand yards to play with.'

He led me out into the passage and down some stairs, and we went on talking as we walked. 'Will there be any landing aids at all?' I asked, with my heart in my mouth. It was the sixty-four thousand dollar question.

'I'm afraid not,' he said apologetically. 'Nor will the pilot be able to use his landing light, except in emergencies. He's got to be able to get in and out without being seen – or heard.'

The Colonel was a tall, distinguished-looking man, and as I listened to him I wondered how many people were walking about Malta who looked so normal, yet were employed in his secret cloak-and-dagger world of fantasy, without anyone knowing. I then realized that they wouldn't be very good at their jobs if they were recognizable, and found it a most uneasy reflection.

At about 11.30 I had collected all the information I needed to do my sums. Before I left the building to find somewhere quiet to concentrate, the AVM told me that he had an important luncheon engagement which he couldn't miss, otherwise he would have offered me a meal.

'If you think of something, I want you to tell me at once. This business takes priority over everything today, and the sooner I make that telephone call the better.'

In the Officers' Club in Valetta the 'Ladies Only' bar had been renamed 'The Snake Pit', and thrown open to both sexes for the duration. It would be empty for at least another hour, and it was never used by the Navy at lunchtime. I wanted to be able to concentrate with a glass of gin in one hand, which I find a great help when doing complicated sums. Apart from the Maltese barman there was nobody there, and I spread my papers out on a table in a corner. I asked for a large gin and water. When he brought it I was busy and failed to notice that he had forgotten the water, and I had to walk to the water jug on the bar.

The barman apologized. 'Take it with you, Señor. We got plenty water jugs this end.'

I gazed at him with delight. Of course! I thanked him effusively, paid for my drink and shot back to the AVM. He had not begun his lunch and came away from his guests at once. 'Have you thought of something?'

'Yes sir – it's simple – I don't take my extra fuel in a big tank, but in ten five-gallon drums. I refuel after landing and there will still be plenty of room for my passengers. I'm on my way back to Hal Far to practise landing and refuelling all the afternoon.'

Hugh Pughe Lloyd stared over my head while his alert brain examined the proposal. Then he nodded briskly. All his movements were brisk and his mind reacted in the same way.

'Good,' he said. 'Take off and land across the airfield at Hal Far, instead of along it – that is, by the shortest route . . . you'll have to work out a very speedy routine, and refuel with your engine running, in case you have to take off in a hurry . . . taxi down-wind, of course, before starting to refuel, for the same reaon . . . be in the Colonel's office at six, for the briefing . . . bring the observer too . . . pick a good one, who can keep his trap shut as well as navigate . . .' He nodded his head, dismissing me. 'See you at six,' he said and went back to his guests.

At Hal Far I invited Sub-Lieutenant (A) J. M. Robertson, RNVR, to come with me as the observer. He was exceptionally intelligent and had come into the Fleet Air Arm from the BBC where he had been one of their backroom wizards in the early days of television development. He had a flaming red beard and a volatile temperament to match, but the plan appealed to his cynical sense of humour.

The Colonel had emphasized the need for us to leave as few signs of our landing as possible, in case the landing-ground was needed again; if we left evidence of our visit there would be a danger of mines in the future. So all empty cans had to be put back in the aircraft, and ditched at sea as soon as we took off; and in case they floated ashore they would have to be riddled with holes. Three sharp spikes were stowed in the rear cockpit for the observer and the two passengers. They wouldn't be able to sit down – or stand in comfort – until they had done it, and it would keep them occupied while we flew through the fighter patrols.

We gradually improved our routine and timing, with practice. The drums were rectangular, and made of a light alloy, which was a help; they were easy to stow and to handle. But a five-gallon can is no mean weight to lift, and by the time we had gone through the routine a few times we were both exhausted. After each landing I had to jump out of the front cockpit and take the cans from Robertson, who passed them down from the rear cockpit. I stacked them on the ground and as soon as they were all out, prised them open with a sharpened spike which I had to take with me in the front cockpit. Meanwhile Robertson clambered out with a spanner and a funnel, straddled the engine cowling with his back to the propeller just behind his head. He undid the filler-cap and inserted the funnel, by which time I had climbed on to the stubplane with a full can. While he was pouring the petrol into the main tank I threw the empty drums into the back and picked up the little metal seals I had prised away from the cans, and tossed these in, too.

Before we began these experiments the ratings had to drain the tank of all but a few gallons, and after they had brought us several loads of full cans, and watched our incredible gymnastics a few times, I am sure that they were convinced that we had taken leave of our senses.

I was particularly concerned that Robertson should know his way up and over the engine cowling in the dark, without hesitation, and without getting tangled up with the prop. I explained to him that I could find my way back to Malta without an observer but not without a propeller.

At the six o'clock briefing I was afraid that his flippant manner might cause misgivings, and as we listened to our orders in an atmosphere heavily charged with cloak-and-dagger, I avoided his eye. But it was soon obvious to him that it was no laughing matter. When I had described our fuelling arrangements the Colonel made Robertson sign for a loaded Mauser, and me for a loaded Browning. He explained that Robertson would have to stand by the port wing-tip, with the Mauser, to challenge all comers. The escapees would sing out the password, which on this occasion was 'Marseillaise'.

'What do I do if someone rushes up and gives the wrong word?'

'Shoot them at once,' said the Colonel, 'and then get into the air as fast as you can. If strangers approach without the password it will mean that your intended passengers have been caught. Their intention will be to shoot you, so the consequences will be conclusive either way.'

Robertson looked at me doubtfully. 'What's he going to be doing with his Browning?' he asked, nodding his head at me.

'Sitting in the front cockpit ready to take off,' said the Colonel. 'But he is armed in case you need assistance.'

'If you are taking pot shots in my direction,' said Robertson to me, 'kindly remember that I'm the one with the red beard.'

There were more surprises to come. The Colonel told us that in the event of a crash or other failure which prevented us from returning under our own power, we were to rendezvous at a certain point on the coast which we had to memorize. We were to be there by eight in the evening of the same day.

'It's not far from Enfidaville, but if you have to lie low for the day, keep out of everyone's sight. The bush telegraph in North Africa is possibly the fastest means of communication in existence. If you are spotted by an Arab – male or female, child or adult – it will be known from Algeria to Tunisia within an hour. You must not be seen by a living soul.'

His next piece of information was so startling that it reduced Robertson to silence. He told us that at this rendezvous we would be picked up by a German Heinkel. 'It is a seaplane and you will have to swim out to it, I expect. It has German markings – a swastika – on the fuselage.'

I could not refrain from asking where it would come from. The AVM looked quietly amused. 'We keep it in the hangar at Kalafrana,' he said. We were learning a lot about Malta which we didn't know, that evening.

We were then issued with French money against our signatures, to be returned when we came back, and a box of escape gear was put on the table and we were told to take what we wanted. There were some fascinating things in that box and I could have played for hours, but contented myself with a compass concealed in a pipe, and a hacksaw blade encased in plastic, which could be inserted into the soles of one's shoes or into shoulder-straps. Then we were made to memorize a number of addresses in Tunisia by heart, of people to whom we could go for help. We promised not to write these names and addresses down. Next we had to be taught a complicated code. 'If you are taken prisoner, by use of this code you will be able to pass information about North Africa to the Ministries at home, or get in touch with us through London; we shall be doing our best to rescue you if the worst happens, so it is essential for you to know this code very well indeed. I am afraid it is going to take you an hour or so to familiarize yourselves with it, but we will get you back to Hal Far in time for some sleep as soon as you think you have mastered it.'

I began to see why the Air Marshal had been so keen for a pilot already in Malta to fly the aircraft that night. There would have been no time to brief a pilot flown out from the UK.

The Colonel then produced his bombshell. He had kept it for last.

'If your passengers fail to materialize, all these efforts will have been wasted. To make sure that the trip is worthwhile, and because it is too good an opportunity to miss, you will be taking two agents with you. They will be delivered to you at Hal Far at midnight.'

We protested at first. Robertson felt that he would be hemmed in with all the petrol in the back as well, and I was worried about petrol consumption and weight.

'They will be hideously uncomfortable, sir,' I said. 'Their heads will be out in the slipstream if they have to sit on top of all that gas, and they will need protective clothing, and helmets and goggles, and so on.'

'It is all being provided,' said the Colonel. 'Plus cushions for them to sit on. These men have a very important job to do and a little discomfort means nothing to *them*.' He accentuated the last word, and I felt rather ashamed of myself for objecting.

After the Air Marshal had left, the Colonel pressed a bell and a very pretty girl came in, with pencil and pad poised, ready for dictation.

'I have to dictate the arrangements in your presence,' he said to me, 'and I'd be obliged if you would add anything you wish.' He then reeled off a summary of the arrangements, item by item, as though drafting a contract, and the secretary took it all down with no sign of interest or emotion. He might have been dictating a shopping list. It was just routine to her.

Later, on our way back to Hal Far, Robertson said: 'Pity.'

'Pity?' I asked. 'About what?'

'That girl,' he sighed. 'Pity we couldn't take her with us. Then she might've shown some interest. If we are pinched and locked up in the bag she would have been a very useful and pleasant companion.'

Our passengers arrived at midnight, shortly after the squadron had taken off, and from the moment of their arrival the whole venture took on a more human note and we felt much more enthusiastic about it. They were a most refreshing pair, and utterly unlike what I had anticipated. I think I had been expecting a pair of supermen, wearing cloaks and beards, but one was a little old man in his sixties, and the other almost a teenager. They were dressed alike, and could have been mistaken for grandfather and grandson in their faded jeans and nondescript shoes and berets; and they were very French. They assured me that they were not related, but the astonishing difference in their ages, and their completely relaxed air, made me ashamed of my fears, and I felt humble at once. If an old man and a youngster could entrust themselves to a complete stranger of different nationality, and go off to face goodness-only-knows what odds, in frightful discomfort, without a murmur of complaint – in fact with eagerness, for they bubbled with excitement at the prospect of a trip in *l'avion* – what right had I to feel that the whole thing was lunacy – which of course it was; because who has ever heard of landing an aircraft in the dark without even a torch to help?

On my way back from the airfield, after I had seen the squadron off for their attack on shipping off Tripoli, I gave myself a terrible fright. On impulse, just to see what landing in the dark would be like, I switched off the car lights. Driving in the blackout, without lights, was quite impossible, and I had to jam on the brakes quickly. The thought of what lay ahead was making my stomach quake, and I had to keep thrusting the thought away.

Looking at those two delightful Frenchmen I realized that I was in the presence of the bravest men I have ever met. I could only pray that I could get them down without killing them.

The two hundred miles to Enfidaville seemed interminable. Strapped in my familiar seat which had all the comfort of a well-worn pair of shoes, the time passed much too slowly. I concentrated on steering a very careful course, and keeping a constant speed and height so that we would arrive at exactly the right spot at exactly the right moment, and went over the Air Vice-Marshal's parting words again and again. He had guessed that I would be worrying about the landing, being a pilot himself, and he had given me some excellent advice in a sympathetic way, in an attempt to ease my mind.

'If I were you I would cross the coast at about two or three thousand feet, so that you have plenty of height to play with. It's only about four miles from the sea to the station, and you don't want to use throttle any more than you can help, though you may have to, in the last stages of your approach. Pass over the railway station as quietly as you can and get your bearings. As the Vichy-French are not officially at war there won't be any blackout, so there should be plenty of lights on the station, and cars meeting the train and so on. The prevailing wind is offshore, from west to east, from the station to the coast, so when you turn you will be facing due east, towards the dawn, and on your down-wind leg there may be a little light on the horizon to help you. At this time of the year, and at that time in the morning, I doubt whether there will be much wind to bother about.'

He was standing very close to me and I could feel strength flowing from him to me. 'Think about those poor devils in the train, and how grateful they will be,' he said with a smile. 'It's not going to be very much different from landing on one of those aircraft carriers of yours in the dark – probably easier!'

As we approached the coast I realized that it was his faith in me that frightened me most of all. I was much more afraid of not living up to his expectations than the consequences to me and my passengers if I did not.

His description of the conditions over the railway station and the field was so accurate that I felt that he was there beside me, helping to fly the aeroplane, and I guessed that at that moment in his official residence in Valetta he was doing just that, probably sitting in his dressing-gown with a cigarette in a long holder, looking at the clock. What none of us had anticipated was an excess of punctuality by the Vichy-French railways. From well out to sea, even at three thousand feet I could see sparks and flames shooting up into the darkness from the steam engine standing at the station. It was as conspicuous as any airfield homing beacon, and gave me a clear indication of what little wind there was – blowing from west to east – as the AVM had forecast. It must have arrived at least ten minutes before schedule. Thanks to that railway engine I was able to turn down-wind before reaching the station.

The glimmering line of grey sky on the eastern horizon was a great help, but the contrast made the darkness immediately below more intense. Then I saw the black silhouette of the hedge quite distinctly, and throttled right back, quickly, before losing sight of it, keeping it in my arc of visibility on the port bow, and losing height in a slow gliding turn. Before I had time to start worrying it was there, right ahead, rushing towards me, and we were gliding over it, and into wind, and the aircraft was nicely stalled, and then we thumped down and rolled across the grassy surface in bumpy jerks and I applied the brakes gently, thinking: 'We are down! We've made it! It's a piece of cake!'

In the dark, most objects seem to be closer and bigger, and the hedge by the road was a great big shadow which was looming towards us fast. I jammed the brakes on hard, and the tail came up and then thumped down, and we stopped. I was sure that we were almost touching the hedge, and leapt out to see if there was room to turn. My feet sank into soft sand; I saw that the wheels were hub-deep, and thought, 'Christ! How are we going to turn?' But the hedge was quite a long way away. I ran back and saw Robertson's helmet, a round dark blob against the night sky. By jumping out at the end of my landing run I had altered our planned routine right away, but I had warned him that we should be prepared for any eventuality, and 'retain fluidity'. This was the opposite condition. The wheels were so deep we were going to have to combat rigidity. I climbed up the side of the fuselage and asked him to bring down a parachute pack and jam it under the port wheel. When he climbed out and peered at the undercarriage he saw the problem at once.

'We shall have to use full throttle to turn, and that's going to make a hell of a noise. Hold back on my port wing-tip when I open the throttle, and when she gives, grab the squashed parachute and chuck it in the back, and then cling to the fuselage when we taxi down-wind. I shall need you on the wing-tip to turn into wind, too.'

I was wasting time. He was so quick-witted that he had seen the problem and its cure at once. He just nodded, and pushed me towards the aircraft.

Back in the front seat I opened the throttle gingerly and then more fully, while he heaved on the wing-tip, and when the aircraft began to turn we were making enough noise to waken anyone within a couple of miles. They must have heard it on the railway station, and I imagined that people would be rushing across the road to see what on earth was happening. While we were turning, the headlights of two cars flashed along the hedge, adding to my tension. But nobody seemed to be interested, or curious. Perhaps the lusty noise of the steam engine puffing away and throwing great showers of sparks up into the air drowned the noise of my engine. Had any one of the drivers or passengers in those cars paused to peer over that hedge they would have got the shock of their lives!

Robertson recovered the squashed parachute, flung it into the rear cockpit and then clung to the fuselage as I taxied down-wind. When I stopped to turn he grabbed the wing-tip again, and hauled back with his heels dug in, until we were facing the railway station and into wind. Then we began our refuelling routine – or tried to. Our passengers had climbed out with stiff legs and were standing patting the sides of the aircraft affectionately, in no hurry to go. We were their last link with safety and civilization, and absence of enmity, and they were being slow to depart. As we could not start refuelling until they were out of the way I turned them round bodily, and pointed them in a southerly direction, so that they wouldn't stumble into the wings, and gave them a gentle push. '*Bonne chance, mes amis,*' I cried, '*mais allez-vous-en, vitement, s'il vous plaît – très vitement – rapidement – vite! vite!*'

It did the trick, and they went off into the darkness rather sadly. I was very sorry to part with them in such an abrupt manner, but daylight was approaching and every second was precious.

I would dearly love to know how they fared, and what happened, but I suppose I shall never find out. The youngster would now be about fifty-five, and perhaps if he reads this and remembers that it was 28 August 1941, I might hear from him.

The fuelling went absolutely according to plan; we had finished in record time and were ready to receive our next passengers. Robertson was manning the wing-tip with his Mauser at the ready, and I was back in the front cockpit strapped in, with my hand on the throttle and my Browning ready on my lap. For what seemed an age I sat staring into the darkness, without a sign of any movement anywhere except for an occasional car when its headlights flickered along the hedge at the far end of the field. I was afraid that my wheels would sink in again, and eventually, when the waiting became unbearable, thinking that perhaps the men were searching for us in the dark, I switched on my navigation lights, dimmed right down with the rheostat. As the minutes passed I turned them up, and up, until they were at full brilliance. Still nothing happened. With every passing moment the dawn was becoming more pronounced, and the sky lighter. Finally, when tension had reached bursting-point, I switched on the landing light, and waved it up and down. It was a great shaft of light, as bright as any searchlight, and I felt as conspicuous as a lighthouse, but time was desperately important and justified any risk.

Then – came an answering flash in the distance. Just a little spark of light, which might have been made by striking a match, but from its very insignificance I knew that it was our quarry, and I turned everything off and sat with my heart thumping as loudly as the engine – or so it seemed – expecting a hail of bullets from the blackness if the men were being pursued. Two shadowy figures came panting out of the night and I saw Robertson challenge them with his Mauser, and then hurry them to the fuselage. By craning my neck I sensed rather than saw when they were all inside; a tap on my shoulder confirmed it and I opened the throttle wide, not caring how much noise I made, and we came unstuck and roared over the stubble and up, over the hedge, and the road, and the railway station, and round, to the coast and out to sea.

When we crossed the coast it was almost daylight and in that sharp, early morning light, when every prominent detail stands out so clearly before the sun has chased away the shadows, the sea looked very clean and friendly. I was flying with a warm feeling of oneupmanship, and a lovely sense of freedom after the tension of waiting. I kept right down, at wave-top height, and knew that the three men in the back would be busy piercing cans and throwing them over the side, and hoped that they would take care to miss the aircraft's tail and rudder.

We had been in the air for about half an hour when I felt a tap on my shoulder again and, turning my head as far as it would go against the cockpit strappings, I saw a hand extended, asking to be shaken. I was unable to see the face behind it but could just reach it, and shake it warmly.

Robertson's voice down the Gosport Tubes said: 'They both want to shake hands with you, to say thank you, but I have explained that it isn't easy. The poor devils look absolutely worn out, but they are exultant – there's no other word for it – and they keep shaking their heads and saying "*les foux Anglais!*" with tremendous admiration!'

'Tell them that it is our privilege, and that we think that they are very brave men,' I said. 'Ask them when they want to go back to North Africa. I'll be delighted to take them!'

'I've given them their sandwiches and coffee,' said Robertson.

Just before we took off my Chief Regulating Petty Officer handed me a few packages wrapped in grease-proof paper, and a couple of Thermos flasks. He grinned and said, 'With the compliments of the Chiefs' Mess, sir. We haven't the slightest idea where you are going, or what you are up to, and we don't want to know; but as we have a feeling that you're off on some picnic we reckoned you might need some food!'

It was elementary, really, and I can't think why we never thought to take food from the officers' mess or the wardroom. I suppose we were just lazy. But I was grateful that night, and so were the agents. I was chewing my sandwiches happily, and sipping some hot coffee from the Thermos flask, when we flew between Pantellaria and Lampedusa; but at only a few feet above the waves, and with plenty of petrol in the tank, there was not a sign of anything which might have given us indigestion – thank God!

On 16 September I was telephoned by a Major with a Welsh surname. He told me that he was deputizing for the Colonel, who was away on duty. I was to report to him in the Colonel's office straight away. I had been sent for many times since August, but it took a little time and patience to explain to him that we had no squadron transport; it had been confiscated by Flag Officer Malta for 'misuse' long before I arrived in Malta. Apparently someone had given some girls a lift in it and that was contrary to regulations. It was a very sore point with me.

'It's too far to walk, Major, so either you send a car or I stay put.'

In the Colonel's office I explained to a taciturn man in khaki, with a major's crowns on his shoulders but no regimental insignia, that the Colonel or the Air Vice-Marshal always sent a car to Hal Far when they wanted anyone from 830 Squadron. I then asked why I had been sent for, and he told me that at dawn the following morning I was to land a VIP on a dry salt lake near Sousse. It was a perfectly straightforward delivery with no complications, but because the salt lake was remote, the VIP would be provided with a bicycle to ride away on.

'A bicycle!' I said, disbelievingly. 'Really?'

The major seemed equally surprised that I found the suggestion strange.

'Yes, why not?'

'Well – it can't be carried inside the aircraft, there isn't room; but I suppose we could strap it on somewhere.' The idea made me laugh.

'What's so funny about it?' asked the major.

'The Swordfish is a three-seater, with open cockpits. It isn't designed to carry bikes. But it has carried practically everything you could think of. Perhaps it has been done before, though I doubt it. But I don't suppose it would prove an aerodynamic impossibility.'

The notion had a strange appeal. These intelligence people sometimes had the strangest ideas and it was not impracticable.

'It will be delivered to you after dark so that it does not arouse any undue curiosity,' he said.

'Don't leave it too late. We may need to experiment, to see where to put it.'

I studied the major's map of the salt lake and its surrounds and was surprised that it was a suitable landing area.

'The Colonel told me that there are very few open spaces in North Africa within range of Malta where an aircraft can land, but if this lake is okay I can't think why we haven't used it before. It's big enough to land a whole squadron in formation!'

'Are you doubting my word?' The major sounded testy and I wondered why.

'Of course not,' I said. I could see that this man and I were not in sympathy, and I am inclined to be offhand with people I don't like, and decided to mollify him. 'Everything the Colonel has laid on from this office has always been spot-on. Now – what about all the other things?'

'What other things?'

'Money, addresses, escape gear, a rendezvous with the Heinkel.'

'This is such a simple task there is no need for any of these things,' he said. At that I dug in, and told him that either I was provided with it all or he must find someone else. He was beginning to look angry and I became suspicious.

'Where is the Colonel, and the AVM, and where is the Colonel's secretary? I'm not at all sure about this trip. You are supposed to be briefing me, but up to date you have displayed remarkable ignorance about these runs. Frankly, I'm not at all happy about it.'

The major interrupted me and it was his turn to be the peacemaker. He agreed that I had every right to be cautious. He assured me that the AVM was away for the day, and the Colonel had been summoned to Egypt to attend a high-powered conference, and his secretary had been given some well-earned leave until he returned.

'I work in a different department,' he said. 'The Colonel left me a note about this trip and said that you would know what was required, so in a minute we will find out where everything is kept.'

I apologized for being so truculent, and together we worked out a rendezvous for the Heinkel, but I had to tell him how to contact the pilot, and where the money was stowed. The escape gear was in its case in the Colonel's wardrobe, and I helped myself. The only item he was unable to supply was a list of addresses, but I felt that this was not so important. The rendezvous with the Heinkel if we failed to return was just off Sousse, in Hammamet Bay, which meant a twenty-five mile walk from the salt lake; but as we would have all day to get there we would only have to achieve about two miles per hour on foot, which seemed reasonable . It was to be a dawn landing which meant taking off long after midnight.

Because Germany had invaded Russia the air raids over Malta were not nearly so frequent or so severe, and we were able to put many more serviceable aircraft into the air now that the afternoon bombing was almost a thing of the past. That night, when I saw the squadron off for a raid on shipping near Lampedusa, there were seventeen Swordfish in the take-off, which was more than we had ever been able to fly at any one time before. I watched them bumbling off into the sky with their torpedoes, and once they had gone, began to worry because the bicycle had failed to turn up and it was one in the morning. The Chief Air Artificer had arranged to lash it to the struts in a normal upright position, with its wheels on the lower mainplane to port, leaving me room to climb in and out of the cockpit. He had agreed to ring me at Hal Far House when it was delivered to the hangar, and it was nearly one-thirty when he did. He spoke in a mystified voice.

'I have never asked you where you go on these trips, sir, and I'm not being nosy, but I think you should come and take a look at this bicycle before we lash it on. I think they have sent you the wrong machine.'

Standing beside him in the hangar a few minutes later we both stared at it in disbelief. On both mudguards, back and front, were heavily embossed British crowns, stamped into the metal. They could not be concealed, and were very conspicuous. On either side of the crossbar, neatly stencilled in white paint, were the two words 'Royal Navy'.

'There isn't time to change it for another,' I said. 'We'd have to be off before the replacement could arrive. I suppose they know what they are doing, but I'm beginning to have my doubts. It will be easy to scrape off the two words, and paint over the marks with black, and you'll just have to paint over the crowns. Use thick enamel and keep painting! It'll dry quickly enough in the air.'

Half an hour later the VIP arrived – a charming middle-aged Frenchman in an elegant tropical suit. His face was vaguely familiar and I realized that I had seen his picture in the newspaper at some time or other, but I was careful not to try to remember who he was. The less I knew about my passengers on these cloak-and-dagger runs the better. But I was surprised, because the Colonel had introduced me to an Arab, dressed in the full regalia of a sheikh, a few days previously, and indicated that he was to be my next passenger. I had been told that the Arab spoke fourteen different languages fluently, but they didn't include English. His forebears had done magnificent work for the British for many generations, and I had been looking forward to taking him across. However, I was merely a taxi-driver, and was not expected to know anything about the organization that I was assisting. It made very little difference to me who was in the back seat. They were all magnificent people whom it was a privilege to carry.

That night I took an underslung long-range tank, which would provide all the extra fuel needed for a straightforward return trip with nobody to pick up. When we flew over the salt lake just before dawn it looked very sinister. In the faint light the surface looked like a frozen sea of ice; little waves of white froth overlapped each other but were quite still, as though the whole area had been stunned into sudden immobility. I hailed Robertson on the voice-pipe.

'It looks very odd to me,' I said, 'and suspiciously moist. Drop a flame-float, please. If it ignites we'll go straight back to Malta.' The flame-float would have been activated by water and a flame would have burned on the surface, throwing out a clear stream of white smoke.

We flew round in a circle, watching and waiting, but nothing happened.

'Drop another,' I said. 'The first may have been a dud.'

When the second had disappeared below and there was no hint of flame or smoke we decided to land. Daylight was approaching rapidly, as it does in the Mediterranean, and I could now see that the lake was surrounded by a thick forest of green pine trees. Once I had slipped down, past their tops, we were committed to the landing.

'We've got to land now,' I said to Robertson, 'but I don't like the look of it at all. However, the major assured me that it was okay, so here goes.'

I eased the aircraft down as flatly as I dared, aiming to touch down as close to the bank as I could. I assumed that the caked surface of salt was only a few inches thick and that when my wheels bore down on to it they would be on a firm surface. I had no means of knowing that the unreal substance stretching ahead with an evil yellow glint concealed eleven feet of treacherous mud, but as we dropped to within a few feet I knew that we were in trouble, and that I should do a pancake landing, like ditching at sea, keeping my wheels above the surface until the last possible moment, in case we somersaulted.

When they touched that piecrust the wind was whistling through the wings in the pleasant sigh of an approaching stall, and the note suddenly changed to a terrible rending sound – a sort of retching, as though thousands of people were being sick. We seemed to plough through hundreds of feet of yellow slime before the wheels embedded themselves deep and the engine and propeller sliced into the mud. The tail flicked upwards and we reared into an over-the-vertical position, and before my face was splashed into the evil-smelling substance I caught a glimpse of two pairs of heels catapulting over my head and thought 'bloody fool Robertson – he's forgotten to do up his jock-strap – and the VIP's!'

The acrid smell was nauseating, and as soon as I had wiped the mud from my eyes I looked upwards and saw the tail and rudder pointing at the sky, and as I looked, more mud squelched on to my face. It was dripping from every inch of the fuselage.

The banks of the lake seemed a long way away, across a sea of this terrible stuff. I remembered that it was exactly two years to the very day that I had dived from the sinking *Courageous*. That had been on 17 September too. Then, I had been able to swim to a destroyer, and I wondered how we were going to negotiate this poisonous substance. But before doing anything else there were two people to be rescued from asphyxiation. I climbed out of the cockpit and stood on the trailing edge of the port lower mainplane and saw that somehow they had struggled to the surface but were lying half submerged, trying to reach the temporary sanctuary of the upended Swordfish. I unlashed the bicycle and tipped it forward so that they could grab a wheel, and they hauled themselves back and clambered out. At least that machine had served one useful purpose. But it seemed a long way to have brought it, just for that!

26
Curtains

Our first responsibility was to our passenger and we had to get him ashore quickly, before attempting to destroy the aircraft. Both would take time, so without delay the three of us set out across the mud in line ahead, with the VIP in the middle, negotiating that cloying morass by using three parachute packs and the navigator's Bigsworth Board as stepping-stones. With each step we sank to our knees, but without those stepping-stones we would have been up to our waists, and I doubt whether we could have moved forward at all.

To start them off, I put the Bigsworth Board in front of me and then stepped on to it from my parachute, whereupon the two behind me moved forward one pace. Then Robertson had the unpleasant task of extricating his parachute from the slimy depths, where he had just been standing, so that he could pass it down the line. Very slowly the bank drew closer, but our progress was painfully slow, and I felt like the helmsman of a small sailing dinghy, beating ashore against wind and tide, when the shore never seems any closer. We took about three-quarters of an hour to do the five hundred yards or so from the upended Swordfish, and throughout this undignified procession, when we were immersed in slime, and on our hands and knees more often than standing up, we were very conscious of a little group of Arabs standing on the bank under the trees, watching us. As we drew closer we saw that they were carrying rifles, and the Frenchman explained that they would be the lake's guards. Neither Robertson nor I could understand why anyone in their senses should want to mount a guard over that inland sea of salty slime, but there was no time to ask for an explanation.

When we scrambled up on to the bank and collapsed, the Arabs stood over us, patting their double-barrelled guns in a significant manner. Each man wore a brass plate engraved with Arabic lettering slung from his neck by a chain. The barrels of their murderous-looking weapons were at least three feet long, and the belligerent expression on their faces left us in no doubt that they considered us their prisoners.

After a short rest, ignoring the guns which were levelled at him, the Frenchman stood up and stripped the flying overalls down over his feet. Apart from his shoes, which were caked in slime, when he had wiped the mud from his face he looked quite respectable, but I was not prepared for the reaction of the Arabs. When he had stepped out of the mud-soaked overalls they lowered their guns and gazed at him with open-mouthed astonishment – almost with awe – and I realized that they knew who he was. Their recognition was instantaneous, and from their manner it was clear that our passenger was indeed a Very Important Person, at least on that side of the Mediterranean. He spoke to them in an authoritative voice in their own language, and then strode off into the woods, a free man. We never saw him again.

When we slid down the bank to go back to the aircraft the Arabs made as if to prevent us, but we ignored them and ploughed out again, back through that awful mud. There was a lot to do before we could leave for our rendezvous. For security reasons we had removed the radar set before taking off, but the fixing aerials on the wing struts had to be destroyed beyond any chance of reconstruction; and we broke them off and splintered them into little pieces, scattering them into the mud in all directions. Then we had to find a way of concealing the bicycle. If we were captured, and it was found, we would have some awkward explaining to do. There was no possibility of taking it ashore, though it would have been very useful. Standing precariously on the trailing edge of the mainplane we hoisted it out of the mud, and with a 'one-two-three', pitched it out as far as we could. It landed not very far from the port wings and sank out of sight immediately, and we hoped that it was far enough away not to be found. Subconsciously, from that moment, and for many days, I began to think up practical reasons for its presence, so that I would not be unprepared when asked why we were carrying it, discarding several novel ideas until I hit on something which sounded reasonably plausible.

In a small waterproof bag stowed in the rear cockpit we had enough hard rations to keep us going for twenty-four hours; and I had my hip flask filled with neat brandy in my pocket, so we were

well equipped for our twenty-five-mile walk. When Robertson
climbed into the up-ended cockpit to retrieve his camera I
reminded him to bring the escape rations, and the Very pistol and
cartridges. 'We'll fire them into the rear cockpit and if that fails to
set the old girl on fire we can shoot at the long-range petrol tank
with live ammunition. But we must get as far away as we can,
because she will blow up when the tank explodes, and we can't run
for cover in this mud!'

When he emerged, Robertson insisted on taking a photograph of
the aircraft before we set it on fire, and one of me standing up to my
knees on the Bigsworth Board in the mud; but time was flashing
past and we still had another frog-like passage to make, to the
shore. We lay in the mud about twenty yards from the aircraft and
fired all the Very cartridges and all our live ammunition at the
aircraft, but it refused to burn. It was drenched with mud, and in
the end we gave up in disgust, comforting our conscience with the
thought that nobody could salvage it from those muddy wastes,
and it would be of little use to them if they did.

Before we started for the shore for the second time, I told
Robertson how I hoped we would be able to escape from the
murderous-looking devils on the bank. 'I spent four years at sea
with Lascars, and I don't suppose the Arabs' reactions differ very
much from theirs. The Lascars could never resist highly coloured
materials, especially silk, which is very popular with their
womenfolk. When we get ashore we'll pull the rip-cord of two of the
parachutes, leaving the third unopened where they can see it. The
moment they see all that yellow silk they'll forget us for a while,
and the minute their attention is diverted we'll run like riggers, to
the north-east. It's a forlorn hope but it might work.'

With two stepping-stones each our progress was much quicker,
and on the banks, when we had rested for a few moments, we
signed to each other and pulled the rip-cords simultaneously. Our
plan worked more efficiently than we had dared to hope; when two
great balloons of yellow silk rippled out across the grass the Arabs
dropped their rifles and made a dive for it. As we ran into the forest
I glanced over my shoulder and saw that our departure had not
even been noticed. Two of the guards were wrestling with each
other for possession of the unopened parachute, and the others
were tearing at the yellow silk in a frenzy.

We ran for at least half an hour before collapsing with
exhaustion. When we had partially recovered I offered Robertson

a swig from my flask, and it was then that we discovered that he had forgotten to bring the escape rations ashore.

We made this unfortunate discovery between seven-thirty and eight in the morning and I made the mistake of cursing him for bringing his camera at the expense of our food. I had selected Malcolm Robertson for these 'spy-runs' because of his quick brain, but I scarcely knew him. I soon discovered that he was extremely obstinate and had a quick temper. There was only four or five years' difference in our ages, but the gap in our experience was more marked than my extra stripe indicated.

'We've got to think this out carefully,' I said, when I had stopped calling him names and had recovered my equanimity, 'and keep our eyes open for something growing, like turnips or carrots, which we can eat. We've got twenty-five miles to walk – perhaps a bit less because we've covered about three already. But allowing for rests, and periods when we shall have to hide, we've got about twelve hours to make good at least two miles per hour.'

'Why bother to hide,' he said. It was a scornful remark, not a question. 'There must be plenty of people about who'll give us some grub if we ask them. After all, they're not at war here.'

I reminded him of the Colonel's warning about the bush telegraph in North Africa, but he dismissed it as 'cloak-and-dagger nonsense'. 'If we behave quite normally, and bluff it out, nobody will notice us; but if we behave like criminals on the run we shall only draw attention to ourselves and be conspicuous. I don't think that Colonel knew what he was talking about.'

'You should see yourself in a mirror!' I said. 'This is Arab country, and your white face covered in mud, and your red beard, make you about as inconspicuous as a nun in a brothel!'

The more I protested the more obstinate he became. I should have realized that he was cross with himself for forgetting the food. By the end of the afternoon our relations were very strained and we were both tired, hungry and short-tempered. The last food we had eaten was in Malta the previous evening, and we had had no proper sleep since the night before. Occasionally, when we saw an Arab leading a bullock at the plough, or a solitary figure moving on the horizon with his camel, I threw myself to the ground, but Robertson refused to take cover and blundered on, scornful of my determination 'to be melodramatic'. In the evening I tried reasoning with him again by pointing out that we were very lucky. 'If we were escaped prisoners-of-war we would be absolutely cock-a-hoop to be where we are now, food or no food. We are in a more populated area and have got to be very cautious. You're crazy to go on behaving as though you owned the bloody country! Just think about it sensibly for a few moments. We are not missing from any roll-call, and nobody is searching for us. In fact, if you'll stop blundering about like a madman, nobody need know we are here. We are making for a previously agreed rendezvous, where an aeroplane is coming to pick us up in an hour or two. They are probably running up their engines at Kalafrana right now. All we've got to do is to keep out of sight and keep going. If we are captured we shall never be in such a fortunate position again; and if we are, it will only be after months of hard work, and writing coded letters, and waiting. For God's sake don't jeopardize everything just because your back's up and you have put yourself in the wrong and won't admit it.'

He was really a fine chap and my approach was entirely wrong. Because of physical exhaustion and hunger, and constant nips from my brandy flask in that blazing sun, neither of us were ourselves. Later in the evening, when we had only a few more miles to do, he plunged through a hedge without even pausing to see what was on the other side, and found himself in a small vegetable garden, behind a single-storey Arab shack. A woman ran screaming into the building, and after that it was only a matter of time before we were rounded up. When we heard her screams we began to run, but we were being pursued by the woman's vindictive little white terrier, with its back hairs stiff with rage, yapping and snarling at our heels. His enthusiasm was infectious, and he was joined by every other dog in the neighbourhood, and for a few unhappy moments I knew how a fox feels when he is being pursued by a pack of hounds in full cry. Then a crowd of Arabs appeared from nowhere, closing in on us from all directions, and we were completely surrounded. They pretended to be friendly but their grasp of our arms was so firm it was painful. They took us into a ramshackle hut where another Arab was squatting on his heels by an open fire, boiling eggs and brewing some sort of concoction which I think was meant to be coffee. We were made to sit down on the earth floor, and were offered a mug of their hot brew and a boiled egg each which we accepted with gratitude. We were both ravenously hungry and delighted to be amongst friends.

We were unaware that everywhere in North Africa there was a guaranteed reward of one thousand francs for the capture of an escaped British or Allied prisoner, and that was almost a year's pay for an unskilled Arab labourer under the Vichy-French. Unbeknown to us while we relaxed, warming our insides, one of the Arabs had slipped away to inform the gendarmes. When French policemen suddenly poured through the door, wearing revolvers and truncheons in the belts of their uniforms, I was agreeing with Robertson, who had just said: 'There you are! I told you that the Arabs would be friendly.' Within seconds we were grabbed unceremoniously and bundled into separate cars, under arrest, and driven to the police station in the main street of Sousse.

Despite his obstinacy that day I have every reason to be grateful to Malcolm Robertson. At times I can be an extremely unpleasant person – this I know – and I am sure that it was my guardian angel who prompted me into provoking his obstinacy. Later that evening, when we were being guarded by two Arabs standing at our cell door with their bayonets fixed, we heard the Heinkel circling round overhead, searching for us, and tried to grin at each other philosophically. Robertson had apologized for his error of judgement, and I for my fiery temper and intolerance, and we were doing our best to make the best of a bad job. When we heard that aircraft we felt sick with frustration and misery, but weeks later we learned that on its way back without us, the Heinkel burst into flames and there were no survivors.

PART V

The Sahara

27
Interrogation

The window of our cell looked down the main street of Sousse, which stretched a very long way into the distance in a perfectly straight line. In the elongated shadows of the warm evening sunshine groups of attractive young people were chatting and laughing together in an atmosphere of peace. It was a strange contrast, seen through the bars of a police cell. They seemed to be completely unaffected by the war raging everywhere else in the Mediterranean, and it was irksome to be unable to join them. In the beginning, the physical and mental transition from freedom to captivity was difficult to accept, and in the first week or two I had to fight against a feeling of savage resentment. The temptation to lash out at some of those smug Frenchmen in their ornate uniforms, smelling of eau-de-Colgone, was almost irresistible.

Our first meal consisted of fish-heads swimming in batter, and the eyes gazing blankly upwards from the plate were most unappetizing. But the coffee was very welcome and after our *repas* we were handed a clean towel each, and a cake of soap, and escorted to *la douche*, to wash off the malodorous mud. At this long-awaited blessing we decided that things were looking up, even when we were taken to an outside yard and found that *la douche* was only a cold tap over a stone trough, similar to the drinking troughs we provide for cart-horses in Britain. But we were grateful for small mercies; at least we were able to rid ourselves of the worst of that dried mud, which had permeated everywhere including our hair and under our fingernails.

The pungent smell lingered with us until the next morning, when our clothes were taken to be washed and repaired. By that time we had been transferred to a cavalry fort on a hill to the west, overlooking Sousse. At daybreak we had been driven across country and up the hill to the picturesque fort. The cars swept through a high archway in a towering wall of stucco and stopped in a cobbled courtyard, where Arab soldiers were waiting with their bayonets fixed. They opened the doors and escorted us up some wooden stairs into a large bare room which somehow contrived to look unfurnished even though it contained two beds, a table and two chairs. Its barred windows were not exactly friendly either.

For two days and nights we were guarded by eight Arabs, with their bayonets fixed at all times, even when we were asleep. They were posted in pairs outside our cell door, at both the top and the bottom of the wooden stairs, and outside our window on the cobbled yard below. We were mystified by this sign of extreme caution, but it seemed that the French were convinced that they had captured the Scarlet Pimpernel and Houdini combined. With knowing winks and confidential nods they did their best to encourage us to talk, and told us that they were aware that we were engaged in '*le mécanisme clandestin*'. They assured us that they were '*sympatiques*' and keen 'Gaullists', and we could speak quite openly to them. They asked us where our *passager* had gone, but we maintained an air of puzzled incomprehension, and refused to be drawn. Our constant reply '*Je ne comprends pas, M'sieur,*' made them angry, and they told us that we were foolish to think that we could continue with our clandestine work against such formidable adversaries as themselves. They expressed grim satisfaction that they had caught us at last – after we had made 'so many trips to their country'. We protested our innocence so frequently and so convincingly that I began to feel indignant that they refused to believe us.

The guard followed us everywhere, even to the lavatory, if one could describe the squalid arrangements in such a grandiose way. There was no need for the guide, who insisted on accompanying us; its presence, and whereabouts, were unmistakable from anywhere in that building. Our introduction to the primitive sanitary arrangements which the Vichy-French never failed to provide, for their prisoners and Arab troops alike, was unforgettable. A small hole in the floor had once been discernible, but was completely covered by the evidence of visitations by dozens of citizens over a long period, whose aim had been casual in the extreme. On either side of this nauseating pile two footplates indicated where the user was expected to crouch. Overhead there was an empty cistern which was non-functional like its chain, which was rusted in the fully-down position. These were the only provisions made for the natural functions of eight Arabs and two British naval officers – and our predecessors. It was not until I was forced to make use of them that I discovered that there was worse to come: Arabs do not use *papier-hygiènique* – I understand that it is against the rules of their religion – and none was provided; and at my first crouched approach a nest of lobster-like scorpions made their appearance. The spectacle of their jointed claws waving only a few inches from my anatomy with the tail reaching upwards to sting was more than enough for me, and I sprang up with a cry of alarm. This upset my Arab guard who had been standing over me with his bayonet pointed at my stomach. He was very startled at my incomprehensible reaction to the commonplace sight of a mere scorpion or two, and was immediately suspicious, and jabbed my stomach with his bayonet, crying '*Attendez!*'

Later, when I complained to a French orderly officer that the sanitary arrangements were entirely inadequate for ten human beings and were in need of immediate overhaul, he shrugged and said, '*C'est la guerre*'. This catchphrase, plus the disclaimer which always followed: '*C'est pareil pour nous,*' was the standard reply to all complaints, on any subject from fleas in the sheets, and bed-bugs in the straw palliasses and pillows, to cockroaches in the food, all of which were a regular, daily part of life under the hospitality of the Vichy-French.

Fortunately, there were some mitigating factors about life in that fort. During our first day we were loaned khaki shorts and rope-soled slippers, like old-fashioned bathing shoes, to wear while our trousers and shirts were being washed. Reluctantly, while we were without shirts, our guards allowed us to catch up on our sleep, and although the grey, unbleached calico sheets crawled with bugs and were hideously stained, and the pillows and mattresses were stuffed with straw and hard balls of camel manure, we managed to sleep the clock round, waking only when a nauseous swill was provided for our consumption in the morning and evening. This was brought to us by a long-skirted Arab who put it down in the middle of the floor in a metal receptacle like a bucket. Enormous bones were swimming about in a greasy brown gravy. I discovered later that they were the ribs of a camel.

These waking intervals enabled us to stagger to the window to breathe in some fresh air, and to indulge in the newly acquired habit of scratching.

When our clothes were returned we were agreeably surprised to find that they had been washed and ironed and repaired very neatly indeed. I was about to take off my borrowed shorts and put on my clean trousers when I caught sight of something unusual inside them; I found a message written in indelible pencil on the lining of a pocket; it read: '*Meilleurs souvenirs d'une demoiselle qui vous a réparé votre pantalons, avec mes baisers les plus foux!*' This enchanting '*billet d'amour*' was signed 'Nelle', and underneath, with her lipstick, she had written the two words '*Bonne chance!*' emerging from a pair of laughing lips which she had sketched in a delectable cupid's bow.

Although I had spent long periods at the window, breathing in the fresh air, I had seen nothing resembling a female, the Arab policeman in his sentry box opposite being the only visible sign of life apart from our guards immediately below. The policeman added a touch of colour to the background of grey cobblestones and battlements. His black face shone under his red rimless hat. It could not be called a tarboosh, which sits on the top of the head and has a tassel. This came down to both ears, and the guard, in his smart khaki tunic and puttees, with a red sash slung across his chest from his right shoulder, looked proud of himself and a good soldier. By grinning at him appreciatively once or twice, I had made him smile, and I liked the white flash of his teeth. As soon as I had read the girl's message I sprang to the window with my trousers in my hand and searched the shadows more carefully. In a doorway quite close to the sentry I could see the dim shape of a girlish form, waving furtively, her hand at waist level. I held up my trousers with a grin. At this she stepped boldly into the sunlight and I saw that she was very pretty. She blew kisses up at my window and I responded with equal enthusiasm, which startled the Arab sentry who thought I was blowing them at him. Then he saw Nelle, and with a flash of his teeth he shouted a playful rebuke and told her to '*Allez – tout de suite!*' As she walked away she held up two fingers in Churchill's V-for-Victory sign and blew a departing kiss, and the sight of her laughing face and the sentry's good-natured grin made me feel better at once.

Amongst the many interrogators who were sent to see if they could wrest an admission of guilt from us was the colonel commanding the fort. He was a wiry little cavalry officer, a Spahi, whose tanned face and lean features were as leathery as his polished riding boots. I think he only came to look at us out of curiosity, but when he extracted a cigarette from his packet of

Bastos Blue, I held out an appealing hand, and he said '*Oui*', twice, through his nose, pronouncing it 'A-wee, A-wee' in two distinct syllables, and gave me the whole packet. I have liked the Spahis ever since.

20 September was my second wedding anniversary. It was also the day that we were moved to El Acuina, the airfield at Tunis, by our new guide and companion, Capitaine Rubin de Cervans of the French Air Force. He had come all the way from Tunis to fetch us.

During our walk from the lake, Robertson and I had agreed to stick to one simple story. The news of the squadron's attack on shipping off Lampedusa would have been broadcast all over Tunisia: we had suffered a petrol leak and I had flown to the nearest point of land to Lampedusa, which was Sousse. In the faint moonlight I had force-landed on the lake because its flat surface was just visible.

For the first forty miles, the road from Sousse to Tunis follows the coastline, across flat open country to the north, and I noticed many stretches of firm grassland where I could have landed our VIP quite easily. A big range of blue mountains bounded our horizon to the west all the way to Tunis, separating the flat plains of the Gulf of Hammamet from the Sahara Desert. At Hammamet we turned to the north-west, to pass through the mountains. The airfield at El Alouina is a few miles south of Tunis on the Carthage road.

We had driven about twenty miles from Sousse when we flashed through Enfidaville, past the field where we had landed in August, but it had passed before either Robertson or I was aware of it, which was just as well perhaps, because Rubin de Cervans was watching us carefully out of the corner of his little pig's eyes. Throughout the whole seventy miles he peppered us with questions – when he wasn't talking about himself –and in the first ten minutes I came to the conclusion that he was one of the most boring and odious individuals I had ever met. His manner was furtive and he was unable to look me in the eye for more than a second or two, when he hurriedly looked away, peering at me suspiciously from the corner of heavy horn-rimmed spectacles. He talked incessantly in idiomatic English which he spoke with a pronounced American accent. It also had a flavour of Cockney about it, and the combination of the two, with the French accent as well, was somehow just as unconvincing as his personality.

He explained to us that he was very pro-British which was why his brother officers mistrusted him. 'Gotta mind me p's and q's an' all that,' he said, shaking his head, which made his chins wobble. 'Can't trust a goddam livin' soul.' He told us that we were going to be looked after by the French Air Force at El Alouina, who were 'grand chaps who'll give you a grand time'. He added, 'I'll do anything I can for you fellas – you've only gotta ask.' Since everything he said on that journey was disproved from the moment we arrived at our destination it was plain that he had expected to extract all the information he needed in the car. Otherwise what was the point of telling us such lies and painting such a rosy picture? We were marched into a brightly-lit cell overlooking the Bay of Tunis in the distance. The open door led onto a balcony where stood the inevitable Arab guards with fixed bayonets. I put him to the test and asked for a toothbrush and a toilet roll, but, of course, neither was forthcoming. 'I'll see wot Oi c'n do,' he said, 'but Oi'd be in trouble if the Deuxième Bureau found out.'

For many days and nights the Arab guards did their best to keep us awake, but because the door onto the balcony was never closed, and the glaring overhead lights were never turned off, the mosquitoes needed very little assistance. Rubin de Cervans was a daily visitor, and his questioning was repetitive, and uninspired, in comparison with the Deuxième Bureau, who took me away for afternoon interrogation, which was done with the assistance of a live wire applied to my person, amongst other refinements even more unpleasant. I asked Rubin if these were the grand chaps who were going to give us such a grand time and he looked even more furtive, and apologized for their behaviour. 'Wish I could do more for you fellas but they're dangerous chaps . . . gotta mind me p's and q's an' all that, you know.'

I was relieved to find that they were sparing Robertson this third-degree treatment, presumably because he had only one stripe and looked very much younger, despite his beard. I was careful not to tell him what was happening in case they decided to have a go at him as well. Until that happened he was spared the agony of waiting for their afternoon visitations. Sometimes it was difficult to refrain from blurting it out, and once, when I found that the pubic hair on the left side of my stomach had turned white overnight, I had to cover myself quickly in case he noticed. Thereafter I was very coy about washing myself from head to foot at our joint basin, keeping a towel around my middle whenever I could.

There were several mitigating factors about this unhappy period. One was a sympathetic French guard, down below our veranda, who insisted on whistling. 'There'll Always Be an England', throughout his watch. It became very monotonous after a while, and although his intentions were good, I would have been pleased if he had whistled the German national anthem for a change. Also, I realized that the Deuxième Bureau were bluffing with some of their threats, and extracted a great deal of personal satisfaction every time I managed to beat them at their own game. They were determined to find out how the squadron managed to sink ships in the pitch dark. They suspected that the Allies had some form of seeing device; but radar for the detection of shipping, or for 'early warning', had only been developed by their enemies, and it was a closed book to them. I was able to grasp some respite by telling them a cock-and-bull story about a listening device which could pick up the sound of a ship's engines from very long range, and hoped that this might encourage them to stop engines more often and at an earlier stage, thereby providing the squadron with even better targets. I allowed them to extract this information from me slowly and gradually, and put on a great act of self-recrimination at having released such valuable information, which was made more realistic by giving way to the pain I was experiencing at the time.

I suspect that it is everybody's secret fear that they will break down under that sort of duress. I had sometimes wondered how I would react, and, if it ever happened, how long I would be able to hold out. I was intrigued to discover that one can be objective about pain, as if it were happening to someone else, though I doubt whether I would have been able to regard it dispassionately had I been given any choice. The greatest mitigating factor of all was the fact that I had no choice. They were trying to establish proof of my complicity in subversive activites, and had they succeeded, the penalties would have been total, and therefore much worse, so I had everything to gain by maintaining silence, and everything to lose if I failed. That knowledge was a tremendous help, and it was really very silly of them to waste so much time and effort. The same applied to a new approach which they tried on two consecutive afternoons; this was very nearly successful because it was more subtle. As I was led into the yard by a group of interrogators, instead of taking me into their headquarters they marched me up and down while they asked questions. Ten Vichy-French soldiers were practising firing-squad drill, and after one complete demonstration, when they fired at a dummy figure propped against the wall, they were stood at ease, and stared at me fixedly as I was paraded in front of them. The implication was obvious, and my knees became very wobbly at first, until I decided that they had nothing to gain but everything to lose by shooting me – unless I admitted complicity and revealed the name of my passenger, which is what they were after. Once I had made up my mind that it was bluff, it was like playing poker; but I held all the cards, including the winning hand, because no matter what they did I was unable to tell them the identity of my VIP since I did not know who he was, even if they should succeed in making me admit to his presence.

Rubin de Cervans startled me one morning by producing a photograph of him. There was no doubt that it was our VIP. With perfect truth I was able to say that I had no idea who he was.

'We know he was with you,' he said, sourly.

'He's a very good-looking chap, whoever he is,' I said admiringly.

'Are you going to tell me that you've never seen him before?'

'I might've done,' I said. 'His face is vaguely familiar. Isn't he a French politician, or a general, or something? I think I've seen his picture in the papers, but I certainly don't know who he is.'

'Bah!' said Rubin in disgust. But his greatest setback was the morning after his scouts had discovered the bicycle. He came bursting into our cell in triumph. When he said: 'We've found your bicycle!' I felt a sensation of relief. I had been preparing for this moment so often, and for so long, that I rather enjoyed the next few minutes, which were the turning-point of our interrogation. It was like the raising of the curtain on a first night after so many weeks of tiresome rehearsal.

'I was afraid you would find that,' I said. 'For God's sake don't report it. You'll get me into serious trouble if you do, and I shall be court martialled when I get home.'

'Whatdya mean?'

'I stole it. It's Government property, as I expect you've noticed. At Malta, the aircraft are dispersed so far from the airfield that it takes me half an hour to walk back for my breakfast. I hate walking.'

'Oh! Pooh-pooh!' he said indignantly, 'You mean to tell me that you carry a bicycle about in your aircraft so's you don't 'ave to walk back for your breakfast?'

'That's right,' I said, and when he shook his head in rank disbelief I trotted out my next ploy, which was designed to suit his own personal psychology. I put on my guilty look, which he would expect from an Englishman admitting to a peccadillo. 'If you must know, I've got a girl-friend in Malta who expects me to turn up on the dot when I have been flying all night. She cooks my breakfast as soon as she hears the aircraft returning, and gets very cross with me if I'm late.'

Being French this made slightly more sense to Rubin who, from his conversation in the car, had let it slip that he had girl-friends all over the place. But he was no fool; since he wore wings on his uniform, presumably he must have flown aeroplanes at some time or other in his life. His little eyes were darting out across to the bay while he thought about this, and before he had time to recognize the aerodynamic improbability of such a fanciful tale, I produced my winning hand.

'Listen,' I said, in an exasperated tone, 'don't get me into trouble for God's sake, or make a fool of yourself by suggesting that the bicycle was provided for some sort of spy. Use your loaf. If you have studied that machine you should have noticed that it has British crowns stamped on each mudguard – front and back – and you're going to look bloody silly if you suggest to your bosses that the British sent a spy over here to ride about on a bike which shouts "Look at me – I am British!" at every passer-by. Come on, Rubin, do use a little common sense for once in your life. Our intelligence chaps wouldn't do anything as silly as that!'

The poor man sat dejected on my bed, and then stood up with a sigh. 'I suppose they wouldn't,' he said dolefully. 'But I don't believe that story of yours about your breakfast – that's a lot of – 'ow you say? – baloney?' He sighed again and fired one last shot.

'This girl of yours, we can check on that – wot's 'er name and where does she live?'

It was my turn to sigh. 'I'm very sorry, Rubin, but you don't seem to understand the British. No Englishman would ever give away the name of his girl-friend, or her address. It would be an unspeakable thing to do. Supposing her husband found out, when your men started nosing round? All I'm prepared to tell you is that she's Maltese, and very pretty, and as jealous as hell. If it's any help to you it takes me nearly half an hour to cycle to her house in the mornings. Without the bike I'd never get to her, and if I left it on the ground while I was flying, some bastard would pinch it.

Bikes are like gold in Malta because of the petrol shortage.'

'Why don't you use a car?' he asked suspiciously. 'You could get plenty of petrol?'

I lowered my voice. 'Tank traps,' I said, confidentially. 'The whole island's covered in them. Nobody can drive about Malta without permission and I can't ask for permission to go and hop into bed with someone else's wife, now can I?'

He accepted my story and I was amazed that the inefficiency of the British Intelligence organization had made it unnecessary for me to face a firing squad after all; and for the first time I felt a slight twinge of gratitude to the major.

Robertson had been an interested listener to the entire conversation, and after Rubin had gone he grinned at me. We were careful not to say anything incriminating to each other because we were sure that the cell was bugged. But he couldn't resist having one little crack.

'I'm tempted to ask you who she is,' he said, 'but I know you wouldn't tell me.'

The Vichy-French had one more trick up their sleeves, and it was only unsuccessful because of their own failure to appreciate the limitations of the human frame. They tried to make capital out of a situation which was forced upon them against their wishes, but I suspect that they were not aware of the activities of the Deuxième Bureau in the afternoons, behind closed doors, and had little idea that I was nearing a state of complete physical exhaustion and collapse.

My brain had never ticked over so fast before, nor had my recuperative powers been so extended. It was as though each physical affront sharpened my wits, out of self-preservation, as it wore down my strength to resist. So far as Rubin de Cervans was concerned I was still a thorn in his flesh, and very much alive, which was perhaps why he did not demur when, at very short notice, he was ordered to bring me to the Commandant's residence in a fit enough state to attend an official dinner. If he considered it an impossible task he gave no sign, but I was too far gone, had he but known. I was to meet the American Vice-Consul. Unbeknown to me he had expressed concern about our welfare, and had to be satisfied that we were still alive.

At that time the position of the United States Vice-Consul in Tunis was fraught with difficulties. Since Tunisia and Algeria and the United States were all supposed to be neutral, the Vichy-French were being very careful not to upset the Americans for fear of bringing that great country into the war against their bosses, the Italians and the Germans. It had not then occurred to the Vichy-French that they might be attacked themselves. German and Italian aircraft were being allowed to use El Alouina all the time, despite the so-called neutrality of Tunis. Standing between two Arab guards, on the balcony outside my cell, I counted the aircraft flying in the circuit with Nazi swastikas painted on their fuselage. While all these activities were going on, quite openly, the presence in Tunis of the American Vice-Consul was a tremendous embarrassment to the Vichy-French and his every move had to be watched. I learned later that he was under 'open arrest' and was more or less confined to his residence, and when he went out he had to be escorted by a Vichy-French guard. But, through diplomatic channels, he was in touch with the outside world, and was therefore a very important person who had to be kept in the dark as much as possible and mollified when he expressed concern about anything he saw.

In 1941 the Allies were preparing the way for the eventual landing in North Africa, which had to come sooner or later since the Vichy-French were co-operating with the Axis powers; and my passengers were the spearhead of that landing. I am certain that one of the first things our VIP had to do was to contact the American Consulate in Tunis, so the Vice-Consul knew all about us, except (at first) where we were. Our disappearance was causing some concern at home; despite many anguished appeals by us we had not been allowed to send cables or telegrams, or even to write letters, and we knew that our next-of-kin would have been told that we were 'missing'.

More than two weeks after our VIP had called on the American Vice-Consul in Tunis that American diplomat had been asked by the British authorities in London to find out what had become of Robertson and me. When he discovered that we were being held in Tunis nearly three weeks after being taken prisoner, he asked why we had not been transferred to the official internment camp for Allied military personnel, which was then at Aumale, just outside Algiers. Until we arrived there, our next-of-kin could not be informed. Dissatisfied with the reply he was given, he insisted on being allowed to see the pilot of the Swordfish, and the Vichy-French hurriedly arranged a dinner as a quick way of showing me to him, at a distance. I was to be produced looking reasonably presentable, and after a quick introduction to the American, Rubin and all the officers present were under orders to keep me as far away from him as possible so that I was unable to talk. All this became obvious in retrospect.

When Rubin burst into my cell that evening he was oozing false sympathy and bonhomie, and was obsequious with bogus apologies. It had all been a terrible mistake, and everyone was desolated, and very, very sorry. The Commandant wanted to make amends, and I was to be given a sumptuous dinner in his residence, to meet all his officers, who wanted to apologize too. Rubin told me that, as a sign of good faith, and so that I would have somebody there who also spoke English, the Commandant had very graciously invited the American Vice-Consul, and I was to hurry, because we had to be there in less than half an hour.

Like a conjurer at a children's party, from behind his back the ridiculous man produced a toilet roll and a toothbrush, and presented them to me with a flourish. I was not impressed. There was something unreal about this invitation, coming straight out of the blue. I told Rubin that it was phoney. 'It's like you, Rubin, phoney, through and through.'

I had long since given up being polite to the insufferable creature. Just to look at him made me feel slightly sick.

'You can go and get stuffed,' I added, 'and tell the Commandant that he can get stuffed too, and the American Vice-Consul. All I want is sleep, and you know it.'

The Deuxième Bureau had given orders that I was not to be allowed to sleep at all until I came clean with them about my passenger. When Rubin burst in with his message I had been awake for seven days and nights and I was almost out of my mind. If I wasn't allowed to sleep soon I knew that I would die. Enforced wakefulness is a worse torment than starvation, and much worse than not being able to clean one's teeth or wipe one's behind, and as we were not being given enough food to sustain life, neither of these pleasant things was as vital as slumber. That afternoon, when I was taken for my walk around the yard, my guards had to support me by either arm, and I dozed off while walking. I could have gone to sleep standing on my head.

Rubin was under orders and tried to be belligerent, but I cut him short. 'Thanks to you French and Italian bastards, I'm in no condition to attend any dinner, or meet anyone. For Christ's sake leave me alone, and tell those bloody Arabs on the balcony to do the same. If your infernal Commandant wants to apologize, that's the way to prove it. I've got to be allowed to sleep or I shall peg out, and I'm not joking.'

The great slab of lard was quivering with fright, and was as nervous as a schoolboy summoned to the headmaster's study. He had been ordered to get me to the Commandant's residence 'tout de suite' and he was going to do so even if he had to use the Arabs and their bayonets. I had no physical strength left to resist, and had to allow him to pull my shirt over my head. I was dizzy with fatigue and scarcely conscious, and on our way to the dinner he had to enlist the aid of a gendarme to take my other arm. Between them they prevented me from lying on the ground, which was all that I wanted to do.

As we approached the house I tried to pull myself together. I was fully aware that the French would have some ulterior motive for this function and I had to be on my guard. In a crowded room I had to shake hands with the Commandant. He was a sharp-featured individual with a poker face. Amongst all those uniformed people the dark suit of the Vice-Consul was conspicuous. He was a small, middle-aged man called Springs with greying hair and watchful eyes, which followed me around the room until I was standing in front of him. When he had shaken hands Rubin tried to lead me away, but the American held on to my wrist and began talking about something quite inconsequential. In the middle of a sentence, without changing the inflexion of his voice, he interjected four words out of context – 'Keep your trap shut' – and then went on talking without a pause.

From that cryptic remark I deduced that he knew all about us and was on our side. It also made the picture quite clear, and revealed the ulterior motive behind the sudden reversal of attitude. By plying me with drinks when exhausted and with an empty belly, the Vichy-French would try to make me say something incriminating in the presence of the official representative of the United States, which would not only justify their criminal behaviour in the last three weeks, but would also provide them with a perfect excuse for any further measures they might take, no matter how violent. It was beautifully done by the Vice-Consul and I was most grateful. I wanted this nice American to know that I was going to disgrace myself at any moment by fainting – I could feel the dizziness overcoming my senses – and was determined that he should know that it was through no fault of my own.

'I'm out on my feet, sir,' I said, which was a phrase I hoped that the watchful Rubin would not readily understand.

'You don't look well.'

'These bastards have kept me awake for over a week and I don't know whether I am coming or going, so don't be shocked when I pass out in a minute or two.'

An angry Rubin tried to drag me away from the American and I had no strength to resist him, but as we moved away the Vice-Consul gave me an understanding nod, which meant, 'OK. Message received and understood.'

The introduction over, and honour satisfied, the Commandant took his place at the table, with the American on his right and with me on his left, so that all three of us were facing in the same direction, and looking away from each other. Rubin made sure that my glass was constantly replenished. I said 'yes please' to everything I was offered, because I wanted to faint before someone involved me in a tricky conversation, and the more I ate and drank the sooner it would happen. My final recollection of that dinner was a feeling of disgust with my hosts that they used the same knife and fork for each course, even at a social function.

When I came to I was back in my cell, and an angry Rubin was standing over me, shaking my shoulder. The sun was high over the balcony and streaming through the window.

'Come on – wake up!' he said sourly. 'I've gotta get both you fellas on to a train for Algiers, and it leaves in less than an hour.'

28
African Journey

On the platform of the railway station at Tunis, Rubin de Cervans handed us over to two gendarmes and a guard of two Arabs armed with their inevitable rifles. They were also wearing tin hats, and as a parting shot I remarked to Rubin that, in a country which was not supposed to be at war with anyone, the fashion of wearing tin hats was rather surprising. 'Your soldiers wear them more than we do in Britain! Perhaps they are afraid of being shot from behind by their officers?'

The gendarmes guided us into a reserved compartment and sat down with us, and the Arabs took up their stations in the corridor outside, presumably to keep other passengers away from our contaminating presence.

We had high hopes of being able to escape during the journey, and had made some rather sketchy plans. Although we had been searched several times our captors had failed to find our French money and other escape equipment. I had a compass, cunningly concealed in a well-smoked pipe, and Robertson had another, hidden in a matching button sewn on his shirt; but most important of all, each of us had five hundred francs, neatly packed under the stiff buckram in our shoulder-straps, together with a hacksaw blade in its hard coating of plastic.

When wearing khaki uniform it is customary for the shoulder-straps, which denote rank, to be made of soft material too; but the gold and black variety, normally worn with white tropical uniform, could be worn with both, and they made a splendid hiding-place for paper money and anything flat. Once inserted under the buckram stiffening all that was needed were a few stitches with black cotton, and the money was well hidden if the sewing was neatly done.

Naturally, when walking to our rendezvous on the first day, we carried the shoulder-straps in our trouser pockets. When we were arrested we produced them as evidence that we were not civilians. The gendarmes were very suspicious about this and so was Rubin de Cervans, who asked us why, if we were not engaged in subversive activities, were we flying dressed as civilians? It was what would be called 'a good question' at the Naval Staff College at Greenwich, when a lecturer is caught out and is seeking time to think of an answer. We explained that they could not be worn under parachute harness without damage, and we had forgotten to put them on again after we landed. That was 'a good staff answer' too.

The money was essential to our plans. Our aim was to get the two gendarmes very drunk, and then jump out of the window in the compartment when the train slowed down at some suitable place near Algiers. The farther west the better, because our ultimate destination was Gibraltar via Spanish Morocco. The single window in our carriage was very big, and before the train left Tunis, Robertson discovered that it opened easily. Muttering something about 'fresh air' he yanked it down in one simple movement. The gendarmes hurried yanked it up again, shaking their heads reprovingly and saying '*Defendu!*'

We had worked out what to say to the policemen to explain why we had so much money. On the correct assumption that they were our guards only for the journey, and were not military officers, we hoped that they would not know that we were supposed to be penniless.

After the train had been under way for about an hour, and we had established friendly relations with the two men, Robertson explained that the American Consul in Tunis had given us some French money to pay for essentials on arrival at the internment camp. 'If you would be kind enough to accompany us to the refreshment car we would like to buy you both a drink or two. We are going to be stuck in this train for a long while, so we might as well try to enjoy it while we can, don't you agree?'

The gendarmes were glad to agree, especially if we were paying, and in the buffet car I asked for ouzo, the aniseed apertif which turns a chalky-white when water is added, and which is just as lethal the next morning, after a glass of water, as it is the night before. They were happy to drink with us providing we kept pace with them and went on paying. Unfortunately Robertson was a teetotaller. To prevent the policemen from becoming suspicious I had to buy Robertson drinks each time too, and when the men were not looking, drink his as well as my own.

At the age of twenty-seven I was foolishly over-confident that I could drink them all under the table. I was wrong. Although I succeeded in getting the gendarmes very drunk indeed, when we returned to the compartment I was by no means sober, and was in no condition to jump out of any window, even if someone held it open for me and guided me through in easy stages. I hoped to have recovered by the time the train arrived somewhere near Algiers, by which time the gendarmes would be tipsy again after drinking their morning coffee.

We had forgotten one essential detail. When their officer came back, reeling along the corridor from side to side, the Arab guards became very suspicious, and at the next stop one of them must have telephoned Constantine, because when we pulled into that border station at midnight, two armed detachments were fallen-in on the platform, one for the two gendarmes and one for us. The Vichy-French were taking no chances of a repetition of this behaviour in Algeria. The Tunisian gendarmes were marched away in disgrace, and we were taken to the local police station for the night.

The streets of Constantine consist of a great number of very steep hills. With our few possessions slung over our shoulders in a pillow-case, and with an armed Arab guard on either side of us, we were jostled up and down those hills in the dark, and by the time we reached the police station it was one in the morning. We were all in a thoroughly bad temper, Arabs and prisoners alike. We were locked up in the main reception room, where a huge sergeant with a very thick neck sat at a desk facing a little window. The floor of the room was cobbled, and apart from the sergeant's table and chair, there was no furniture in the room whatever.

A diminutive Vichy-French orderly officer had been roused from his bed in the barracks at the other end of the town to come and deal with us. He was feeling pretty sore too, and told us that we would have to stay in that room for the rest of the night, sleeping on the stone floor. At this I lost my temper. The combination of jostling Arabs marching us through the streets in an undignified manner at dead of night, and the failure of our plans to escape, now that the boozy gendarmes had been taken away, was too much for me, and I allowed the ouzo to take command of the situation.

Picking up the little French officer by his elbows I gave him a good shake.

'When do we go on to Algiers?' I asked, fiercely.

'*Lâchez-moi! Immédiatement! Tout de suite!* he cried, kicking his heels.

'Not until you tell me,' I said, giving him another little shake.

'*A huit heures du matin,*' he said, spitting the words into my face. I put him down while I thought about this. I had no intention of spending the night in a room with a cobbled floor and no furniture, and asked to be shown to a cell, where at least I would be provided with a mattress. This was refused. I then demanded an audience with the little man's CO, and when this was refused I picked him up again, and shook him more vigorously. Unfortunately, the big sergeant then intervened and I had to put him down again. But this behaviour had achieved what we wanted. Enraged at being plucked from the floor in the middle of the night, the orderly officer telephoned his CO, and once again we were marched through the hilly streets of Constantine. We were shown into an office where we found an irate Colonel sitting behind a desk under an enormous picture of Marshal Pétain. There followed a quite ridiculous altercation, with everyone shouting at each other, and poor Robertson trying to pacify them. The Colonel had several rows of decorations, and medal ribbons galore, on his chest, and at one point in the childish scene he drew my attention to them.

'*Regardez!*' he shouted. 'I have seen action! You have not!' – and he pointed at my left shoulder where, of course, there were no signs of valour. Then he waved a lofty hand at Pétain's picture on the wall above his head.

'*C'est mon père!*' he said. I was so taken aback by this allegorical rhetoric that I couldn't refrain from saying that the King of England was my uncle, which was patently untrue. The Colonel took me up on it at once, and was unforgivably rude.

'*Vous – un Anglais – vous n'avez pas un père – Churchill seulement – et votre roi – et ils ne sont rien – rien de tout.*'

I then made a tactical error which I have often regretted. I leaned over the desk and made a disdainful sweeping gesture, with my fingertips and the back of my right hand, above his row of medal ribbons.

'*Pouf!*' I said scornfully. '*Il n'importe. Il est rien de tout, aussi! Parce que vous êtes Vichy-Français!*'

Inflamed with anger the Colonel clasped the arms of his chair and raised himself enough to slap my face.

All the indignities of the last three weeks and of that night boiled up in one spate of overwhelming rising gorge, and I had to hit him. Nothing could have prevented me. It was a short right-hand punch which only travelled about six inches, but I tried to hit him harder than I have ever managed to hit anyone in the boxing ring. The blow lifted him out of his chair and his head struck the wall behind him with a resounding thump, and as he slid down to the floor with his eyes closed I was fascinated to note that he was actually snoring. Before that incident I thought that snores only occurred in the middle of a deep sleep, as a sign of contentment. But that man was snoring before I had unclenched my fist.

Babel was then let loose. Half a dozen Arabs beat me about the head and neck with their muskets, and succeeded in displacing a number of discs, and I have suffered from spondylosis ever since, and shall have to attend for continual treatment for the rest of my life; but even had I known that the consequences were going to be permanent I could not have refrained from hitting that man. It was almost worth it.

The immediate effect was very satisfactory. By striking the Frenchman I had qualified for a cell in the barracks until the train left the next morning, which saved Robertson and me another walk up and down those Constantine hills; and the cell was far more comfortable than the cobbled floor of the police station.

29
Aumale

The first men to be taken prisoner by the Vichy-French in North Africa were a number of army privates who had struggled to Marseilles after the fall of Dunkirk, and had then managed to cross the Mediterranean, thinking that they would be repatriated from Algeria, which was both unoccupied and neutral; but Marshal Pétain had set up his Vichy-French Government, and thrown in his lot with the Axis powers, and the poor fellows were locked up.

To begin with they had been under house-arrest in Algiers, where they lived fairly comfortably in a small boarding-house, while a full-scale internment camp, with barbed-wire fencing and machine-gun posts, was being built at Laghouat, an oasis out in the Sahara desert. When the numbers became too many for the boarding-house they were moved to Aumale until Laghouat was ready.

While in that boarding-house their meals had been brought to them by a buxom Arab waitress who was very friendly. She spoke no English, so the privates taught her some polite phrases, including one thing to say to English-speaking visitors when she took them their early morning tea. I wondered what happened to that poor girl when senior British officers were billeted there, later in the war. Each morning with a beaming smile, she greeted her customers with the phrase: 'Pees off, you geeve me the sheets!'

Aumale is a pretty little suburban town, sixty miles from Algiers and the Mediterranean coast. While there, many attempts to escape were partially successful; some prisoners managed to get away from the building, but the Mediterranean was a bar to further proceedings and nobody ever succeeded in getting away altogether. When we were moved to Laghouat it became an impossibility. There was every incentive to escape from Aumale because the conditions were vile. Only the Vichy-French could have selected the site as a suitable place to house human beings. Some sixty officers and men of all three services existed in the top storey of a huge barn-like building above a lunatic asylum for Arab females. The entire ground floor was occupied by these unfortunate ladies, who were all incurably mad. Many of them were not allowed any clothing at all in case they hanged themselves, and during their exercise periods they performed all their natural functions – and many which were unnatural – below our barred windows in the nude. The poor things were hideously ugly, but their appearance was not nearly as off-putting as the sound and fury of their habits, which were indescribable. Many of them screamed throughout the night.

The tall building had started life as a single-storey warehouse, but at some stage a permanent floor had been laid across the rafters, and wooden walls had been nailed to them to divide the roof into small storage compartments. Windows, fitted with strong iron bars, had been put into the outside brick wall under the eaves. The bars were originally to prevent thieves breaking in; they were now very effective in preventing us from breaking out, though we managed to do so at times.

A staircase led up to the centre of this weird home amongst the rafters, dividing it in half. For sleeping purposes one half was used by ratings and the other by officers, but we intermingled freely, especially at the two daily 'Appels' when the French tried hard to keep us apart. To confuse them, we often swopped places at these roll-calls, and if a man could manage to slip from one side to the other during Appel, so that he was counted twice, the subsequent confusion kept us extremely amused and drove our captors into a frenzy of rage. At these times there was little to choose between the Vichy-French officers and the ladies down below.

Outside, at the back of the building, was *la douche* – four cold water taps above stone troughs. At Aumale there were no hot water showers or any other form of ablutions. The only sanitary arrangements for sixty prisoners were three holes in the floor of an outhouse above three metal drums which were supposed to be emptied once a week. They should have been emptied daily, because the majority of the men were suffering from dysentery, sandfly fever, and almost continuous bouts of jaundice. The drums were in constant use, and when they were taken away they resembled enormous chocolate ice-cream cornets.

The building was surrounded by a high wall, where Arab guards were spaced about twenty yards apart. Anyone seen attempting to escape was shot at, at once, which was indefensible when one remembers that we were 'internees' in a neutral country, and could not even be referred to as 'prisoners-of-war'. Because of this status we were entitled to send cables and telegrams, and the Vichy-French had to allow this whether they liked it or not. One of the first things I did was to send a cable to Jo, telling her that I was safe but a prisoner; it was a relief to be able to do so at long last.

In the mornings, before the first Appel, we were brought tureens of ersatz 'coffee' made from date-stones. It was dark blue in colour, but after a few days I found that I could drink it without wanting to spit it out, and after a few weeks actually looked forward to it, and found it reasonably palatable. It was warming and sweet – two characteristics which we seldom experienced, during the days and nights in that scabrous wooden home under the roof. The same did not apply to the food. Twice daily, large urns of some unspeakable mess were dumped on the floor at the top of the stairs. The contents were even more obnoxious than the food which had been given to us in the Fort at Sousse.

When this pig-swill was brought to us, the Arab porters were always accompanied by the Vichy-French duty officer. The Commandant at Aumale was an out-and-out sadist who liked to watch the starving men scramble for their obnoxious food. Those who had been locked up the longest had been forced by circumstances to acclimatize themselves to eating it, and they were so hungry that there was often a rather undignified scramble around the urn when it arrived. When he stood watching this pathetic display, the Vichy-French Commandant always made the same remark: with an expression of disgust he would turn to the duty officer and say: '*Les Anglais! Comme les cochons.*'

Before I arrived he had sentenced the entire community, officers and men, to a period of confinement in a single cell, all incarcerated together, so cramped that they had to stand up, taking it in turns to sit down. With no sanitary arrangements or exercise, it is a wonder that they did not go out of their minds.

The majority of the internees had a private supply of French money which they managed to hide on their persons during searches, and by lowering a bucket on the end of a rope we could buy tins of sardines, and dates, and mushrooms, from Arab black market vendors. The guards extracted a levy for allowing this, which added to the inflated cost. There was also a legitimate market once a week, in the courtyard, organized by the Vichy-French, when we were encouraged to buy cigarattes and eau-de-vie, and other alcoholic beverages. The French made a handsome profit out of our purchases and the more we drank the less likely we were to want to escape. We had to pay cash to the black marketeers, but at the organized market, sums spent were deducted from our monthly allowance.

Although we were never supposed to be in possession of actual money we were allowed a monthly credit of 1000 francs per head. This was paid to the French, in cash, by the American Vice-Consul in Algiers and Tunis – who was the man who was so helpful to me. This arrangement was part of 'Lease-Lend', and over the years it must have amounted to a sizeable sum. When I returned to the United Kingdom and made inquiries, I discovered that the Americans never asked for it to be repaid. In fact they wrote it off as something they would gladly pay towards the cost of the war in the years before they took part. I have often wondered whether this was appreciated by the other prisoners. It was a wonderfully kind gesture, and typical of the relationship built up between the United States and Great Britain by Roosevelt and Churchill. Without that monthly allowance there would have been many more deaths from starvation than there were, and during the year which followed our stay at Aumale, although we lost a percentage of men who needed special diets which were unobtainable, and who had no resistance when they became seriously ill, the majority survived because of the food that they were able to buy on the black market – thanks to the Americans.

Clothes and footwear were commodities we could not buy at all. There was a terrible shortage of both throughout North Africa, and all the internees had to manage with the clothes and shoes that they were wearing when they were taken prisoner. As a result, we were a very scruffy group of individuals, many of whom were forced to go about in their bare feet. Because I had learned how to sew canvas in the Merchant Service and it had become a lifelong hobby, I was quite handy with a needle. I became one of the camp tailors, and spent many hours trying to patch up the men's clothes, which was sometimes almost impossible when the material had worn very thin. But we did our best. Also, I became one of the camp barbers; there was no need to hurry, and through lack of skill I generally took an hour at least to cut each head of hair.

Each inmate was provided with a bed and a set of grey calico sheets I had first met at Sousse. Once a month the sheets were changed, and when replacements arrived from the laundry it was essential to straighten any folded edges which were turned over and smooth out creases, or lift any fold which had been ironed flat, because lurking underneath there were bound to be colonies of bed-bugs, seeking obscurity. After the initial shock, one had to try to accept this as an occupational hazard, but I never approached the task without a shudder of horrific anticipation. Our own clothes became infested, too, no matter how careful we were. It was an unequal battle because the walls of the barn were crawling with bugs and cockroaches. Whenever we smoked a cigarette it became routine to search out and stab our own live-stock with the lighted end while we sat around and talked.

On our arrival in this Dante's Inferno, Robertson and I were so exhausted that we slept for nearly a week, waking only for Appels and when some kind person offered us sardines. The first people I saw as we walked through the barn-like doors were Cooper and Davies, the pilots of the Hudson which had been shot down by Robin Kilroy on the day that *Illustrious* joined the Mediterranean Fleet. When we had recovered from the shock of seeing each other, I asked them why they were there. 'Dai' Davies said, 'We were shot down by the bloody Fleet Air Arm!' Then it all came out, and they were amazed at the coincidence, that I was only a few hundred yards away in my Swordfish when it happened, and was able to tell them the name of the pilot who fired the offending burst from his Fulmar. I did my best to show them that it was not Robin's fault, and we had many months ahead to discuss it from every aspect. They were not bitter, but Davies had a daughter then aged nearly two whom he had never seen, and it was a subject we avoided after a while.

Amongst the other prisoners were the pilot and observer of the Skua which ran out of fuel on its way back to *Ark Royal* after escorting Hurricanes to Malta. There were also many Swordfish crews who had been taken prisoner flying from Malta in 830 Squadron.

When I had caught up with my sleep and was able to take an intelligent interest in my surroundings, I decided to go into training and get as fit as possible. To escape was every man's dream, and a high standard of physical fitness was essential. I made myself a punch-bag and a skipping-rope and began a serious training routine. My antics on the heavy bag – moving round it to my right, away from my 'opponent's' right hand, and stepping in with body punching, and in and out with a quick left hand – were watched by a crowd of interested spectators who asked me to give them boxing lessons. The Vice-Consul had already supplied a set of eight-ounce gloves, and I began what was to become an institution; those boxing lessons, every morning, were a feature of life in that community, and became very popular. One of the men I taught from scratch became the featherweight champion of the Royal Air Force when he returned to the United Kingdom, which gave me a big thrill.

The community needed more than that to take themselves in hand. For the first month or two I was a spectator, and became alarmed at the future. Listening to the news, edited by the Vichy-French, it seemed that Britain was losing her lonely war, and if we were to remain prisoners for years to come, few would survive. Their sense of humour was still simmering under the surface but was becoming warped, which was understandable – but very frightening. When the soldier and sailor and airman can't find something to laugh about, it is almost as dangerous as it is when they can find nothing to complain about. At Aumale there was too much of the latter and not enough of the former. Their favourite pastime, when they became bored and angry, was to bait the Arab guards and the Vichy-French, who were easy to arouse. All we had to do to start a riot was to sing 'Oh! Vive de Gaulle', which was a catchy tune with some offensive words, ending in a crescendo with the line, 'Darlan! – You Bastard!' Whenever the Arabs heard this song they fired volleys of bullets through the windows. Before breaking into song we sat with our backs to the wall beneath the windows, armed with sticks. A hat or piece of cloth balanced on the end of the stick and held up to the window was immediately shot to ribbons. The Arabs were very good shots indeed.

Strangely enough, another song which never failed to provoke them into opening fire was the hymn, 'All Things Bright and Beautiful'. Why they found it offensive I shall never know – perhaps because we always sang it after 'Vive de Gaulle' – but it was at the end of the second line, 'All creatures great and small – all – all . . .' on a rising note, that the fusillade came rattling through the windows. Now, when I sing that hymn in church, I still find that I want to duck down in the pew at the word 'small'.

Although I had more reason than most of them for disliking the Vichy-French, I thought these riots were fun while they lasted.

When they took place the population of Aumale used to gather in the road outside, and they must have thought that the British prisoners in their midst were a very strange lot. These demonstrations of hate and independence made the ill-feeling between captor and captive much worse, and in my opinion did no good whatever. They also terrified the poor women down below. Because of the effect on the women, I managed to dissuade my companions occasionally, but not always. They had to have some means of letting off steam in Aumale, or go mad.

My influence, for good or bad, was removed from the community after I had been there for only a few weeks. At one of the morning Appels the Commandant read out a warrant sentencing me to seventy days' solitary, for striking a French officer, which was greeted with loud cheers by the British as I was marched off to the cells. I was still there two months later when the camp was moved to the oasis in the Sahara, and I was only released on a temporary basis to rejoin the others for the move. At Laghouat I had to go back to cells to complete my sentence. If anything, the cells at Laghouat were better than at Aumale. Although they were completely without light, the Arab guards were more friendly, and would sometimes sit and chat with the door open. At Aumale there was enough light to see but not to read. A light shone down outside the bars of my cell window and by putting my hands through them, I could hold a book and read through the bars. But I only did it once. Some French soldiers on the floor above saw what I was doing and emptied the contents of a urinal onto the book, which splashed up in my face, and I was not prepared to take the risk again. It made the book rather smelly to read.

In the Aumale cell a black market Arab vendor was allowed to visit me on one occasion. He was a confectioner, and sold me a vast supply of gâteaux. They looked most attractive, and being very hungry indeed, I fell on them, devouring a number in double-quick time. I think I had eaten about five before I noticed the cockroach legs sticking out of the middle. Every single one had a big cockroach inserted into the centre. They could not have been there by chance.

Seventy days is a long time to be shut up on one's own. Like the famous Bruce, at Laghouat I became very friendly with a huge spider, which was nesting in a skylight overhead. He rode out a sirocco, and when the storm abated and he reappeared and started rebuilding his web, I found that I was crying in relief. I was afraid he had succumbed to the storm, and he was my only companion. At those tears I realized that if I wasn't very careful I would soon be round the bend, like the poor girls at Aumale.

The sound of an aircraft engine overhead, followed by a gun-salute, and shortly afterwards the same in reverse, puzzled me at the time, in the darkness of my cell. When I was released I was told what had happened. General Huntziger had flown in with a group of Vichy-French politicians. At the orders of the Slug – the Foreign Legion Colonel in command of the garrison at Laghouat – all British prisoners were fallen-in in readiness for an address by the General.

On 21 June 1940, General Huntziger was the head of the French delegation of four who sat in a dining-car in the Forest of Compiègne, with Hitler, Raeder, von Ribbentrop, Keitel, Brauchitsch, and Hess, to discuss the terms of the French surrender. On Saturday, 22 June, on behalf of Marshal Pétain, Huntziger signed the surrender of his country. He then flew to Rome, and on Monday, 24 June, signed the Italian Armistice. The terms of both were pitiless, and as Churchill said in the House of Commons, 'They amounted to nothing less than the complete capitulation of France, and from being a powerful ally France had been converted into an enemy.'

Huntziger's visit, and his address to the British prisoners at Laghouat, were the result of my striking the French colonel on my way to the camp, at Constantine. 'Only because I hope for friendly relations with Britain after the war have I refrained from sentencing that officer to six months' imprisonment,' he said. When he walked away, the Slug stayed behind to deliver a parting shot of his own. 'The Arab population of North Africa have been told that the reward for the recapture of an escaped British prisoner is one thousand francs. I have altered this. It remains at one thousand francs if you are brought back alive, but they will receive two thousand francs if you are brought back dead.'

Shortly after these stirring words the General's aircraft took off to fly him back to Algiers, and then to France. It crashed after a few moments, somewhere in the Sahara, and all the occupants were killed.

French officers 'in the field' can be sentenced by their command-ing officers without court martial, or an inquiry. Under any other system the fact that the Colonel insulted the King of England, and the British Prime Minister, would have emerged in evidence – not as an excuse for my unpardonable conduct, but in mitigation of my crime. Presumably, under French military law the Colonel also had the right to slap my face, if he so wished. To a young lieutenant in the Royal Navy, aged twenty-seven, all his actions were indefensible, and although mine were incorrect, in the same circumstance I would do the same thing again, only perhaps a bit harder.

At the time, I put everything I could into that short right-hand punch, but I had had very little sleep for some weeks, and very little food either, and it was not one of my best. However, the fact that indirectly it caused the death of the man who had signed the surrender of France makes up for its lack of power.

30
Laghouat

When we left Aumale for Laghouat we travelled by train to Djelfa, the most southerly point in Algeria which can be reached by rail. It is deep into the Sahara and when the railway came to an end it seemed that we had left civilization far behind. For the last hour, at least, the train had been rattling across open desert where there was no sign of life.

Outside that lonely station we were packed into lorries and driven a further seventy-five miles to the south; with each mile our spirits sank and our hopes of escape were swallowed by the unending vistas of sand. If it took us so long by rail and lorry to reach our destination, how could we expect to return along this route by our own resources?

The next morning, when Lieutenant Martin and his Tirailleurs marched us to the top of a hill on the outskirts of that bleak garrison, our feelings of isolation deepened. Martin had been bombarded by the British Fleet in Syria, and he was coldly hostile in all his dealings with us as a result. He waited until we had been completely surrounded by his Arab soldiers and then drew our attention to the endless tracts of desert which stretched in all directions to a completely circular horizon. He seemed very satisfied with this view. With an ironic sweep of his hand he said, *'Voilà! Regardez,'* and speaking in halting English gave us a picture of our new environment. His message was stark and uncompromising.

'Djelfa is the nearest water supply. To get there you must cross one hundred kilometres of open desert, without cover. Just in case any of you hope to catch a train there, let me warn you that every stranger who appears on that station is going to be locked up. They will be under arrest and will not be released until they have been checked by someone from Laghouat. So, if you are determined to escape, you will face a journey of three hundred and fifty kilometres to Algiers, mostly on foot. The first two hundred will be across the desert in the burning sun.

'For myself, I would not attempt it and I have had many years' experience of the Sahara.

'Here, in Laghouat, there is one battalion of Tirailleurs – who are sharpshooters – and the Premier Spahis – who are the best cavalrymen in the French army. All these soldiers are here to make sure that you do not escape, and to search for you, and find you, if you do. On their horses they will find you, before you have been able to walk more than a few kilometres, and the Arab Spahis are very fierce soldiers.'

Once again he waved his hand in a wide circle at the empty horizon.

'*Regardez!*' he said grimly. '*Vous avez la bonne chance.*'

My own opinions of the hopelessness of our position were echoed by his words, but I would not have admitted to those feelings to anyone. Sad to say, they were borne out in practice; in the year which followed, although many people escaped from the compound, and some lost their lives in doing so, I believe that 'Le Camp des Internées Britannique', at Laghouat, was the only military prison in the whole of Europe where not one single prisoner ever got away altogether. All who managed to set off across that open desert were brought back by the Spahis, generally in grim circumstances. Before doing the fifteen days' solitary in Arab cells, which followed an escape as surely as day follows night, it was generally necessary for them to recuperate in hospital.

Our domestic quarters were designed for Arabs and had been used by them for decades. The men were housed in single-storey dormitories which bore a plaque on the door saying 'Vingt-cinq hommes'. Our numbers had been increasing week by week, and on arrival at Laghouat there were at least forty men per dormitory. During the year this number was to swell to more than double, when conditions became unspeakable and survival problematical; but to be fair to the Vichy-French no other accommodation was available.

The officers were allocated a separate block which was also single-storey, containing a number of small rooms leading one into the other. From the bugs and cockroaches which infested the walls it was clear that these had been Arab quarters too. My two RAF friends, Flight-Lieutenants Davies and Cooper, occupied an inside room, with two beds, but no outside door, so that they had to walk through two little rooms to get to their own. The first of these was the home of Monty, an army captain who had spent most of his life in the Argentine. He was a tall, bearded man who spoke in whispers and shuffled about his little room in carpet slippers. I think he was the scruffiest individual I have ever met, but he was a very pleasant fellow, none the less. One afternoon I noticed dried lentils in his beard and when I pointed them out he gave it a little tug, and a number of them rattled onto the floor. We then stared at each other thinking the same thought: it was more than a week since we had eaten lentils!

I occupied the little room between Monty and the two flight-lieutenants; it was therefore a passage between the two rooms, but it had two doors which I could close at night in the winter, when the nights were very cold indeed, or when I needed brief privacy to talk to someone. Privacy was essential sometimes.

When we first arrived I was only allowed a few days to settle in before being taken off to cells to finish my sentence. Apart from the darkness, my main objection to solitary confinement was the tin 'milk churn', which was the sole concession made by the French to the natural functions of the occupant. One could not describe it as being for sanitary purposes because it was most insanitary, and was seldom emptied, even when there was a change of occupant.

The Vichy-French suffered from three main shortages: firstly, although they prattled about '*l'honneur de France*' they had no sense of honour at all, but were prepared to jump on any band-wagon which would lead to victory, even if it meant dishonouring their friends. Secondly, they had no sense of humour; they had a pronounced sense of satire, but that is a very different kettle of fish altogether. They could never bear a joke against themselves, and any race of people who are unable to laugh at themselves is sick indeed; and thirdly – and perhaps the worst of all – they had absolutely no sense of sanitation.

I made these observations to the Slug one day, when on my way to start yet another fifteen days' solitary, which was one time when one could indulge one's temper because one had nothing more to lose. I told him that if the opportunity ever occurred for me to go to war against them, I would be delighted; but instead of dropping bombs or torpedoes, I would drop lavatory seats and toilet rolls.

Whenever I was sentenced to solitary in Laghouat, which happened three times, I was in the charge of a cheerful little Arab guard whose name was pronounced 'Ay-ee-sa'. I have no idea how it was spelt, and he was unable to tell me because he could neither read nor write. He was a swashbuckling little rogue of a man, with a flowing moustache and a twinkle in two very dishonest eyes. He had a pronounced taste for wine and women, both of which were denied to him, officially, by his religion. Although we could only converse in halting French, we became very good friends.

Every British prisoner was issued with a litre of Algerian wine each day, because the water was strictly rationed, and in any case it was unfit for consumption until it had been boiled. The wine was the umpteenth press, and the left-overs, after the French had received their ration. It was very coarse, rough wine, and a taste I did not acquire for many months; but Ayeesa was devoted to it, and by giving him daily dollops in my mug I managed to persuade him to empty my churn from time to time. One afternoon, when he had drunk far more than was good for him, he regaled me with a deliciously funny story of how he incurred a stretch of 'solitaire' in that selfsame cell. It took him about half an hour to tell me, which was splendid because my door was open all the time, and fresh air was pouring in, and his imitations of his officers were worthy of Mike Yarwood. Fortunately I can tell his story in one sentence: he was found in bed with one of the French officers' wives.

The door of my cell was secured by a very solid three-pronged bolt, which could never be forced open from the inside. Every time it was clanged home I laughed, because the French had failed to notice a little iron grille, at floor level, just beside the door, through which the sanitary milk-churn should have been passed when it was emptied. Because this so seldom happened – and when it did it was much easier to carry it through the door – the tiny padlock securing the grille had rusted in the locked position. During my first week I managed to saw through the hasp with my hacksaw, and was glad of an opportunity of using it. Afterwards, a little carefully placed mud and dust concealed the cut in the metal, and the padlock remained locked until I wanted to use it. From my previous experience in Egypt and Libya I knew that outside help was essential and I was keeping this up my sleeve until a proper escape could be organized.

In December 1941, when I was back in the main camp, I received a telegram from my wife telling me that I had been awarded the DSC, which I heard later was for operations in Albania. All telegrams were read very carefully by the French before they were delivered, and at Appel, the Slug called me out, and demanded to know the reason for this honour. The Vichy-French at Aumale and Laghouat had all been fully briefed about my alleged subversive activities, and they were very suspicious.

'*Pourquoi?*' he demanded, obviously assuming that it was a reward for anti-Vichy-French adventures. The reason had not been stated on the cable.

'*Je ne sais quoi, M'sieur,*' I replied, quite truthfully at the time.

'*Quinze jours de rigueur en cellule, toute de suite!*' he ordered, and once again I found myself being looked after by Ayeesa, in my cell.

One month later, in January 1942, I received another telegram from my Josephine, saying 'Am bursting with pride. You have been awarded the DSO,' and I was again summoned from the ranks.

'*Pourquoi?*' demanded the Slug.

This time it was for successful attacks on Rommel's shipping, but I saw no reason for telling the Slug. It was a private matter between my Monarch and myself. In any case we had established a routine and I had no wish to break with tradition.

'*Je ne sais quoi, M'sieur.*'

I am afraid that he disliked my manner.

'*Quinze jours de rigueur en cellule, tout de suite!*' he roared, his eyes glinting with rage. Ayeesa was delighted to see me, and asked me if I had got myself a season ticket. It would be untruthful to pretend that I was pleased to see him. I was getting very tired of being locked up in the dark in a smelly cell, and by then the other ranks and ratings in Laghouat had elected me their 'Adjutant', and I was responsible for their wellbeing and discipline, and the two things added up to survival, and there was a major job of work to do. I was tempted to send a cable to His Majesty at Buckingham Palace, saying 'Please, no more!' but decided it might be considered presumptuous.

I know of nobody else who has received a sentence of fifteen days' solitary with each award, and when I met His Majesty, King George VI, I would have liked to have told him. He had a tremendous sense of humour and would have thought it very funny. But the opportunity never occurred.

To while away the days, in the total of one hundred days that I had to do in a dark cell, I used the ample time to think about all sorts of things I had never bothered to think about before. Because I was worried about money matters, I retraced all my experiences since diving from *Courageous* in September 1939, so that I could work out where the money had gone and how much I had received in 'casual payments'. I had not been allowed to make a claim for leaving my clothes behind in Athens because I was 'fleeing from the enemy'. According to Paymaster-Commander Lucy Waters, at Dekheila, if you take such avoiding action you forfeit your right to make a claim. My pay papers had never caught up with me, but the bill for the beer which we took into the Albanian mountains had. The NAAFI manager was one of the few who managed to get out of Athens with all his bills before the Germans took over. When this bill arrived at Hal Far I went to the Paymaster's offices in St Angelo, to point out to the Pussers that it was a squadron debt, and that half the chaps were now dead, and most of the others were prisoners, or scattered about the desert fighting Rommel, and there would be no chance of getting them to stump up; but the Pussers said: 'You signed for thirty-six crates of beer and you must pay,' and that was that. I had inadvertently paid the entire squadron's mess bill at Paramythia for nearly two months!

Eighteen months before the war, when Jo and I announced our engagement in the newspapers, I had just changed back into naval uniform from the RAF, and some of the naval lieutenants who were co-students with me on the same nine-month observers' course did their best to persuade me that nobody could possibly keep a wife on his naval pay alone. Over the centuries the majority of naval officers had vast family estates, double-barrelled names, and substantial private incomes. They regarded their pay as pocket money, to meet incidental expenses like monthly mess bills, and their monthly allotment of a few pounds to Gieves, the naval tailors. It was also used to pay their annual subscriptions to a military club in London, and if there was anything left over, it paid for the occasional bottle of wine when they dined ashore.

In their opinion it was quite impossible to marry without private means. The normal naval wedding only took place after a marriage settlement had been agreed with the bride's parents, involving a large capital sum; and to my companions a marriage without this settlement was unthinkable. No lieutenant ever received as much as one pound a day throughout his eight years.

All that I could afford was the annual premium for an endowment policy, and even that was stretching my elastic more than somewhat. The premiums for life policies for aircraft pilots were high. We were not considered a good risk at Lloyd's.

Three delightful RN lieutenants took me to Liphook Golf Club in an expensive car, ostensibly to play a foursome. They were all in the same well-heeled income bracket, and all the way around those pleasant eighteen holes, when we met on the greens after battling our separate ways from the tees, they did their best to explain, as tactfully as they could, that it was impossible to keep oneself on one's naval pay – let alone a wife. Between putts I argued that if I had to wait until I could afford a wife I would never get married. It was unlikely that I would reach senior rank after re-entering the Navy through a back door; but even if I did achieve a brass hat, if I waited until then, the best years of our lives would have passed, and we would have to bring up a family in our old age.

'You don't measure love in pounds, shillings and pence,' I declared, waving my putter at them. 'I've found the right girl and I'm damned if I'm going to let her slip through my hands just to marry some landed gent like one of you, who can afford to smother her in diamonds!'

'No,' they said, 'but she will probably want to eat!'

At that time they were quite right. Their Lordships of the Admiralty were fully aware that the pay was inadequate, and assumed that all officers had private means. Today this no longer applies.

The Navy's aviators always flew into harbour before the Fleet arrived, and rejoined their carriers after the Fleet had sailed; we were therefore the first in and the last out, which made us very popular with the ladies, but rather unpopular with the rest of the Fleet. This, plus our 'flying pay', caused our non-flying brethren much anguished toothsucking. In their opinion we were grossly overpaid, and they were inclined to refer to us, scathingly, as the 'glamour boys', which was pure sour grapes on their part. This was not assuaged when we explained that because of our longer time in port we needed the extra money, which only amounted to five shillings a day anyway.

Marriage allowance could not be paid to an officer until he reached the age of twenty-five, and in official eyes anyone who had the temerity to marry before being entitled to marriage allowance was 'living in sin'. Before announcing their engagement, officers were expected to apply to their commanding officers for permission to marry, and this was seldom granted willingly to anyone below the stipulated age. When I broached the subject to my CO I was twenty-four, and he said: 'By all means announce your engagement, but I advise you to wait another year at least before you take your bride to the altar.'

It was sound advice, because in any case we couldn't afford to wed until I was eligible for marriage allowance. I achieved my twenty-fifth birthday six months before the war and so, when *Courageous* sank, we didn't hesitate. It was then or never.

A monthly allotment to my wife, through 'the ledger', made sure that her allowance was paid into our joint account at the bank without fail, even though my pay papers were missing, on the vain supposition that she would be able to draw it out before I could spend it. What was left over had not gone very far during our essential breaks from the war, in Alexandria and Athens.

While thinking these thoughts and doing these sums in my cell at Laghouat, I sat watching the huge spider over my head, scrabbling about in his thick web in the tiny skylight ventilator which was my only area of light. I added up all the 'casual payments' I had received, to buy clothes after being sunk in *Courageous* and bombed in *Illustrious*, plus the cost of replacing everything after our flight from Greece, when I had not been allowed to make a claim, and then added the cost of the beer I had been forced to pay for, and tried to remember other expensive outgoings. Unfortunately, there were too many; in that smelly Arab cell this mental arithmetic revealed that I would have to remain a prisoner for at least a year if I was to be all square when I emerged.

That thought did nothing to lighten the surrounding darkness.

All this retracing of the past did not provide an answer to my financial problems, but at least it enabled me to remember everything very clearly, as though it had happened yesterday, which is why I have been able to write this book. There is nothing which prompts the exercise of memory so implacably as one hundred days in the dark, with nothing to do but think.

The newcomers who arrived at Laghouat almost weekly were mostly RAF aircrew who had come down in the sea and had suffered fearful privations, sometimes for very long periods, before being rescued and then interned; and so we were all startled when two RNVR lieutenants and the crews of two Motor Torpedo Boats were brought into the camp. They were in the best of health, and had with them practically all their possessions – clothing, a library of books, gramophones, records – which from our point of view were all heaven-sent. They brought with them all the music from

Ivor Novello's 'The Dancing Years' and several of Paul Robeson's blues, including 'My Curly-headed Babbie', which tore at our heartstrings in the quiet of the hot tropical nights.

I was able to cadge some clothes from the captain of one MTB, a Lieutenant Strang, from the Clyde, and this made a lot of difference to my outlook. The story of this MTB was most disturbing, and afterwards I spent hours composing a coded letter, reporting the facts to Whitehall. In accordance with the terms of the Geneva Convention, Strang had taken his MTB into Algiers accompanied by another boat, claiming twenty-four hours to do essential repairs. Although he was entitled to stay for that period of time, the Vichy-French paid no attention to such refinements as the Geneva Convention. The RNVRs found themselves under arrest as soon as they had made fast alongside, when their vessels were impounded. As Strang remarked, their reception could not have been more hostile in a German port.

The only benefit we derived from being internees and not prisoners of war was that we could not be prevented from sending as many letters and cables as we could afford, and being a neutral country, not at war, letters took only a few weeks to reach their destination. The code I had been taught in Malta was to prove invaluable in Laghouat. It was very complicated and the letters were difficult to compose, so I was kept happily occupied for days on end. In the main they consisted of instructions to 'my stockbroker' in London to buy and sell mythical shares. In August, when being taught its complexities, I had been asked to provide the name and address of someone who could be trusted to forward my letters to the War Office without question, and without opening them. I had nominated a Mr A. P. Maggs, a close friend, much older than myself, whose family owned a famous bookshop, then in Conduit Street until being bombed, but now in Berkeley Square.

A. P. Maggs was in Scotland that autumn, when he was very startled to be run to earth by a uniformed army officer; but he readily agreed to the arrangement, especially when the officer explained that my letters would be returned to him after they had been decoded, with the relevant parts blacked out by the censor. 'At least I shall hear from him more regularly than usual!' he said, with the cynicism of a close friend.

Another arrival, which I had to report by coded letter – very quickly – was the Arab sheikh whom I had met in Malta. He came striding in, accompanied by two Royal Marine sergeants who were Commandos, and who had rowed him ashore from a submarine. The Arab had shaved off his beard and moustache, and was dressed in a nondescript civilian suit, and called himself 'Second-Lieutenant Dick Jones'. When I remarked that I understood that English was one of the few languages he could not speak very well, he pointed out that he had only adopted that name and title because he had been caught, and his only chance of survival was to become a military prisoner.

After a briefing by the major, he and the two Royal Marine Commandos had gone to a previously arranged rendezvous, where they expected to be met by other agents. Instead, they found gendarmes awaiting them, and they were caught red-handed. It was then that he told me about the Heinkel bursting into flames on its way back after searching for Robertson and me.

It seemed to me that the background of 'the major' – and the absence of the Colonel at our briefing – needed a little research; and that was the theme of my coded letter, which I sent off the next day. However, the trouble with the cloak and dagger world is that one never hears the final story, and to this day I do not know whether the major was just grossly inefficient, or a very clever man working for the other side. I would prefer to think the latter, because it would be most disturbing if our intelligence people were as inefficient as that major appeared to be, and I have been gently pursuing this ever since, so far without result.

I told 'Dick Jones' about the broken padlock in the cell, and tried to persuade him to get himself sentenced to solitary so that he could make use of it, but he agreed with my assessment – that escape would only be possible with outside assistance. Although an Arab, he would not attempt the desert walk.

He made no pretence of being anything other than a devout Moslem, in front of our guards, who were startled when he produced a mat and prayed to Allah on his knees, using all the right phrases and responses. Something about his actions made them aware that he was a sheikh, and they treated him with great respect. He was only with us for two weeks, before he and the two Royal Marine sergeants were taken away, presumably to be shot, since they had been caught with maps and other incriminating evidence.

To keep track of what was happening in the outside world I interviewed all new arrivals the moment they walked into the camp, preferably before they were taken off to the hospital, if they were in need of treatment. At this point their stories were usually true. Later, when they had had time to think, the truth was sometimes obscured, particularly if they felt guilty about any aspect of their survival. When trying to evade capture it was often necessary to steal food, and it was a help to me to know in advance if visitations by the French police, or the Deuxiènne Bureau, were liable to occur.

When only three of a bomber's crew of four arrived, after nearly three weeks afloat in a dinghy, I was allowed to visit them in hospital on their first day. They had been carried from Djelfa in an ambulance, and were in a very weak condition. Their survival had been a miracle, and I asked them what had happened to their pilot. The three men were all from the Commonwealth, and were the aircraft's navigator, wireless operator, and gunner. They admitted that there had been a difference of opinion between them and the pilot. They had stopped at Gibraltar for temporary repairs, and the crew thought that the repairs were inadequate, and tried to prevent the pilot from taking off again. When they came down in the sea, rather naturally they blamed the pilot.

'He died in the dinghy,' said the navigator, uneasily.

'You buried him at sea?' I asked, and there was a long silence, and then a haggard face looked at me from a pillow, through hollow eyes.

'We ate the bastard!' he groaned, closing his eyes as though the picture filled him with pain.

Later, when they had recovered, and were out of hospital, they tried to retract their statement, and said that they were joking.

'Nobody confesses to cannibalism, even in jest,' I said, and there was a long period of silence which was an admission of guilt on their part. Then one of them asked me what I was going to do about it.

'Nothing,' I said. 'I'm by no means the senior officer here, and am only doing this job at the request of the more senior ratings, who wanted some discipline and order injected into the community. If I thought that it was important I would make a report to the senior officer, but I have no intention of doing so – unless you start murdering the other prisoners!' I thought about it, while we all sat in silence, and then said: 'I'm in no position to pass judgement, and I don't see how anyone who hasn't experienced the extremes of starvation could be expected to judge either.

You've got to live with this thing for the rest of your lives, and in my opinion that's punishment enough.'

Hunger does strange things to people. It certainly altered our values. When men are at the knife-edge of starvation, the theft of a piece of bread can be almost as heinous a crime as murder. Hunger can also remove people's will to live. I had an early example of this when a fine Chief Petty Officer, wearing the DSM, called on me after he had been in the camp for a few days. He wanted me to confirm that what he had seen was the permanent state of affairs.

'Tell me if I'm wrong, sir,' he said. 'The daily food consists of one loaf of bread between four, and the loaf isn't any bigger than a saucer. Apart from the blue coffee in the morning there is only one meal – some sort of ghastly soup. Water, for washing, only comes on at five-thirty in the morning for half an hour. There are three drums which are 'the heads' for over a thousand men. If we want to walk out of this place we are shot. Is that correct?'

I said that I was afraid that it was. 'It sounds dreadful, I know, but you'd be surprised how quickly you can get used to it.'

'Not me,' he said, shaking his head. 'It isn't just dreadful, it's downright criminal. These bastards aren't even at war, and we are supposed to be internees! We have to sleep on the floor in Arab quarters that are limited to twenty-five of them, and there are over forty of us. Only three men are allowed to walk across to the heads in the dark. If you start off without knowing how many buggers are already out there you're liable to get your head blown off by a trigger-happy Arab. Why go on living?'

'Because sooner or later we'll be out of this place and fighting the war again, that's why. You'll be a great help to me,' I said. 'I could do with a few Chiefs with DSMs.'

He went off to find somewhere reasonably quiet to lie down and never got up. A day or two later someone turned him over and he was dead.

I had no idea that it is possible to 'opt out' like that, and a man must be in great mental stress, and at a very low ebb, to be able to lie down and die. Perhaps his wife had let him down, or he had private family problems. This applied to a number of the chaps in the camp, and I provided a shoulder for them to lean on, and dished out advice to them, designed to keep them from going round the bend. But we had our work cut out to save those who wanted to live, and if a man gave up, and could not strive, even on his own account, then it was his decision and there was little we could do.

Unfortunately there are often few outward signs of mental sickness.

It was perhaps fortunate that starvation kills all thoughts of sex. Lack of food – and the overcrowded conditions – made such thoughts an impossibility. When a man is starving, sex is the last thing he thinks about. It comes a poor fourth in priority, in basic needs. Thirst comes first; to a man dying of thirst a drink takes priority over all things. Thirst is followed by sleep, which to the exhausted is more important than food. Food is definitely third, and only then, when all three of the basic priorities have been satisfied, does sex creep in at all.

This truism takes time to discover, and newcomers, whose bellies were still full, would sometimes regale us with lurid tales of what they would have been doing to some female, 'that very moment', if they had not been taken prisoner. In the end, the inevitable question would be put to them, by someone who had been a prisoner for some time. Usually just as the raconteur reached what I call 'the crotch of the story' somebody would interrupt and say, 'What were you going to give her to eat?'

Hunger in Laghouat provided me with one of the most exquisite moments of my whole life which I shall always treasure. It happened when Ayeesa was escorting me back to the camp after I had completed a sentence of solitary. He always took me back, and carried my small sack of gear for me, bless him. We passed the Spahi galley, and – trusting me – he nipped inside, and came out with a huge chunk of bread and dripping, which he gave to me with a big grin. Nothing I have ever eaten surpassed that piece of simple food, and nothing has ever tasted so good again. Meals at the Savoy, Christmas turkey, smoked salmon – no matter what – nothing can ever transcend the sharp flavour of that heavenly bread and dripping, that morning. I can taste it to this day.

The three barbed-wire fences which surrounded the three internal sides of the compound, from a long outer wall at the back, were parallel with each other, and eleven feet high. Between them were rolls of hooped wire, piled one on top of the other. Machine-gun and searchlight platforms were mounted at strategic points all around the barricade and along the wall, and there was at least one on the roof of each building.

We discovered that it took eighteen minutes to crawl through that fence. Sergeant Belcher, a black-bearded New Zealand farmer, had found one spot which was out of sight of the searchlight platforms. He was a 'cat who walks by himself', a silent man whose arms reached well below his knees. He had thought it out very carefully, and while he crawled through, on his face, inch by inch, we provided a diversioin by conducting a noisy sing-song on the other side of the compound. Belcher stayed out longer than anyone else and achieved the greatest distance. He managed to stow away under a van all the way to Djelfa; but later, after walking for days, he took off his boots to relieve his swollen feet before going to sleep under a railway bridge, and when he awoke they had been stolen. Without boots he was unable to continue and had to give himself up.

No escape ever took place without reprisals, and after Belcher's triumph, the Slug banned all gatherings outside the buildings other than Appels; and the Arabs were instructed to open fire if more than three people were seen standing together in a group. This meant that without special dispensation we would have to discontinue our church services on Sundays, which I had organized at the request of some of the NCOs. The services were very well attended, being entirely voluntary, and I was delighted to be 'about my father's business' for once. My father had always been disappointed that I had not followed in his footsteps and become a parson, and I looked forward to shooting him a bit of a line about these services. Thinking about it, and wondering what he would have recommended, I asked for an interview with 'M'sieur le Commandant', and in company with Robairre, a French-Canadian prisoner, to act as interpreter, I was granted a short session with the redoubtable Slug of the Foreign Legion.

'Every man has a right to sing a hymn on Sunday morning if he wishes,' I said, 'and it puts heart into the men to raise their voices in unison once a week. Can you perhaps apply the same principle to church services that apply to Appels?'

'*Non*,' said the Slug.

'You have no right to prevent men from worshipping God,' I said. 'I must insist that this order does not apply to our church services.'

'*Non*,' said the Slug. The Foreign Legion rogues had very little to say for themselves, and he was never a very chatty person.

'Then I shall ignore the order on Sunday morning,' I said defiantly.

'*Vu*,' said the Slug.

I asked Robairre to find out what he meant by 'noted', and there followed a short conversation between them in French involving a good deal of shoulder-shrugging and gesticulating on both sides. The Slug's white shapeless face became more like putty with every word, and his eyes were pink slits of venom.

'He says that it may only be necessary to shoot you!' said Robairre, cheerfully.

When I relayed the gist of this conversation to the men, on Sunday morning the entire camp turned out in force and formed a circle around me. As we sang 'Eternal Father Strong to Save' I hoped most sincerely that He would – because the Arabs were shouting excitedly, and pointing their guns at me with their fingers on the trigger. However, the men had formed a strong bodyguard, and they were in the line of fire too, and I doubted whether even the Slug would allow us to become Christian martyrs at his expense. He would have gone down to posterity as the Pontius Pilate of the Second World War!

The day was saved by the Commanding Officer of the Premier Spahis, Commandant Jeunechamp, who walked through the main gate in his immaculate uniform and stood at the back of the circle with his hat off. He then joined in the singing, and the Arabs were unable to open fire.

It was a courageous action on his part, in more ways than one. Although he could plead that he had done it to save his Commanding Officer's face, he was already under suspicion of being a *collaborateur*. He had admitted to me, privately, that he had a son flying with the US Air Force: and that during the First World War he had been a prisoner of the Germans, sharing a camp with the British; and he had extended many little kindnesses to the camp as a whole, which he had asked me to keep to myself. From then onwards he was a marked man with the other Vichy-French officers, who were all distinctly pro-Hitler and Pétain.

We had only been at Laghouat for a few weeks when Monty and I made a remarkable discovery, quite by chance. One morning we were sitting at a table outside his door, in the arched passage where we played poker most evenings, when I noticed a tiny little air-vent at the foot of his exterior wall. When I drew his attention to it, my interest was purely idle.

'I wonder what that is for?' I said. 'I've never noticed it before. Why does your room have a ventilator at ground level?'

Monty studied it for the first time too, and grew very excited.

Grabbing me by the arm he took me into his room, and studied the floor levels, and we saw – also for the first time – that the level of the outside passage was slightly lower than the floor level of the rooms. By scraping very carefully around the sealing of a big flagstone under his bed, and then by inserting levers under it, we managed to lift one side, and found ourselves looking down into an enormous cellar. It was exactly fifteen feet deep, and the sides fifteen feet square. It was an ideal spot to start a tunnel, because it was on the side of the building farthest away from the outside wall, and nobody would expect tunnelling operations to start from the greatest distance away: I am quite certain that the Vichy-French knew nothing about the existence of that cellar, or they would have been on the lookout: and in the following seven months, when digging took place almost without a break, they would have discovered it on many occasions.

Working in watches we logged a total of 1750 hours digging at the 'Face', and when it was finished it was sixty-eight yards long, a metre tall and a metre wide, and every bit of earth had been hauled back in *crachoirs* attached to ropes, and packed down in that cellar. Since the tunnel was fifteen feet below ground we were able to make almost as much noise as we liked, and the entrance to it, wired with stolen equipment, filched from every dormitory and room in the camp in small bits and pieces so that it would not be noticed, looked like the entrance to Piccadilly Circus Underground Station.

The word tunnel was forbidden, at all times. It was known as the poker school, and a game was always in progress outside Monty's door, which faced the main entrance to the compound, so that we could not only see people coming in through the main gate, but for several hundreds of yards, as they approached up the long drive from the garrison. It was simple to replace the flagstone quickly, and fill in the cracks with a mixture of dates and dust, always kept ready to hand. The entrance to the tunnel could never be found unless the seeker knew of its existence, and where to look.

A team of experts were kept busy, full-time, making candles and ventilators and sharpening digging implements. Others were busy forging passes and identity cards and travel permits. Other specialists in magnetism were hard at work making compasses in empty boot-polish tins, and the like. In every community of fighting men, there are always experts to be found for any task.

Ventilation became our main problem. When we had reached

thirty yards the air was fetid, and there was insufficient oxygen. The candles would flicker for a moment or two and then die. So our technicians soldered together any number of Klim milk tins, with their bottoms removed, making a mobile pipe; and under the very eyes of the Arab guards on the roof, while pretending to dig a sanitary trench, the pipe was sunk to a depth of fifteen feet. Eventually, when we managed to get tunnel and pipe to meet, the problem was quite different: there was so much air in the tunnel that the blasted candles blew out!

To prevent any misguided Arab from putting the trench to the purpose for which it was supposedly intended, we filled it with large stones, and spread the buzz that it was a urinary trench only, by making a pretence of peeing into it ourselves. This had to be done with one's back to the sentry on the roof, and facing the wall, which was too far away for the wall sentries to spot the duplicity. Unfortunately, some of the Arabs followed our example and made use of it themselves, but as Dai Davies remarked, we could scarcely complain to the Slug that his soldiers were peeing into our tunnel!

We had to find out what was on the other side of the wall, in case when we dug upwards we found that we were under a building, or in the middle of someone's garden; and a number of us signed our parole to go on an organized walk outside the compound. We had made a firm rule that nobody would ever give his parole, at any time; but by general agreement the rule had to be relaxed for this vital purpose. One or two purists objected, saying that we were giving it improperly, since we were doing so to obtain information in connection with an escape; but the giving of parole means that the donor promises not to escape while on parole, and there is nothing to prevent him from admiring the view!

The Roman Catholic Church in Laghouat was in the direction we needed, and so, one Sunday, a number of us insisted that we had changed our religion overnight, and wished to attend Mass. The church was fascinating, being a baroque combination of Spanish, French, Moroccan and Algerian architecture. We were relieved to note (as we happened to glance in that direction on our way back to the camp) that there was a nice stretch of open ground outside the big wall, very suitable for amateur gardeners.

Although I knew that nobody would survive the walk across the desert unaided, digging a tunnel made sense, because it provided wonderful occupational therapy for everyone, and gave us all a feeling of oneupmanship. In any event, outside help might be forthcoming by the time we finished it. I had managed to get in touch with Malta about an aircraft, using the code, and had been asked for information about possible landing areas near to the camp, and a plan to rescue a maximum of five prisoners was being considered. General Huntziger had managed to land there, and it was simple to find out where.

There was plenty of room outside the oasis for quite big aircraft to land, or even a whole formation of two-seaters, like Beaufighters, if their reception was organized as a proper military operation at our end. If for any reason the Malta team had to withdraw, Johnny Hyde was going to try to arrange a squadron-landing of Beaufighters. We had been in touch, using a schoolboy code which Jo knew too. It was very simple, but good enough to get past the Vichy-French censors.

Johnny had been chosen by the Air Ministry to play the lead in a film called 'Coastal Command', and he had been promised his own choice of command afterwards as an inducement to get him on to the film set and away from his Sunderland. To me he made it clear that he had asked for Beaufighters because he intended to land at Laghouat in the autumn. In my reply I indicated that other arrangements were in hand 'locally', and that he should stick to his boats. That was my last message to him. The next communication was from Jo, telling me that he had been shot down during a Beaufighter raid on the Germans in Norway, and had been buried on the top of a mountain near Tromso. In the same letter she told me of the death of Darby Welland, then flying in the desert.

After this shattering news I went through a bad patch, and found myself becoming short-tempered and intolerant. Every escape attempt at Laghouat was prefaced by childish bickering and squabbling, when individuals tried to prove that their return to the United Kingdon was more important to the war effort than anyone else's. To put an end to this childish behaviour I appointed an Escape Committee, giving them power to decide on who should go and who should stay. They also took charge of all escape equipment and money, and vetted everyone's plans. This should not have been necessary, but human nature in the raw, at close quarters, can be singularly unprepossessing at times.

Then, two things happened, one after the other. The first was ludicrous, but it upset me more than I cared to admit, perhaps because I was so distressed at the news of Johnny's death. I was certainly not in the mood for sheer lunacy. In a Forces programme on the BBC, run by that great man, Freddy Grisewood, wives were given the opportunity of speaking to their husbands serving overseas, and Jo had arranged to speak to me from London. I had been forced to appeal in writing, officially, for special dispensation in order to listen, because our electricity was switched off in the evenings before the programme was due, and our set ran from the mains. As a result the entire camp was listening.

It was wonderful to hear her voice after all that time. She had to be careful to make no mention that I was a prisoner, but said, 'I never expected to be able to speak to you in your oasis!' Freddy Grisewood then asked her to choose a piece of music which we both liked, and she chose the Dwarfs' Marching Song, from Snow White, explaining that it was a film we had seen just before I left, at Littlehampton, shortly after Dunkirk.

We had strolled down a road holding hands and swinging along to the music, and in Laghouat I listened with real delight. The little men marched along with their picks over their shoulders singing 'We dig – dig – dig – dig, dig – dig – dig, We dig the whole night through', when to my utter astonishment an army captain flew at me, with both fists flailing, hitting me in the face. Thinking the poor chap was out of his mind, or very drunk – or both – I resisted the temptation to hit him back, and bent over with my back to him, so that his blows fell harmlessly on my shoulders. He was hysterical, and took some time to calm down. Then he accused me of jeopardizing the tunnel. 'How else could she have chosen that song? You must have told her about it in a letter home.'

That incident was only worrying because it proved that officers were going slightly mad. The second was much more important and worried me enormously. One of the key men in my own escape plans, who was a person we all relied upon for his intelligence and ability to keep calm in emergencies, suddenly went berserk one evening, and tried to strangle one of his best friends. He very nearly succeeded, and it took half a dozen of us to drag him away from his victim. I was relying on this chap to lie out in the desert with me, after we had got out of the compound, in order to flash a torch at intervals as part of the guide-path for the aircraft.

After these two incidents I began to have my doubts about the wisdom of my plans, since everyone was in such a highly-strung state, and I had no wish to risk valuable pilots and aircraft in a rescue attempt which might fail. Then the last straw came. After seven months of digging that tunnel we reached our target, and all that remained was to dig upwards. It so happened that the night we finished was the hottest day in the year in the Sahara. A number of people expressed their intention of going straight away. I appealed to them to seal it up for a few weeks until the weather was less cruel, and until outside assistance had been arranged, but my appeal fell on deaf ears. The majority agreed with me, but we were powerless and unable to stop them. Their response implied a criticism of us for not going to. '*We* are not going to spend another night in this awful place when there is a means of escaping,' they said.

Fortunately, my own project was not dependent upon the tunnel, though it would have been easier to accomplish had it been available; but it did depend on the silent co-operation of the whole camp, and I was relying on some very close teamwork by five specially selected people, some of whom were amongst the twenty-nine who went through the tunnel on that boiling hot night. One of the men I hoped to take with me when we escaped was an elderly officer who was beset with family problems, and who seldom slept. There had been opposition to this because he would have been rather a dead weight to carry, but I was worried about him. Before the mass exodus he came to me in tears, and explained that if the tunnel was going to be used he would have to go too, because it might be his only opportunity. I said that in my opinion he stood a better chance with me, but I could see that his mind was made up, albeit reluctantly, and because the shoes he was wearing were falling to bits I gave him my treasured escape boots, which I had 'acquired' with Ayeesa's help, while in cells. I wished him luck, and that was the last coherent conversation we enjoyed, because during his walk in the desert he was badly affected by sunstroke and never recovered his mental health. I heard later that he spent the last ten years of his life in an asylum.

Because of these signs of mental disorder amongst even the most responsible people, I felt that I could not risk the aircraft and pilots, and cancelled my operational organization. I had been provided with a simple method of cancellation for emergencies. All that I had to do was to send a single-word telegram to my 'stockbroker' in London, saying, 'Sell'.

When I told the escape committee what I had done I was very unpopular with certain groups, who waited their opportunity and pounced on me in the dark one night and gave me a thorough going-over. I had two lovely black eyes and a swollen face which stayed with me for nearly a fortnight, but this made me more convinced than ever that I had done the right thing. In retrospect I have never had the slightest doubt about it.

The mass exodus through that tunnel had its moments of humour. Before he was taken away from us we had gained a lot of valuable information from 'Dick Jones', the Arab sheikh, particularly about the customs and traditions of his own race. We had discussed tunnelling with him, and he told us that when the surface of the earth is disturbed, Arabs have the quaint custom of leaving their visiting cards on the freshly turned soil in the form of their own human manure, so that the soil will prosper. He suggested that if we ever succeeded in digging a tunnel we should do the same, because the Vichy-French would search for signs of tunnelling outside the camp after an escape, and they would not expect us to know about that Arabian custom. They might be fooled by a clear indication that the ground had been disturbed by Arabs, and that might delay their discovery.

On the night in question a number of young officers drew lots for this privilege. Whoever won would be the last man out, and his task would be to fill in the escaping end of the tunnel with displaced earth and do everything he could to disguise the fact that a great many people had recently poured through it, by scuffling over any footprints, and so on. Only then should he leave his Arab-type visiting cards.

There were many volunteers for this task, from people who had no escape plans, but who would enjoy a night of freedom. It would be fun, and worth fifteen days. A tall good-looking sub-lieutenant RN drew the winning number. He had no intention of trying to cross the desert, but he had somehow managed to make an assignation with the barmaid in Laghouat's only hotel, the Hotel Saharienne, and after doing all that was required of him, leaped into bed with a hugely delighted girl. He was arrested the next morning, and after fifteen days in cells came back to camp looking much refreshed.

Appel the next morning was interesting. The Slug was not there. Unfortunately Jeunechamp was in charge, but Lieutenant Martin did the counting. He repeated his count three times, and became more and more pale with each one. In the end we were told to remain fallen-in, while the two Frenchmen searched the camp in case the twenty-nine absentees were hiding somewhere. When they came back, Jeunechamp grinned at me, and said, *'Bien joué!'* which was very sporting of him, since it meant a great deal of future trouble for him. Martin made no such gesture, but stalked out of the camp with his head high. I watched him walking along under the arches, and as soon as he thought he was out of sight he leaned against the wall, his head on his forearm, in despair. He had been on duty during the night and it meant a court martial for him, and perhaps a reduction in rank.

After the sub-lieutenant had filled in the hole our scientific experts laid any number of traps along the tunnel, on the assumption that the French would find it from the outside by searching for the disturbed earth. They were quite correct. The sub-lieutenant's visiting card fooled nobody, and they dug their way down. By the time they emerged in Monty's cabin, they were very cross indeed. Trays of treacle, explosive devices, rat traps, *crachoirs* full of water, overhead booby traps – all manner of obstacles had been left for them to stumble into before they could reach the tunnel's beginning; and then they had to shout for help, so that someone on deck could lift the flagstone.

Twenty-nine men had taken less than a quarter of an hour to file through into the night, but they were back in Laghouat within twenty-four hours, which to my way of thinking was rather a waste of seven months' work.

31
Sahara Psychiatry

The 11th April 1942 happened to be my twenty-eight birthday, and on that day I received a present I would gladly have done without. Long after sunset the entire ship's company of HMS *Havock* came streaming through the main gate. She was a Fleet destroyer with a famous record and only one member of her crew was missing. He had been killed when she ran aground at 26 knots off Cape Bon and tore out her bottom.

With them were two distinguished passengers, Commander R.F. (Dick) Jessel, DSO, lately the captain of HMS *Legion*, and his engineer officer, Tim Sayers. After fighting one of the most noteworthy destroyer battles of all time – when Jessel ignored a signal in true Nelsonian manner and turned towards an enemy battleship instead of away, putting a torpedo into her – the *Legion* had been bombed from under their feet when alongside in Malta. He and Sayers had a broken leg apiece, encased in plaster, and were taking passage home in the *Havock* when she ran aground.

Jessel's other leg had been severely injured in Malta before the war, by no less a person than the Prince of Wales himself. The Prince was at the wheel of a speedboat, and at dusk failed to see Jessel's head in the water until it was too late. The swimmer dived quickly, but one leg was churned up by the boat's propellers. At the request of the Prince he was rushed home to hospital in a cruiser.

From the moment of *Havock*'s arrival Lieutenant Martin's enmity became even more pronounced, because *Havock* was the ship which had bombarded him in Syria. On the night of their arrival he was on duty, and when I pleaded with him for extra food and coffee, and for straw mattresses, and some forks, knives and spoons and plates, all he would say wasy, '*Demain – peutêtre.*' With no additional bedding, or mess traps, the night was a headache;

but we managed somehow, and the men rallied round by making innumerable cups of tea, and scratched out some morsels from their Red Cross stores. We had to break a few hearts in the process. The old-timers in Laghouat had collected an assortment of plates, cups, and cutlery, which were precious to them, being their only earthly possessions which had been 'acquired' the hard way over the years, by stealth and cunning. I had to appeal to them to part with everything they could spare, keeping the bare minimum for themselves, and in this I was ably assisted by my RPOs.

In January, when the men had asked me to inject some semblance of discipline into their lives, I had appointed three senior NCOs as the camp's Regulating Petty Officers, partly to fulfil the function of internal police, but also to protect the men from the Arabs and the Vichy-French by acting as the official go-between. I chose one from each service for their qualities of leadership and their sense of humour, which was more important than anything else in that environment. Sergeant 'Rudy' Knight for the Army; Flight Sergeant Stevens for the RAF – a gigantic man with a patriarch's beard and tremendous energy; and Petty Officer Charles Wines for the Royal Navy. All three were born leaders. With their assistance I had introduced 'Requestmen and Defaulters' and appointed Divisional Officers. To my knowledge it was the first time in military history that officers and men had been locked up together in the same prison camp, and we had no means of enforcing discipline other than by persuasion and example. In a letter to the Admiralty I pointed out that as we intended to introduce our own discipline, and apply internal punishments for 'crimes against the community', we must also be in a position to deal with requests for advancement when they became due.

By stating our intentions we relieved the Admiralty of the need to make a decision. It would have been customary for me to use the word 'propose', but I knew that the civil servants would probably argue about it for ever, and rightly or wrongly we had made the decision for them. I asked Their Lordships to inform the Air Ministry and the War Office accordingly, and it is to their everlasting credit that all three Ministries gave us their backing. They ratified every recommendation that we made, and accepted the *fait accompli* when it was presented to them. The Admiralty even processed our recommendations after we had been released. Before Commander Jessel arrived I had written a report on Petty Officer Wines, stating that he was setting a fine example to officers and men alike – and to the enemy – and I had recommended him for promotion to commissioned rank. Years later, when I ran into him quite by chance, I was gratified to see that he was dressed as a Lieutenant-Commander.

To make sure that all our letters were received, we sent them by three different mails, marked Copy Number One, Two and Three.

The health of the community was growing visibly worse, week by week, and the only news we received was strained through Vichy-French filters, who told us that the British public were starving, and the future looked very black. This was having a terrible effect on all the prisoners, who were shrinking, despite our PT classes and games. The PT had to be very gentle, and I would never let anyone box more than one-minute rounds. An outbreak of polio killed quite a few, the first victim being *Havock*'s medical officer, who was the first doctor we had ever had amongst us. The Vichy-French had confiscated all his medical equipment, but just having a doctor in the camp made a difference. On my way to the heads, one night, I heard him groaning, and found him lying stiffly, with a cigarette burning on the floor. He asked me to put it out, and to turn him on one side. In the morning the French sent for an aircraft to fly him to an iron lung in Algiers, but he died on the aircraft. He was the first of quite a few to take that dreaded air passage in the next few weeks. Only a small percentage survived. Everyone who had come into close contact with the sick men was put into isolation, and on my second morning of this I awoke with a terribly stiff neck and nearly died of fright! It turned out to be spondylosis, the result of the Arabs in Constantine, and all was well; but I went through some rather agonizing moments.

With this background it is understandable that many of the young officers objected to being forced to do a Divisional Officer's job. Some complained at being locked up in the same prison as ratings, and pointed out that it was contrary to the Geneva Convention – as if I didn't know! 'How could they be expected to behave like officers when they were in the same rags and tatters, and had nothing to offer, and were in their bare feet too, and sharing the same bugs and lice and fleas, and squatting over the same disgusting oil drums?'

With some, I did my best to be patient, but with others I agreed: 'If you need all the trimmings, like a uniform, and a Master-at-Arms, to prove that you are an officer, perhaps you aren't; and if you like, I will recommend that you are reduced to the ranks? Then you'll have nothing to complain about.' But that brutal reply was only needed occasionally. When I suggested that for once they had the opportunity of really doing something for their men, if only by putting heart into them, they nearly always responded. It came up so often that I had a staff answer, all ready to trot out. 'I doubt whether you will ever get another opportunity like this to prove to your own satisfaction that you don't need a uniform to be recognized as an officer.'

As they lived a life of involuntary compulsion through no fault of their own I disliked telling an officer or a man to do anything which was against his wishes. The parade 'Requestmen and Defaulters' was our only mandatory event, but even that simple occasion was often most peculiar. Quite often Dick Jessel would look round for the Divisional Officer, to hear what he had to say about the candidate on the other side of the table, and the man himself would say, 'Sorry, sir – my Divisional Officer is doing fifteen days' cells.'

Because I had been given the task by the men themselves, and had taken it on reluctantly, there was seldom an occasion when my authority as 'Adjutant' was challenged, but when it was I was always available in the boxing ring in the mornings. Never before had my interest in boxing proved such a boon. I often breathed a little prayer of thanks that there wasn't a real boxer amongst the others who could have seen me off without trouble. Every morning I climbed into the ring and anyone could 'take a poke at the bloody Adjutant' if he wished, and a lot of them did; but it is surprising what a simple straight left can achieve to stop a would-be aggressor without really hurting him. One morning I heard a delicious conversation about this: a newcomer was complaining about the conditions to Private Ballard, one of the pioneer prisoners who had struggled across the Mediterranean from Dunkirk. He was one of my favourite people, and I persuaded him to give a magnificent lecture one evening about his civilian occupation. It was most instructive because at his home in Kent he was a professional poacher. To the newcomer he said: 'You can always take a poke at the bloody Adjutant if you don't like the way he runs things, but I don't advise it. The bugger'll probably knock your bleedin' block off!'

A few days after *Havock*'s ship's company arrived we had a full-scale mutiny, and I thanked God for Dick Jessel and his wisdom. It was my first and last experience of such an eventuality, luckily, but it taught me a sharp lesson in many ways. It was caused by a misunderstanding brought about by the violent change in environment which had not been fully appreciated by the *Havock's* captain, a lieutenant. His men were by no means in the majority, and by losing his ship and bringing his men into a prison camp he had surrendered his control over them without realizing it. Naturally, they came under the central command of the senior officer, now Dick Jessel, who alone had the right to punish, apart from me, and I nearly always consulted him, or remanded a man for his report, if punishment was necessary. The captain of *Havock* decided that my PT session in the early mornings – designed to get the men up for the short time the water was available for washing afterwards – was to be obligatory where his men were concerned. When they grumbled at being made to turn out, the old-timers said, 'You don't have to go if you don't want to – it's entirely voluntary,' and so they all climbed back into their sacks. Their captain was understandably cross about this, since he had given an order, and as a 'mild form of punishment' stopped their coffee the following morning. The Arab porters had no means of differentiating between one group of men and another and when they were told that no coffee was to be served to a section of the community they decided to bring none at all. This infuriated the old-timers, and none of the prisoners turned out for Appel.

When I heard what had happened I explained to the captain of *Havock* that because we were all starving we never interfered with the men's food in any circumstances, and stopping the men's coffee was far from being a mild punishment. He was a very nice chap and realized his error at once and apologized, but the damage had been done, and the Slug stalked into Jessel's cabin immediately, demanding disciplinary measures at the top of his voice. Jessel sent him on his way very summarily and then sent for me. I was given my instructions and I learned how to deal with a muntiy in one easy lesson, which I have never forgotten.

At Appels, the men were fallen-in by Divisions, three deep, in a double-L formation, like a capital E without the central column.

'Tell the men that I am sorry that their coffee was stopped and explain that it was a mistake and it won't happen again,' he said. 'At the same time tell them that I would like to address them after tomorrow's Appel, and say that I shall be obliged if they will kindly turn out. When the French have finished their count and you and the Slug have exchanged salutes, I want you to get them into one long line, still three deep. Wheel the wing columns outwards, right and left, until they are abreast the central column. Then turn them about so that they are all facing the same way in one long column of three ranks. Got it? Right. Then march the whole column of three lines towards you and halt them when they are about five paces away from the French. Then turn them about so that they have their backs to you . . .'

'What for, sir?' I asked, fascinated by this dynamic man.

He smiled, and being a Jew his smile conveyed a wealth of gentle understanding. 'When you finally turn them about I shall be there, facing them. When you have to deal with a mutiny it's always the rear ranks you should talk to. The wrong 'uns always gravitate to the back.'

I have only met a few seafaring Jews and they have all been wonderful people and exceptional leaders, but Dick Jessel was quite the most outstanding of them all. In the rush of disembarking from a sinking ship he had lost his uniform cap with gold leaf around its peak, but my experts had made him another – out of a margarine tin. Their workmanship was exquisite and from a distance the gold leaf might have been sewn by seamstresses at the Royal College of Needlework.

When I turned the men about, after frightening the French by marching the men towards them in a belligerent manner, Jessel was standing still in the fierce sunshine, in white shorts and a white shirt with shoulder-straps. These, and his brass hat, were glinting in the sun. His black beard was jutting out aggressively, and altogether he was an arresting spectacle, which came as a shock to the men when made to face the wrong way. With one leg in plaster of Paris, and the other looking more like an elephant's trunk than a leg, he looked what he was – a tough warrior – out for their blood. The men stood absolutely still in stunned silence. The timing was perfect.

He studied them quietly for a pregnant moment. Then he said: 'We are on display here, all the time, like animals at the zoo, with a lot of bloody Frogs and Arabs looking at us through the bars of our cage, hoping that we will crack up. If we can't behave like disciplined men, so that our spectators recognize that we are British, and proud of it, then we should be ashamed of ourselves.' He then called to me over their heads. 'You will now oblige me by taking them in PT for the next twenty minutes.'

He stalked away on two stiff legs and I signed to the men to form their usual circle around me and wondered how they would react. There were close on five or six hundred of them and a few minutes before they had been sullen and angry. Now they were grinning, and they did their PT as though they were enjoying it.

Sailors, soldiers and airmen are all the same under the skin: they like a man who can put the fear of God into them, and when they know that they have a real Chieftain-Amongst-Men at their head, they will put up with anything – even twenty minutes of PT from 'the bloody Adjutant!'

We managed to keep ourselves informed of world affairs and the progress of the war by listening to the only radio we were allowed; and in case something happened which the enemy might try to conceal from us we kept a duty roster of officers who took it in turn to listen to every overseas news bulletin by the BBC. This helped to counteract the biased news we were fed by the Vichy-French.

Also, we found out the true picture from newcomers, and it was surprising how often new prisoners would arrive who had taken part in recent battles which had been headline news, some even from as far away as the Pacific war. When this happened I always did my best to persuade the individual to give a general lecture on the theme, 'I was there, and this is what really happened.'

Our newcomers sometimes arrived unostentatiously and melted into the background, and after a while it was difficult to remember a time when they had not been there. One such was Lieutenant-Commander Pinson Wilmot Bennitt, DSC, RN (Retired), who had been taking passage in a merchant ship which had been sunk off the Algerian coast. He told us that he was the most senior lieutenant-commander in the official list of retired officers, and for the last seventeen years of his retirement he had been the First Lieutenant of the Duke of Westminster's private yacht. He was an amusing old boy and whenever the Vichy-French did anything beastly he puzzled them by complaining with statements like 'His Grace wouldn't care for that one little bit!' or 'That wouldn't do for the Duke!'

Being in his early sixties he was the only one of his generation in the camp, and was rather a lonely figure, because his conversation revolved around an era which had ended before most of us had been born; but he was very useful at settling arguments. He had a remarkable, photographic memory, and was a walking encyclopedia of useless information. When asked some ridiculous question, like who won the boat race in the year so-and-so, or which team won the Cup . . . one eye would roll upwards and become much bigger than the other while he searched for the answer. He was never wrong.

Because he was a lonely and rather pathetic figure we were all pleased, for his sake, when he was allowed to keep a scruffy mongrel bitch he had befriended. Lieutenant Martin argued with Jeunechamp about this, but we promised that nobody else would ask to be allowed to keep a pet. For some months the pair were inseparable, and when the bitch became pregnant I was sure Bennitt was sacrificing his own meagre rations to feed the animal. When the litter arrived he was as happy as a lark – until Martin stalked into the camp and shot the mother and had the puppies destroyed. It was a senseless action which shocked the whole community.

I found the old man sitting in the shadows, quietly weeping.

'I wish he had shot me instead,' he said, and I knew how he felt.

Lieutenant Martin's vindictiveness had always been lurking in the background, but after the arrival of the *Havock*'s ship's company he displayed it openly. The arrival of Red Cross parcels was a joyful occasion, but Martin made the Arabs stack them in the sun, on their side of the barricade, sometimes for days, and when they were delivered they had to be opened in front of guards who had orders to pierce all canned food with their bayonets – 'in case they are kept for escape attempts'. The only way to stop them doing this to something which would perish at once, was to cry '*C'est cochon!*' On religious grounds they would not pierce anything which was remotely connected with the pig.

When he took to stacking the mailbags on the other side of the fence I demanded an interview with the Slug, or Jeunechamp, but Martin had introduced a new assistant named Rossignol, a young officer-cadet who spoke English rather well, and all he would say in reply was '*Vu*'. Since the hymn-singing incident, Jeunechamp was kept away from us almost entirely, and under Martin, relations were becoming strained. The last straw was the cancellation of our weekly showers. We had been marched to the Arabs' wash-house once a week, but Martin said: 'There are now too many British and you use too much water. Besides, you all have jaundice and are in quarantine.'

In fact, the showers were a mixed blessing. It was not very pleasant to stand in the nude with an Arab's bayonet pointing at one's anatomy, and they had a habit of waiting until a group of men were covered with soap and then turning off the water shouting '*Finis*'. To draw our discontent to the notice of the Slug we organized a riot, and made both regiments stay on duty for a whole night to control it. After that we were able to demand more humane treatment. The riot resulted in the usual 'sanctions' of course, but we had prepared for this beforehand.

Whenever the Vichy-French were angry with us, they applied' these 'sanctions'. Naturally we knew in advance when this was going to happen, which gave us the advantage. The Vichy-French officers and their armed Arabs would stalk into the camp, and remove all *papier-hygiènique* and confiscate our radio. The removal of toilet paper did present a problem because any sort of paper was hard to come by, but we hid away as much as we could beforehand, and substituted the dummy radio for the one which worked. Our experts had made a duplicate, and the two sets were identical. Although they confiscated it on many occasions they never discovered that it was a non-functional dummy.

Towards the end of July our affairs took a definite turn for the better. Months before, I had written in code asking for at least five hundred pairs of strong Army boots to be sent as soon as possible as a 'morale-booster'. In early August we were able to march on parade for Appel, and when the men came swinging across the hard sand with crisp steps, I halted them very close to the Vichy-French, who were cowering backwards. The men came to the halt with a bang like the explosion of a cannon. Any spectator might have been fooled into thinking them a fit body of men. Knowing how frail they were I found the spectacle rather moving. But it was surprising what a boost to morale those boots were.

On 11 August, when a vital convoy was battling its way from Gibraltar to Malta, the cruiser *Manchester* was hit by two torpedoes, and a few days later, half the ship's company arrived in Laghouat. The other half had been ferried by destroyer to Gibraltar. Overnight, our total figure shot up to over a thousand, and from then onwards there were over a hundred Allied troops in each dormitory designed for twenty-five Arabs. The conditions in the camp were appalling, and were so unsanitary that they were dangerous.

The *Manchester*'s ship's company were not very happy to be in prison. In that convoy a tanker named *Ohio* was carrying the oil without which Malta would have been forced to surrender, and she was attacked continuously, all the way. For the last few miles she was towed by two destroyers, at a speed of one knot, and when she reached Grand Harbour she was still on fire and most of her officers and crew were dead. But the oil got through. It is an epic story, of unusual interest because the *Ohio* was an American

Liberty ship and some of the officers and crew were American. The Captain was an Englishman and some of the problems which faced him must have been incredible. His name was D. W. Mason, and for his efforts he was awarded the George Cross.

The entire population of Malta turned out to watch her arrival. Until the ship was safely inside the harbour the Maltese stood in taut silence, but as the destroyers towed her through the harbour entrance the huge crowd went mad with joy. Their cheers were muted with tears – but they were tears of happiness that their island had been saved.

Commander Clifford Gill was the navigating officer of *Manchester* and when I discovered that he had also been the pilot of HMS *Repulse* when she and the battleship *Prince of Wales* were sunk by the Japanese off Singapore in December, I persuaded him to give a general talk to the camp. We had listened to the Vichy-French version of this when it happened, but the BBC had said very little about it, and it was fascinating to hear the whole story from somebody who had been there.

In the unlikely surroundings of an oasis in the Sahara he transplanted us to the Pacific. The graphic description of the way that his captain guided the ship's company along the gaping deck by talking to them through a megaphone is something I shall never forget. The men had to be moved forward, step by step, and Captain Tennant sat on the bridge looking aft, talking to them quietly. 'One pace forward – now, one pace inboard – now forward again.' And as the ship began to roll over, he said, 'And now step into the sea and good luck to you all.'

Clifford Gill told us that he was so spellbound by this display of magical command that he had forgotten that he and the Captain had to abandon ship too – until Tennant said, 'Come on Pilot! It's time we left,' and they found themselves in the sea as the ship rolled over on top of them.

August was a month full of incident at Laghouat. On the 19th the duty officer, keeping a listening watch on the radio, heard the news of the Dieppe landing. He rushed around the camp bellowing the news that the Allies had landed in France, and we were all overjoyed. The next day we heard how the Canadians had fought against overwhelming odds, and we settled down to an uncertain future, feeling even more depressed than ever. The next time that the same thing happened, everyone was very suspicious. It was 7 November 1942, and early one morning a Sub-Lieutenant Donald

Grant, whose home was in Birmingham, ran from building to building, shouting that we were free. When we managed to calm him down he told us that the Allies had captured Algiers, and that he had heard an American voice broadcasting from Blida, near Algiers, asking everyone to keep calm, that Eisenhower had landed in North Africa, and Algiers had surrendered.

This time everyone turned out, to cheer and to dance and to shout, and nothing could stop them. Our imprisonment was nearly over and this time it was true.

The next few hours were amongst the most remarkable I shall ever experience. In their beds in the Laghouat Garrison, the Vichy-French heard the clamour and were very puzzled. All telephone lines from Algiers had been cut and they had no knowledge that the landing had taken place. Since it was during a period when our radio was in their keeping they could not understand what we were celebrating, and an angry Slug put on his red cloak and peaked hat, and stalked into the camp with the officer-cadet interpreter, demanding an explanation. Most of the inmates were outside their quarters packing their few possessions ready to leave!

I fell-in beside Rossignol, and accompanied them to the Captain's room. The senior officer was now the captain of *Manchester*, but I was still the Adjutant, and attended all meetings. When told the news, the Slug began to ask how we had heard, and then bit back the question. *Manchester*'s captain had said that we had heard the announcement on the radio and there was no point in pursuing that aspect, at this stage. With the curt remark that he would return shortly, the Slug stalked out again, but was back a few minutes later with paper and pen. Through his interpreter he demanded a signed statement from the Senior Officer that it was not a leg-pull. Armed with this, he swept out again to consult with his officers.

It was some hours before there were any further broadcasts, by which time the Armistice of Algiers had been signed. Throughout that period the Vichy-French in Laghouat had no communication with the outside world, and had to rely on our word. Nevertheless, their next proposal was almost unbelievable. About a dozen people were crowded into that small room, most of them British, and we stared at each other in sheer disbelief as Rossignol explained the Slug's demands. I feel sure that never before had such an outrageous proposition been put to their prisoners by the armed forces of any race of people in the history of mankind. Through the young officer-cadet, the Foreign Legion Colonel made himself clear: he explained that all the Arab troops in the garrison hated their French officers.

'I am forced, because of the honour of France, to defend this garrison if it is attacked,' he said, and the words *'l'honneur de France'* slipped from his throat as glibly and easily as a Colchester oyster would slip down mine. 'But while we defend, it is probable that our Arab troops will shoot us. From being an anti-French hate, it will become an anti-white hate, and they will shoot you too.'

When asked what he wanted us to do about this, he said that he would arm us, if we would agree to protect the French officers from the rear, and stop the Arabs from shooting them, and thus ourselves.

This took some time to assimilate and after asking him to clarify the proposal, the *Manchester*'s captain spoke slowly to Rossignol.

'Please ask the Commandant if I have understood him correctly, by saying either yes or no to the following questions: one – is he offering to provide us with arms and ammunition in order that we should stop his men from killing their officers?'

The answer to this was 'yes'.

'Two – does he seriously expect us to assist him in repelling an attack by our own forces?'

The answer to this was also 'yes', but with the added rider that the alternative was the certain death of all white men in the oasis before the Allies could enter the garrison.

'If that is so,' said the captain, 'then why does he not surrender instead of defending a lost cause?'

The answer to that was 'the honour of France'.

At this point *Manchester*'s captain asked the French to withdraw while he discussed it with his officers. As soon as they had gone, we all looked at each other and tried not to laugh, because the two Frenchmen were standing just outside the door.

'I find this very difficult to believe!' said the senior officer. I wished that Commander Jessel had been there, but he was in the hospital nursing his broken leg.

'Sir,' I said. 'I think I can follow the corkscrew thinking behind this. He knows that the minute he gives us arms we will say to him "Right – hands up, you've had it!" I'm sure that that is what he wants us to do. Then he can say that he was forced to surrender, *"force majeure"*. He knows that, being mad Englishmen, we will stop his Arabs shooting him, and if he has surrendered to us he will not have to defend the garrison – *"l'honneur de France"* or not. His honour will be saved as well as his greasy neck. It's a heaven-sent answer to a lot of problems,' I said, 'but if we give some of these chaps a rifle and a few rounds of ammunition, it might be a case of who shoots the bastard first – the Arabs or the British!'

'But if we accept arms from him, and then arrest him, he will say that we have dishonoured a promise,' protested the captain.

'He wouldn't be around for very long if he did,' I said. 'You weren't here when he doubled the reward to the Arabs if we were brought back dead. One peep out of the Slug and our chaps would string him up to the nearest palm tree.'

'Precisely,' said the senior officer and, calling to the Frenchmen to enter, he declined the offer.

Perhaps it was just as well. There might have been a proper old holocaust if my chaps had been given arms. Ill-feeling was running particularly high at the time. Without consulting anyone, a young stoker from the *Manchester* had tried to bribe an Arab guard with his gold watch to let him crawl through the barricade; the Arab had accepted the watch, but as soon as the stoker had stretched himself out under the hooped wire he had been shot dead. There had been a riot over this, which was why we were supposed to have no radio, but in the end the Slug had been forced to take action and the Arab had been searched. When the watch was found in his possession he was put under arrest, but the tension, inside and out, was inflammable, and the Slug might have been the first victim of his own bizarre thinking.

Although we had begun to feel that we were forgotten men, our immediate release was Item Two on the agenda of the Armistice of Algeria, and in a matter of thirty-six hours the old-timers were climbing on board those lorries on their way back to Djelfa. During the intervening period my wicked RPOs had a lot of fun at Rossignol's expense. We were still guarded – more closely than ever – because the French were taking no chances on reprisals – and whenever the young officer-cadet had to come into the camp he was followed by Flight Sergeant Stevens, and Petty Officer Wines, and Sergeant 'Rudy' Knight, and the rest, in sinister, crouching attitudes, drawing their fingers across their throats in a threatening manner. The boy surrounded himself with an armed guard and was in tears most of the time. In fact, they were only pulling his leg, but they looked terribly sinister, and by the time we left, the young man was a nervous wreck.

32
The Voyage Home

When the lorries were drawn up for the first consignment, the French were taking no chances, and we were complimented by being provided with an armed guard for every two prisoners. This was good thinking by the Vichy-French because they knew that some of the prisoners who had been locked up for two years or more would be keen to settle old scores. To the cheers of those who were left behind to follow later, we were marched down the drive. I saw Jeunechamp standing in the background, watching us go, and walked across to him and shook his hand. I thanked him for doing his best for us in very difficult circumstances, and wished him luck, but I could see that he was as nervous as a choirboy about to sing his first solo, and I asked him what was wrong.

'For you, the war is only just beginning,' he said, 'but for me it is over.' From that remark, and his pale face, I knew that he was facing a trial from the arch-villain of all, Admiral Darlan, whose arrival in Algeria the day before had received much publicity. Darlan was breathing fire, and threats of capital punishment, to all Vichy-Frenchmen who capitulated to the Allies.

When the lorries moved off the motion made me feel slightly dizzy; and I looked at Cooper and Davies in amazement, and saw that they were experiencing the same sensation. We had not been in a moving vehicle for nearly a year and it took us a mile or two to get used to it. There were many more shocks to come.

The next morning we were made to leave the train at a station on the outskirts of Algiers, and were marched through the back streets to the docks. We were being taken on board a troopship, HMS *Keren*, and as soon as we had embarked, the ship's Master had orders to hoist the brow and anchor outside Algiers, in the roads. None of us were to be allowed ashore. I suspect that hints had been dropped that we were a bunch of desperadoes, and we certainly looked the part. In the dockyard I saw a very smartly dressed naval officer striding along in our direction, whose face was vaguely familiar, and as we drew closer I saw that it was none other than Alfie Sutton, the Senior Observer of 815 Squadron, whom I had last seen in Crete. I shouted 'Alfie!' at the top of my voice, and a puzzled Lieutenant-Commander A. W. F. Sutton DSC (and two bars), stopped in his tracks and said 'Good God!' rather primly. Apart from the shock of seeing me, I suspect that he was staggered at our motley appearance. We had been awake all night in the train, without an opportunity to wash properly, so we must have looked terrible.

The Arab guards began to mutter when I stopped, because the whole party had to stop too; but I had had enough of Arabs, and used a colloquial phrase of 'Laghouatese' which meant a variety of things, amongst them 'pipe down' and 'get lost'. I explained our immediate future to Sutton, who said, 'What utter nonsense! As soon as you have anchored I will send a boat for you. You must come and have lunch with me on board the *Bulolo*.' His ship was the C-in-C's staff vessel, which had led the attack on Algiers.

My first meal after so long was an unforgettable experience. In my decrepit khaki rags I felt abashed, but Sutton introduced me to everyone in the wardroom as though I were an honoured guest. The table linen was so white, and the silver and glass sparkled, and the bread was white too, and there was water to drink, and real food. After a glass of gin I made the painful discovery – which all the long-term prisoners experienced that day – that my stomach had shrunk, and I couldn't eat at all. Two mouthfuls, and I felt sick. But I was relieved to find that my insides were more than willing to receive the occasional drop of alcohol.

Sutton was very disappointed with me. At lunch he offered me the command of a small squadron of aircraft. He was the staff officer Operations to Flag Officer Aircraft Carriers, who was flying his flag on board HMS *Victorious*. I was astonished to learn that the Admiral was Lumley Lyster, who had been relieved as Fifth Sea Lord by Denis Boyd.

'The squadron has half a dozen Swordfish, three Hurricanes, and a couple of Walrus amphibians. It's an all-purpose outfit. You can get some of your own back, and beat up some of your Vichy-French friends!'

'Be reasonable, Alfie,' I said. 'I haven't seen my wife for two and a quarter years; I haven't flown an aircraft for a year and a half, and was nearly sick when travelling in a confounded lorry, yesterday, out in the Sahara. I weigh less than eight stone, am covered in boils, and can't eat. Besides, I have had no leave since September 1939! I'm on my way home, and nothing is going to stop me!'

I was astonished to find that he was making me a serious offer, and pointed out that observers always assume that their 'front-man' has a very simple task in comparison with their own. Few of them ever understood the basic facts of life about flying. When out of practice it would be madness to climb into the cockpit of any aircraft without some refresher flying first, including dual instruction. He was disappointed when we parted, but assured me that he understood, which I think he did.

The *Keren* was an old, ex-British India steamship, now painted battleship grey, and flying the White Ensign. She had landed some American troops for their first active service attack, and because Americans were never allowed alcohol on board ship, there was no bar. The prospect of taking passage home in an old steamer capable of ten knots at the most, which was a 'dry' ship, filled me with horror. Sutton had told me that the approaches to the Mediterranean were stiff with German U-boats, hunting in packs. We would be sailing from Gibraltar with a naval escort, but on 'evasive' routing – zig-zagging about the Atlantic to avoid giving our destination away – in a 'seven-knot convoy' so it would be weeks before we arrived in the UK. He suggested that on arrival in Gibraltar I report to Admiral Lyster, on board *Victorious*, in case any of the HM ships were going home.

In the evening, before the *Keren* was due to sail, I slipped up on to the boat deck to look across the water at the lights of Algiers. Imprisonment had been an interesting experience, and I had learned more about human nature, and the vagaries of life, than most people can learn in a lifetime. It had all been concentrated in a small arena, where everything that could possibly happen to a community without women had happened with a vengeance. Greed, lust, hate, vanity, murder – yet all those men had come through it, and most of them would benefit from the experience. I realized that I had grown up in that camp, and ever afterwards would have to guard against a tendency to try to measure people with an unfair yardstick: 'How would he behave in Laghouat?' All the evils had been couterbalanced – and superseded – by the shining examples of man's humanity to man, and his never-failing sense of humour, without which none of them would have survived. But I was glad that it was over, and that I would no longer be required to play at being God.

At a tap on my shoulder I turned, and saw one of my favourite people standing in the dark. He was one of the originals, who had experienced it all from the very beginning, long before my arrival. He was holding out a letter.

'Will you post this for me when you get to England, sir?' he asked. 'It's to my wife.'

'You'll be there before the letter. But if you can't go straight home, why not post it yourself?'

He shook his head. 'I'm not coming with you. I'm going back to Aumale. I made a vow.'

'What are you talking about?'

'I swore that I would cut that bastard's throat before I left the country, if it's the last thing I do.'

'It may well be, if you are serious,' I said. He was a fine chap, and I knew that he wasn't joking. Somehow I had to try to persuade him to change his mind. I tried every approach, but his mind was made up, and he kept saying 'I made a vow!'

'Suppose you succeed,' I said. 'You'll be arrested and charged with murder. It's my guess that the Allies will be trying to make friends with the Vichy-French now, otherwise they're going to have one hell of a bloody battle on their hands before they can get through to Monty and the Eighth Army in the Libyan desert. So, if you do slaughter that sadistic bastard, you'll be very unpopular with everyone, including your own chaps at home. But if you stay in the ship with me and come home, we can all make protests about some of these Vichy-French scum, and see that justice is done.'

'I made a vow,' he said, and that was the end of the matter for him. There was no point in continuing the discussion. 'Post the letter for me, won't you?' He thrust it into my hand and, before I had realized what he intended to do, he had climbed over the rail and dived into the sea. That in itself was no mean feat, because the boat deck was about fifty feet above sea level. I craned over the side and could just make out the splashes as he swam towards the shore.

A group of ex-prisoners strolled up to me. They had been admiring the view too.

'What was that splash?' one of them asked.

'Perhaps it was someone who wants to go back to Laghouat or

Aumale, instead of going home,' I suggested, which raised a very big laugh.

My friend succeeded in fulfilling his vow, but the storm over his action was drowned by the tremendous storm which resulted from the assassination of Admiral Darlan later that month, and he was flown home quickly. I have a shrewd idea that he got home before we did, but I posted his letter in Glasgow. Later, because he had given my name as a reference, I received a letter from the main headquarters of his fine service, asking me for my opinion of him as a man. He had informed them that I was the 'Adjutant', and could therefore speak with authority. I replied that he had done what we all wanted to do, but we had lacked his determination and courage. I offered to speak for him if he was to be court martialled, when I would have pleasure in suggesting to the court that he deserved a medal, not punishment. I was able to refer them to a letter I had written about him, many months previously, in which I had said that he had shown fine qualities of an outstanding character, and that I recommended him for promotion as soon as he was eligible.

I don't think that he got a medal, but I did hear that he had been promoted – eventually.

The Officer of the Watch in the aircraft carrier *Victorious*, in Gibraltar, had every right to view me with suspicion when I walked up the officers' brow in sandals and faded khaki trousers. I had bought an old reefer and uniform cap in Laghouat, from one of the RNVR officers from the MTBs, and although I had spent many hours straightening out the wavy RNVR rings on the sleeves, the result looked very peculiar and unorthodox. I knew that I looked like a cross between some foreign naval officer and a bus conductor, and did my best to explain that I had just been released from a prison camp, and that I would like to report to Admiral Lyster. At this request the OOW looked even more doubtful. I realized that my aim was too high, and lowered my sights accordingly.

'If you are not prepared to pass my name to the Admiral, perhaps you would be kind enough to ask your Commander Flying if he would spare me a moment? I'm afraid I don't know who he is.'

'His name is Commander Figuls Price,' I was told.

'I have heard of him, but we have never met. But I am sure he will know that I am not phoney!'

When the Commander Flying appeared after a few moments he

was charm itself. Everyone over the age of twenty-five knew all about everyone else in the Fleet Air Arm, and he insisted on taking me straight down to the cuddy to the Admiral, notwithstanding my scruffy appearance.

Admiral Lyster greeted me like a prodigal son. The *Victorious* was sailing that night, to escort a big convoy through the U-boats to the Clyde, so I had struck lucky. The ship was meeting up with the convoy outside the Straits of Gibraltar after dark. When he offered to take me home, I asked whether he would be willing to offer a passage to Robin Kilroy's victims from the *Hudson*, and the Admiral was delighted. 'Of course – it's the least we can do – and we'll give them a wonderful passage home.' He turned to the Commander Flying. 'I would like a reception committee waiting, to look after them, and please make a broadcast to the ship's company about their presence on board, and the back history.' Then he turned to me again and told me to take his barge back to the *Keren*. 'Collect your gear and make sure you bring those two RAF pilots with you.'

Cooper was too frail and ill to face a boisterous naval passage, and elected to stay in his bunk in the *Keren*. He was obviously rather relieved that he was going to have the small cabin all to himself for the rest of the passage home. Dai Davies came back with me, and I am sure that by the time he reached the United Kingdom the officers and men in *Victorious* had done their best to persuade him to forgive the Fleet Air Arm for shooting him down in 1940.

The following morning, at sea, the Admiral piped for me to report to his bridge, where he invited me to join him and his staff for Bovril and sherry; and when the hot drinks were brought by the same Marine Wright who had been the Admiral's personal attendant in *Illustrious*, we shook hands warmly, and I congratulated him on surviving for so long in what must have been a very arduous task.

'Come on, stop nattering,' said the Admiral. 'Let's have those drinks.' But when the Marine had gone, he said, 'I'm glad you remembered Wright – it will cheer him up. I think he knows I'm going to sack him when we get in.'

Captain Charles Coke, his Chief of Staff, was aghast.

'Sack Wright, sir? I thought that you were devoted to each other?'

The Admiral grunted. 'He's too familiar,' he said gruffly, but from his manner I suspected that he was not really being serious. 'D'you remember that we were being dive-bombed the other day, off Algiers? The pom-pom crews were missing everything, and firing in every direction except the right one. I nipped out on the wing of the bridge and yelled at them to pull their fingers out, and blow-me-down if that bloody fellow Wright didn't come out after me, and grab the tail of my jacket. He started trying to pull me back inside, and shouted, "Come inside, you silly old fool!" '

The Admiral pretended to glare at us as we shouted with laughter.

My mind leaped back to Laghouat, and the Vichy-French. Under their régime the hapless Wright would have been clapped in cells before he had had time to think, and the Vichy-French officers would have found the situation anything but funny. But, of course, none of their officers could have engendered such loyalty that a man would be capable of expressing himself so openly and bluntly out of affection for his chief. It couldn't happen to any of the Axis powers, and in a flash of inspiration I saw that it was this sense of loyalty and humour and the friendly relationship between officer and man which was going to defeat the enemy and bring victory to the Allies in the end. It was unbeatable.

During our passage through the Bay of Biscay a German U-boat was brought to the surface by one of the escorting destroyers, and the captain and crew were transferred to *Victorious* where there was more room for them. The German skipper was very arrogant to start with, and insisted that all the ships in the convoy would be sunk before we reached our destination. Each morning, when he was brought up on to the quarter-deck for air and given the opportunity to count all the ships, we enjoyed watching his expression become increasingly bewildered. Every morning there were the same number of ships, sailing along in apparent serenity. They all arrived safely, despite the warning of an attack by a German Condor as we approached the southern tip of Ireland. The opportunity of shooting down one of those very long-range bombers, which carried such a gigantic bomb load, was too tempting for our fierce Admiral, who turned the convoy seaward again in the hope of enticing the bomber into range of the aircraft carrier's fighters, but I was relieved that he avoided the bait. All I wanted to do was to get home, as quickly as possible, with the least excitement and danger. I was looking forward to a long leave, away from ships and aircraft and guns.

Just before we anchored off Greenock, at the Tail o' the Bank, in the Clyde, the Admiral sent for me again.

'I've had a message from the Fifth Sea Lord – Admiral Sir Denis Boyd,' he said. 'When the *Keren* arrives here in a day or two, we have got to send all the ex-prisoners to Portsmouth for a thorough medical examination, and for an address by the Prime Minister himself. They are not to be allowed to circulate amongst the public until this has happened, in their own interests, and the interests of the war in North Africa. I have reported that you are not carrying any infectious disease – according to our PMO who has examined you on board – but as you and Davies have escaped the net, you do not have to go to Portsmouth. I am arranging for Flight-Lieutenant Davies to go straight to the Air Ministry, and you are to report to the Fifth Sea Lord as soon as you arrive in London. His offices are in Rex House, in Lower Regent Street. I am to warn you that you are not to talk to anyone, including your wife, about your prison experiences, or your other activities in North Africa, until you have seen Admiral Boyd. Understood?'

I assured him that I did.

'You will be given a full "air medical" at Queen Anne's Mansions, in St James's Park, after you have seen the Fifth; and when you have done all this, I want you to go to the Park Lane Hotel, in Piccadilly, and book a double room for yourself and your wife for the night of the fifth of December. I should book it for two nights if I were you.'

'What for, sir?' I asked. The Park Lane Hotel was rather beyond my pocket, but I refrained from saying so, and the Admiral grinned.

'You will be able to claim normal expenses,' he said. 'I shall be staying there on the fifth, and I want to meet your wife.'

I was very complimented by this, but hesitated. I hadn't seen my wife for over two years and it seemed rather presumptuous to be organizing her affairs after such a long interval without consulting her first.

'Of course, sir,' I said, 'but I can't be sure that my wife will be there. She is in charge of the feeding of all the people who make Wellworthy piston rings – it's quite a big job – there are one or two factories.'

'She knows about it already,' he said pleasantly. 'She'll be there. She has been invited to Buckingham Palace on the morning of the sixth. So have you. Admiral Boyd and I are attending an investiture that morning, and arrangements have been made for you to attend the same one.'

I stammered my appreciation of this tremendous compliment, but he dismissed it airily. 'I wish all the other young men from the Mediterranean Swordfish squadrons could come as well, but most of them are either dead, or still in jail. We all earned these things together, and the more of us who can collect them together, from the Monarch, the better. It was Admiral Boyd's idea, and his office has made all the arrangements, so you'd better thank him when you see him. Don't thank me, but be at the Park Lane on the fifth. I shall be in civilian clothes and very late. You can go to bed early if you want to, but I'm keen to meet your better half.'

Both of those Admirals were constantly springing surprises, with their magical touches of humanity. A few months later, without telling him, one of Admiral Lyster's daughters joined the WRNS, and he came face to face with her during an inspection. He looked her up and down, and said 'Oh yes – I know your mother!'

After being locked up under constant guard for a long while it takes time to grow accustomed to being free to do as one pleases, and just walking about without being challenged was a delight; but being able to pick up a telephone and ring my wife and family really brought home my new-found freedom more clearly than anything else. When I was put through to Jo from the Glasgow station hotel, it was such a wonderful moment that it was difficult to know what to say after a gap of nearly two and a half years. We fell back on the easy gambit of talking about our immediate plans, but I found it difficult to concentrate at first because I was listening to her voice more than to what she was saying.

She agreed to catch a train to Waterloo the following evening, by which time I would have been able to book a double room somewhere, and do all the other things required of me. I explained that I had to report to the Fifth Sea Lord in the morning before doing anything else.

'I'm expecting a fairly substantial chunk of leave, if only to learn how to eat again . . .'

'Are you all right?' she asked.

'Yes, but I'm a bit thin, so be prepared for a shock. But to hell with your factory workers, it's me that needs feeding from now onwards!'

We discussed the forthcoming investiture and she told me that I was allowed two guests at the Palace and that she had arranged for my mother to go with her. I told her about Admiral Lyster and the Park Lane Hotel and she suggested that I booked the room the next day to make sure. It was very nice to have someone to help me do the thinking and planning after so long.

'We'll give a lunch party after the investiture, for the entire family,' she said. 'You'd better arrange that too!'

The next morning in the Fifth Sea Lord's offices in Lower Regent Street, Arthur Sowman greeted me with a pretence of the dignity and decorum required of a very senior officer: I was tickled to see that now his boss was a Sea Lord he was wearing four stripes.

'I shall expect a lot more respect from you in the future,' he said, but the haughty voice was belied by the grin from under his bent nose. 'I have to wet-nurse you all the morning and hand you over to the Admiral in the Piccadilly Hotel at noon.'

It seemed an odd arrangement until he explained that the Admiral would be approaching from the west, up Piccadilly. I had to accompany him somewhere else, in the Whitehall area, at noon sharp, but Sowman wasn't sure where.

'I think some VIP wants to de-brief you about North Africa. It's the focal spot of everyone's attention at the moment.' He invited me to sit by his desk. 'Now – we've got to make arrangements for you to be medically examined this afternoon before you spread some hideous tropical disease all over the place . . .'

On the stroke of noon a smiling Admiral Boyd joined us in the lounge of the Piccadilly Hotel. I stood to attention and he shook hands with me, but his greeting was unflattering.

'Don't expect any sympathy from me for being locked up all this time! I sent you to Malta to sink Rommel's shipping, and it served you right for not sticking to your aim.'

He led me out into Piccadilly and we climbed into the back of a big chauffeur-driven Humber, flying his flag on its bonnet. We were whisked off in the direction of Piccadilly Circus leaving Arthur Sowman saluting on the pavement. At the traffic lights outside the Haymarket Theatre I asked the Admiral where we were going.

'To Admiralty House,' he said with a sideways grin at me. 'To avoid being a known target the Prime Minister seldom uses Number Ten . . .'

I gaped at him. 'I'm going to meet Mr Winston Churchill, sir?'

'Yes, but only for a few moments. He is going to address all the other ex-prisoners from North Africa when they arrive, and as you are the first to get here he wants to ask you a few questions.' Then his face became serious again. 'It is a great honour for you,' he said, and in my state of numbed shock I thought that it was the most unnecessary and silly remark that he had ever made.

I was so shaken by this staggering news that I was unable to speak for the rest of the short trip round Trafalgar Square and under Admiralty Arch. Things were happening too fast and I was unable to take it all in; and I was still in a daze when I found myself shaking hands with the man I admired more than anyone else alive, whose voice had stirred the world. The next few moments passed in a kind of haze, as if I were dreaming, although every second has remained in my memory as clearly as though my brain was photographing it all.

After shaking my hand the great man growled, 'I don't usually waste time talking to lieutenants! But I want to know one or two things about the country you have just left and the conditions in your prison.' He fired some questions at me about the Vichy-French and I did my best to answer sensibly.

'Tell me exactly what the conditions were like – in a few words,' he ordered.

'They were bloody, sir,' I said. I then explained that there had been insufficient food to sustain life properly, and that the sanitary arrangements for over a thousand white men would have been inadequate for the handful of Arabs for which they had been designed, and that the Vichy-French had stirred up a lot of hate for themselves. After these few sentences I dried up, because it was difficult enough to be standing in the presence of this great man without the added strain of speaking to him.

The Prime Minister grunted with dissatisfaction.

'I'm not going to ask you or your companions to tell lies,' he said, 'and we shall do our best to punish the guilty men; but I'm going to appeal to you all to exercise restraint in what you say. The battle in North Africa is in full swing and its progress will be hazarded if we antagonize the French-speaking people. We must persuade them to side with us, not against us, otherwise hundreds of lives will be lost. The progress of the battle is more important than retribution.' He looked at me searchingly. 'Do you think that the Vichy-French will side with the Allies, young man?'

'They will climb on the band-wagon, sir. If we are winning they will side with us.'

'In other words we can't afford to lose any battles in the early stages.' Churchill nodded at Admiral Boyd and the interview was over. As we withdrew he said, 'Your own story must never be told, do you understand? Not for many years. You did well, and I congratulate you, but like this meeting with me you must forget that it ever happened.'

'That's not going to be easy, sir!' I grinned, and he flashed-me an appreciative smile. The puckish expression on his face at that moment has remained with me ever since.

After what seemed a very thorough medical examination that afternoon, at Queen Anne's Mansions, a consortium of medical officers told me that, basically, my health was sound. 'There is nothing wrong with you fundamentally that a few weeks' rest and some good food won't put right, and you are bound to get at least two months' leave. On that assumption we are prepared to pass you fit for full flying duties now, to save you having to return for another medical at the end of your leave. Naturally if anything goes wrong you must report without delay.'

Armed with my medical chit, stating that I was 'AIB' – which is the highest medical category of all – I called on the Commander responsible for appointing aviators, to whom I had to apply for leave. His offices were in Rex House, in Lower Regent Street, too, at that time. He congratulated me on retaining my original medical category.

'I'm going to give you ten days' leave,' he said, 'and then the command of a minelaying squadron operating from Manston, in Kent.'

I did my best to explain about the medical officers' proviso, but he cut me short.

'How do these MOs know what leave you are going to get? If you are "AIB" there is nothing wrong with you. I decide how much leave you will be given, not the bloody Medical Branch!'

'Their assessment was dependent upon my getting two months' leave at least, sir,' I said doggedly. 'I'm at least a couple of stone under weight, and I still can't eat properly because my stomach has shrunk . . .'

'Then they shouldn't have passed you fit for flying,' he snapped. He was beginning to get angry with me, and I began to lose my temper too.

'I haven't had any proper leave since the *Courageous* sank, sir, in the first month of the war. I haven't seen my wife since the summer of 1940. In any case I wouldn't dream of flying any aeroplane until

I've had some refresher dual – it would be crazy!'

'You've lost your nerve, have you?' he asked unpleasantly, and that remark was the last straw. I reached for my cap, because at any moment I was going to say or do something I would always regret, and the best thing to do was to leave quickly. I realized that the medical officers were right: I did need that two months' leave. I don't think I had ever been so angry before in my life. I put my cap under my arm and walked to the door. Then I paused.

'If you ring the Examination Board at Queen Anne's they will confirm what I have just said,' I suggested, trying to control my temper. I meant the remark as a sensible way out for us both, but it sounded impertinent, and the Commander exploded with wrath.

'Don't come here telling me what to do!' He was really angry, which was a pity, because I was a great admirer of his. He had fought a very hard war himself a year previously, and standing at his door I wondered whether he had been polishing the seat of his pants on an Admiralty chair since then, and had lost his sense of proportion. Nothing drives a man round the bend so quickly as being forced to sit at an Admiralty desk in wartime, especially when his task was to send others to the front line. I tried to explain that I had made the suggestion to prove to him that I had been speaking the truth, but he cut me short.

'Good God!' he exclaimed. 'By the way some of you young chaps behave when you come to this office anyone would think we are running a bloody picnic, not a war!'

Not trusting myself to reply I walked out. Later, when I had recovered some sense, I realized that his remarks were made in the heat of the moment, without thought, but for an hour or two while I was waiting for Jo to arrive I was so angry that I was near to tears. I knew that the Medical branch should not have passed me 'AIB' and that the fault was theirs as much as the Commander's, and that all I had to do was to report back to Queen Anne's, and ask them to telephone him; but my pride had been bludgeoned into insensibility and when I went to Waterloo to meet Jo I was still smarting. But the sight of her put all other thoughts out of mind, and instead of needing comfort myself, I found that I had to work swiftly to comfort her. When she saw how much weight I had lost she burst into tears, and I soon forgot about 'bloody picnics'.

In the main bar of the Park Lane Hotel on the night of 5 December, Jo and I sat waiting for Admiral Lyster until the bar closed, when Jo insisted on going to bed. I promised that I would join her within half an hour if the Admiral had not arrived, and settled in the residents' lounge for a nightcap. During the war the Park Lane Hotel was favoured by officers of the Canadian forces, and one or two of them came with me from the bar. They knew that I was waiting for an Admiral and were keen to meet him. When he came stalking in, wearing an old naval raincoat with a brown trilby on the back of his head, he looked more like an elderly Warrant Officer on the booze than a Flag Officer. He strode up to my table and asked me what had happened to my wife. I explained that she had gone to bed and introduced him to the Canadians. One of them said, 'Say! Are you really an Admiral?' and Sir Lumley grinned down at him and said 'Yeah! I guess I am,' with a distinct Canadian accent. Then he beckoned a page-boy and told him to fetch my wife at once.

'Tell her that I'm not going to let her husband go to bed until she has appeared. She can come down in her nightie if she chooses!' He then sat down at the table and ordered drinks all round.

A few moments later Jo arrived in a quilted dressing-gown looking delicious, but trying hard to appear firm. The Admiral reached for her hand and she gazed down at him reprovingly.

'Are you Admiral Lyster?' she asked, and then she said, 'Well! You really should be ashamed of yourself! It's high time you were in bed in view of what is happening in the morning!'

He patted the seat beside him invitingly, and signed for the night waiter. It was nearly two in the morning before we retired.

In Buckingham Palace, the next morning, I was standing beside Admiral Boyd, by a big fireplace in an ante-room, when I was kicked, quite hard, in the seat of my pants, and nearly fell into the fire. It was most un-Flag-Officer-like behaviour in those august surroundings, but nothing ever daunted the irrepressible Admiral Sir Lumley Lyster.

'That'll teach you not to get Admirals to Buck House with a hangover in future!' he said.

Before we left the ante-room the Lord Chamberlain gave us last-minute instructions not to talk to the King. 'Just answer yes or no,' he said. 'There are a great many people to be decorated and we shall be running short of time.'

We then filed into the Ballroom, where the Yeomen of the Guard were standing discreetly in the background behind the rows of silent spectators, and an orchestra was playing soft music. The Lord Chamberlain was beside the Monarch, calling out names, and when it was my turn to walk up the small gangway on to the dais, to face my King, I took a pace forward as instructed, to put myself within reach. After he had shaken my hand the King startled me by asking a question.

'I understand that you have been a prisoner?' Because of a slight stammer King George VI spoke rather hesitantly, pausing between each word.

'Yes, your Majesty,' I said.

'Where – were – you – a prisoner?' he asked.

'In French North Africa, sire,' I said, glancing rather uneasily at the Lord Chamberlain. I couldn't answer that with a yes or no!

The King looked surprised. 'Oh!' he said. 'You mean – the other day – then you have only just been released?'

'Yes, sire,' I said, and stood still while he pinned things to my chest. Then we shook hands again.

'I hope – that I am among the very first – to welcome you home,' he said, and at that moment I would gladly have gone back to Laghouat had he asked.

33
The Biter Bitten

After a short spell of refresher flying from an icy airfield in Scotland in January, I was glad to be sent south again, to Lee-on-Solent, to form a new squadron. It was to be a combined 'anti-submarine and attack' outfit, with six Swordfish and six Hurricanes, destined for a 'Woolworth' carrier in the Atlantic.

After fourteen months in the Sahara I was suffering from the violent change of climate. Crail, on the north-east coast of Scotland, had been a cruelly cold place to spend January. Food was still difficult to swallow and I had put on only a few pounds, and I knew that I should have demanded more leave. The fact that the Fleet Air Arm was desperately short of experienced pilots was common knowledge, and it was impossible to ask for more time to recover. The need for absolute silence at sea, after carrier operations, had resulted in the Navy's aviation being one of the most taciturn branches of the Silent Service, and the only news about us which ever hit the headlines seemed to be justified criticisms that we flew obsolete aircraft. This had a marked effect on recruitment, and every intelligent boy with the urge to fly went straight into the RAF without giving the Fleet Air Arm a thought, and nobody could blame them. Our pipeline was non-existent, and the need was becoming desperate.

Lee-on-Solent was our headquarters, and after a few weeks, when the Admiral asked me to give a lecture to all officers, it was a command not an invitation. Lee's huge barracks were commanded by a commodore, and when I saw that he, and the Admiral, and their combined staffs were in the audience, I plucked up courage and hammered home the need for a new pipeline, pointing out that the same pilots who had been flying at the beginning of the war were still struggling on, without hope of relief, and were rapidly reaching the end of their tether if they had been lucky enough to survive and keep out of prison.

The next morning I had booked the target range for the squadron, and was about to go out to the aircraft on the tarmac, where all the pilots were waiting for me with their engines running, when the phone rang on my desk. A voice said, 'Surgeon-Captain, Central Air Medical Board speaking' and I interrupted him.

'Sorry, sir, but I've got to leap into the air – I'll ring you back when I land.'

'You are to come and see me now,' said the voice, and so I muttered something unrepeatable, and replaced the receiver, cursing all medical officers. An hour or so later, when we flew back from the range, I found an officer waiting for me with a car and driver. I was to be taken before the Commodore for being rude to the Surgeon-Captain and disobeying an order. The Commodore ordered me to go and apologize at once.

The Central Air Medical Board was housed in a little red-brick villa on Lee's promenade, and I was greeted by a stout Surgeon-Captain who exuded joviality. When I tried to apologize he roared with laughter.

'That's a very nasty temper you have,' he grinned. 'I think we shall have to do something about it! I listened to your talk last night with great interest. Sit down. There are one or two things I would like to ask you. For example, how much leave were you given when you came home from that prison camp, last month?'

I tried to explain what had happened, and he sat shaking his head, saying, 'Ridiculous', every time I paused. I appealed to him to forget the whole thing. 'I am CO of my own squadron, sir, and it's coming along well, and I'm very content. I want to take them to their carrier when they are ready in a few weeks.'

'Okay,' he said cheerfully. 'But I'm going to give you a thorough medical examination today and if you really are AIB I won't interfere.' He then did something extraordinary: he reached across the desk and grabbed my hand, opening up the fingers and peering between them.

'What are these scars?' he asked, and sat listening while I explained. In the last few months of imprisonment the old-timers became more and more thin and our stomachs became distended, and we began to lose our sense of touch. When holding a lighted cigarette I had burned my fingers several times without feeling it. The first indication was often the smell of burning flesh.

'Didn't you think that a bit gruesome and strange?'

'Everything was gruesome and strange in that place,' I said. 'But it didn't last. As soon as the Red Cross parcels arrived we regained our sense of touch, and I always assumed that it had something to do with malnutrition.'

'It had,' he said, and escorted me through to the changing room. For the rest of the day I was subjected to exhaustive examinations, and at the end of the afternoon the jovial Surgeon-Captain invited me to join him for a cup of tea in his office, when he broke the news to me that I was grounded for a year.

'Your eyesight is terrible, and you shouldn't be flying; your eardrums have both popped – probably because of the violent change in climatic conditions; and when you are stronger and have had some proper leave you must have about nine teeth extracted. Those scars on your fingers made it clear to me that you had a touch of beri-beri in that prison. We found the same symptoms amongst some of your co-prisoners when they came to Portsmouth – which you managed to dodge.'

I was sent on two months' leave without the option, that day, and when I began to argue he said, 'You are underweight and I would have grounded you for that alone. Kindly allow me to know my own business.'

When I first arrived back in London in November, my 'adopted godfather', who was a famous actor, had offered me his cottage on the coast of Dorset. His name was Leslie Banks, and when I told him that I was off on two months' leave he pointed out that he was playing the lead in Congreve's *Love for Love* at London's Phoenix Theatre, and would not be needing his cottage for a long while. 'Take Jo, and stay for as long as you like,' he said. As well as being a wonderful actor he was a very kind man, and after two months in that adorable cottage at Worth Matravers, on the Isle of Purbeck, overlooking the Channel, I reported back to the fat Surgeon-Captain, feeling very fit indeed.

'Good,' he said, 'because you are now going to have nine teeth extracted!' He explained that I was about to be sent on a twelve-month lecture tour of Britain's schools, and it was essential to have this done first.

On my way to the Command Dental Surgeon, Commander Luck, I called on the Admiral to find out about this lecturing nonsense, but he confirmed the news.

'You can now go and start that pipeline you were talking about,' he said. 'Your first talk is at Eton in a fortnight, when you have to report to the headmaster, Mr. C. A. Elliott. Make sure that you have some nice new teeth by then!'

When he had extracted all nine, Commander Luck apologized that he was not allowed to supply new teeth free of charge because I had enough of my own to chew my food. 'I have to abide by the regulations,' he said.

'If their Lordships won't pay for them I won't have any,' I remarked. Commander Luck was very shocked. 'You can't walk about like that!' he exclaimed. 'You look terrible!'

I agreed, and told him about my proposed lecture tour.

'I can always explain to the headmaster at Eton and all the other schools that the Admiralty refuse to supply teeth to ex-prisoners; and I'm quite prepared to lecture to the Etonians about the effing F-f-f-f-f-leet Air Arm,' I said politely.

When I reported with my free Admiralty teeth to Mr Elliott, in his house at Eton College, they must have been a reasonably good fit because he made me stay with him for three days, and a large number of boys opted to join the Fleet Air Arm, the Royal Navy, and the Royal Marines.

At the end of the year I had discovered that schoolboys are the most wonderful audience of all, and after taking them up into the Albanian mountains and introducing them to King Peter of Jugoslavia and his alcoholic Prime Minister, and then through that tunnel at Laghouat, they flocked to join. A really exciting story, no matter how tough, is a much better recruiting draw than 'beating the drum'. Hundreds of first-class chaps came into the Fleet Air Arm and flew aeroplanes from carriers. All those audiences in 1943 would now be in their early fifties, and I doubt whether any of them will remember; but the tour was a great success.

Towards the end of the year, when I was tired of the sound of my own voice and had regained two stone in weight, I tried hard to have my medical category reassessed so that I could fly again, but the rulings of the CAMB were irrefutable and I could not persuade any medical officer to examine me until the statutory year was over. In the end I cheated, by jumping the gun. At Yeovilton I persuaded the Commander Flying to lend me one of his Grumman Martlets, so that I could do the requisite number of dummy deck landings to be qualified to take it on to the decks of a carrier. He was Commander Alan Black, with whom I had shared a little office at Máleme airfield in Crete, and his Captain was Connolly Abel-Smith who had been my Commander Flying in *Courageous* when she sank. Neither of them knew that I had been grounded, so I was taking advantage of their friendship. Afterwards, armed with a chit signed by Alan Black to say that I was qualified to deck-land Martlets, it was simple to persuade the Commander Flying in HMS *Argus* to let me do half a dozen deck-landings. I then admitted that I had been flying illegally, and the cat was amongst the pigeons, and a number of courts martial might have taken place. I suggested that it would be tidier for everyone if my medical category could be changed, and made retrospective, and just before Christmas 1943 I was classified 'fit for full flying duties' again, and in January 1944 I was back at sea.

The two big aircraft carriers, *Indefatigable* and *Implacable*, were nearing completion on the Clyde. *Indefatigable* had started building three months before her sister ship, *Implacable*, and therefore was commissioned first, from John Brown's yard. Three months later *Implacable* was commissioned at Fairfields, in Govan (Captain Lachlan Mackintosh of Mackintosh) and Their Lordships tried out an experiment in *Implacable*. Some of the Fleet carriers had not been very happy ships and to make sure that *Implacable* got off to a good start, every officer and man who could be found who had served under Denis Boyd in *Illustrious* in 1940 was sent to the ship. Charles Evans was the head of the Air Department with the new title 'Commander (Air)' and he invited me to be his assistant, the Lieutenant-Commander Flying in charge of the operations in the hangars and on the flight-deck. The ship's first commander had been the gunnery officer in *Illustrious*, Alfie Sutton was the Commander Operations, we had the same PMO, Surgeon-Commander Keevil, DSO, and Bosun, the redoubtable Mr Howe, and wherever one went in the ship men would pop out of doorways and say, 'Hello, sir – remember me?' It was a splendid arrangement, and the ship's future was assured from the word go.

A few days after *Indefatigable* had sailed from John Brown's yard, my opposite number in that ship – her Lieutenant-Commander Flying – was involved in a serious accident, and I was sent in his place, on loan; and spent three months on her flight-deck in the Arctic, during several attacks on the *Tirpitz* and other equally attractive targets in north Norway. The ship was unlucky, and suffered many tedious breakdowns owing to technical faults; and on the day that *Implacable* came storming down the Clyde on her acceptance trials, with her Royal Marine Band playing, the *Indefatigable* was lying at the Tail o' the Bank with all her aircraft disembarked, and her arrester gear in need of repair. I was due to return to *Implacable* in a few days and watched her sail past from *Indefatigable*'s quarter-deck with great admiration. Her appearance was not so welcome on board the decks of her rival. As she went past, *Implacable*'s Royal Marine band struck up the mournful music of 'John Brown's Body', and for a moment I feared that the *Indefatigable* was about to open fire.

A few days later I went back to *Implacable* and we left for the Arctic for our '*Tirpitz*-runs'; and at the end of the year we returned to Rosyth for a refit before sailing for the Pacific to fight the Japanese. Captain Mackintosh was promoted to Rear-Admiral and relieved by Captain Charles Hughes-Hallett. Just before we sailed, His Majesty King Geroge VI and the Queen came on board to see us off. With them were the two Princesses.

On parade for a Royal inspection, when I reported my Division to King George VI, I had no reason to know that he had recently toured HMS *Victorious*. He had been shown round the Air Department of that great ship by her Lieutenant-Commander Flying, E. W. ('Bill') Sykes, a stout friend of mine who was a complete extrovert and who was known throughout the Fleet Air Arm for his air of prosperous urbanity. Apparently he had given the King a thorough grounding in the problems of handling, stowing, and operating aircraft in carriers, with particular emphasis on the tremendous responsibilities of the Lieutenant-Commander Flying.

'What Division did you say this was?' asked His Majesty, and when I repeated the phrase, 'The Flight-deck Division, sir,' he smiled knowingly.

'Then you must be the Lieutenant-Commander Flying!' he exclaimed.

'Yes sir,' I said, puzzled by his air of amusement.

'Ah!' said the King, 'Then you are the man who does most of the work and gets none of the credit!'

I gaped at this amazing evidence of royal perspicacity and said, 'How on earth did you know that, sir?'

We both laughed, and when the King turned his head to go on inspecting the men he was still smiling, but I was grinning all over my face. At that precise moment the photographers from the

Scotsman newspaper took the photograph which my family have called 'The Monarch and I' ever since.

The humorous situation did not end there: a carrier's flight-deck division consists of the men who are exposed to extremes of weather at all times, more than any of the men in the other divisions on board, and after six months or more in the Arctic they were deeply bronzed in comparison. During inspections I did my best to make them look upwards at the topmast, or the funnel, so that their chins were held high, and I must admit that on those occasions when smartly turned out in their Number Ones they were a very fine-looking bunch of men.

At the end of his inspection His Majesty congratulated me.

'The smartest men in the ship,' he said in a clear voice. I thanked him and when he had moved on I turned to my one hundred and ninety Welshmen and studied them scathingly. They were looking unbearably smug.

'Did you hear what the King said?' I asked, in an amazed voice, and at this they looked even more complacent and gave a pleased little murmur of assent.

I grunted and said, 'I wish I could say the same!' and they emitted a little groan, which was more of a quiet boo, their eyes pointing heavenwards. It resounded across the flight-deck and the Captain and Commander turned quickly and frowned at me warningly; but I am afraid I was still grinning with pleasure. So were my men.

The entire royal visit was enjoyed by everyone on board. Her Majesty had launched *Implacable* at Fairfields when the ship had finished building, and had a personal interest in her; and during a delightfully cosy conversation with her in the ante-room after Divisions I remarked that it gave me a lot of pleasure to think that the King had welcomed me home after my last sojourn overseas, and was now wishing us all God-speed as we set out to fight the Japanese.

'It is a happy coincidence, Ma'am,' I said, and she thought so too, and said that she would tell him. Then, presumably to make conversation, she asked me if my wife had been up in Scotland during our refit.

'Yes, Ma'am,' I said.

'Where has she been staying?'

I mentioned the name of a famous Inn, on the other side of the Firth of Forth by the Queensferry car ferry, and then looked at her doubtfully. It had a peculiar name and I thought it wise to explain how it was spelt. Her Majesty the Queen – now the Queen Mother – put her head back and gave a tinkling laugh.

'How do you think I would spell it?' she asked.

The name of that famous hostelry is, of course, 'The Hawes Inn'.

I told Jo in the evening before we sailed and she thought it was very funny too.

34
The End of the Story

HMS *Implacable* arrived in Sydney, Australia, on V-E Day, 8 May 1945, the day that the Germans surrendered. We were about to become part of the British Pacific Feet, which was almost entirely aircraft carriers, the main ships being *Victorious, Formidable, Indomitable, Indefatigable*, and now us, to take the place of *Illustrious*, which was then on her way home. On 15 June we were to do a solo operation against the Japanese island of Truk, and at two in the morning on the 15th I went below for a bath, having ranged twenty-four Avengers, eighteen Fireflies and twelve Seafires for a free take-off at dawn. In the upper hangar, armed and ready for ranging and catapulting, were six Fireflies to be launched before the main strike for a reconnaissance of Truk; and another six to be catapulted after the reconnaissance aircraft had gone.

On board this great ship we had a total of eighty-two aircraft. There were over three thousand men on board, and in my opinion she was the most efficient vessel that had ever flown the White Ensign. She was also a very happy ship, and of course the two things are concomitant.

When I went below for my bath I should have turned in for a couple of hours, but I knew that I was about to be either killed or severely injured, and it seemed more sensible to take a bath. In any case, I had to write to my wife and my mother, and settle all my bills by writing out cheques. I had no doubt about this. After nearly six years of fighting one can become psychic before operations, and in my bath I admired my anatomy and thought what a pity it was that at last it was to be despoiled. I cannot explain what made me so certain. I had never felt like this before, in much more hazardous situations. Caldecott-Smith had felt the same before he was taken prisoner, and I had met others who had admitted to similar traumatic feelings before they were written off.

Then I remembered that unexpended bullet in my parachute at Paramythia, and reassessed the situation. It was unlikely that I would be killed – that bullet had my name written on it and I had survived that. No, at the worst I was about to be badly injured.

At 0400, in clean underclothes and fresh tropical khaki, I went back to the flight-deck to dispatch the six reconnaissance Fireflies, and when they returned after a brief sortie, there were seven on the radar plot. The seventh aircraft was obviously a Kamikaze suicide bomber, following the six back to the ship. Since the deck was covered with aircraft, loaded with bombs and other weapons, 'dispatch was necessary', and we began to catapult the rest of the Fireflies quickly, so that we could fly off the remainder and clear the deck.

The drill was quite normal, and under Charles Evans's leadership, had always to be done with the minimum of delay. I knew that the ship's fighter directors would have sent the returning aircraft away on 'evasive routing' to give us time; and I lowered my Lucite wand when the fourth pilot gave me the 'okay' sign, so that the flight-deck engineer could release the catapult machinery, and I half turned, to duck under his wing as the pilot was blasted off. At that moment I was struck an incredible blow which shattered my right leg, and in the half-light saw that the aircraft had not gone, but was in a nose-down attitude. I realized that his wooden prop had hit the iron deck and broken off at the boss, and I can remember changing the green light for red so that the launch was stopped. The next few seconds were rather confused and I don't know whether I was sitting down or standing up, but I can recall telling my 'doggie' – Leading Aircraftman Hall – to go to the island door to get a stretcher, and four hands for a stretcher party.

'What for?' he asked, and I called him by a very impolite name, and told him that it was for me. After that I certainly was sitting, because my right leg was behind me somewhere, and I had to pull it round into a normal position, and discovered what felt like a lot of pieces of wet fish lying about the deck, and thought 'Good God! – these are part of me!' and stuffed them all back into the hole in my trousers, in case they were needed.

There was no pain. The human anatomy has been designed very cleverly, so that when something really terrible happens, the shock overrides the agony. I had discovered the same thing under interrogation in Algeria – or was it Tunisia? My thoughts were disturbed by Charles Evans's voice on the bullhorn. It was getting lighter and he could see me, stretched out on the deck.

'This is one hell of a time to take a rest!' he bellowed, and before I could find someone to tell him what had happened I heard him say to the Aircraft Handling Party, 'Come on you chaps, don't just stand there gaping, we've got to clear the flight-deck. If he's dead we're very very sorry; but pull him out of the way and mop up the blood.'

A flight-deck doctor with a soft Scottish voice peered at me from the dark and asked me what was wrong.

'I've broken my leg,' I said.

'Are you sure?'

'Quite.'

'Well, don't go away,' he said, darting off to get help.

He need not have worried. It was nearly two years before I could walk again.

I was heaved over to the starboard side by a lot of my sailors, and I tried to talk to them because it was obvious that they thought I was dead: the silly, sentimental sods were crying. On the flight-deck there were 190 of them, all from Wales, and we had a delightful love-hate relationship. I used to swop punches with them when they did anything silly, and as a result we never had to waste time attending 'Requestmen and Defaulters' in harbour. We merely slugged it out on the flight-deck, with Charles Evans encouraging them on the bullhorn from the bridge, shouting to them to hit me back. The Captain was very shocked by it all, and warned me that he would always take the men's part if any of them complained. Then Charles imported Johnny King to the flight-deck party – the European bantam-weight champion, and a splendid little pro – and after that the silors used to shout 'King!' whenever I threatened them, and in every lull in the flying they used to make us put the gloves on together. He was very difficult to hit, and as quick as lighting, and we all loved him dearly.

Trevor David, my assistant, appeared out of the darkness, and I said something to him about taking over, but he appeared not to be able to understand what I was saying. Then Mr Howe, the Bosun, appeared, with an old canvas sail, and some firebars, and his funeral party – and I thought, 'Jesus Christ, they're going to sew me up, and toss me over the side!' Somehow I managed to sit up for a second, and Trevor said, 'He's not dead, so shove off, Bosun.' After that I don't remember anything very clearly, except occasional moments of consciousness in sick bay, where I found that fresh blood and plasma were being poured into both my arms; but it was running out again, from my leg, into a bucket. Apparently I used up the ship's entire supply, and the PMO had to make a broadcast to the ship's company asking for volunteers to give fresh blood, and by the time he got back to sick bay, after making the broadcast from the bridge, there was a queue of men stretching the entire length of the ship, and curling round the quarter-deck. Charles Evans told me about this on one of his many visits to sick bay, and it made me pipe my eye. I apologized and explained that normally I only cry when I find myself looking at an empty bottle, late at night.

'The PMO telephoned the Captain this morning,' he said, about four days later, 'and asked him to reduce speed to cut out the vibration, so that he could amputate your leg, but I dissuaded him by pointing out that you are severely handicapped already, on account you have no brains, and therefore it would be a great mistake to cut your effing leg off!'

'You bastard,' I said. 'Was he really going to amputate?'

Evans grinned, and shook his head. 'No, the young Surgeon-Lieutenant RNVR has taken you over. He's a Fellow of the Royal College of Surgeons, and only just qualified, so he knows all the tricks. You are in good hands.'

I awoke to hear the tail-end of a discussion about it, between Fergusson, the young Surgeon-Lieutenant, and the PMO. They thought I was unconscious. I heard Fergusson say, 'If you amputate you will be sentencing him to crutches for the rest of his life. It will have to be done at the hip, and he'll have no stump.' That piece of information was very useful in the next year or so, whenever some bright spark suggested amputation, because it helped me to resist the temptation.

When the ship returned to Manus, in the Admiralty Islands, I was put into a Tobruk Splint and lowered over the side into a lighter, to be taken to the US Navy's jungle hospital. I was very hurt that none of my sailors had been anywhere near me, and when the ship's Commander came along, to take charge of the lowering himself, I asked him where they all were. He said, 'You're on the danger list, chum, and nobody except Charles has been allowed near you. They wanted the Royal Marine band to play that silly song they sing on the flight-deck, but the PMO said that excitement is bad for you. I hope that makes you feel better?'

I thanked him, because it did. As I swung outwards, away from the ship's side, I stared upwards and saw an unending row of heads peering over the starboard side of the flight-deck in silence: hundreds of them, stretching the entire length of the ship. We had shared the hurly-burly of the gale-force winds, and the slipstream, on the flight-deck, for exactly a year and a half, and we had come a long way – from the Arctic to the Pacific. It had been fun to work with sailors instead of officers all the time. I raised an arm and waved farewell, and they all stood up and cheered. It was very moving, and I cursed myself for piping my eye again, and thought, 'Thank God they didn't get the band!' Their silly song was 'Friendship', from *The Dubarry*, but they substituted my name in each line, because it rhymed – 'If you're ever in a jam, go to Lamb! If you're ever in a jam, Lamb's your man.' I used to curse them, and tell them to pipe down, but it seldom had any effect, and Evans used to encourage them.

For nearly five months I was the only Englishman in the US Navy Base Hospital Number Fifteen, Manus, where I became known as 'that goddam Limey'. Everything that happened in the United Kingdom, such as the ousting of Churchill in the post-war election to 'reverse Lease-Lend', was my fault, and I was expected to explain. When V-J Day arrived, after the Hiroshima bomb went off – 'just up the road from here Command-er!' – I wrote a notice which was pinned to the foot of my bed at my request. On it I had written, 'I know that you won the war and I am very grateful.' I thought it might prevent any argument, but it seemed to have the opposite effect on the US Navy patients.

The American surgeons in that jungle hospital were the best in the States, and the equipment and nursing were unbelievably good. Without any doubt they saved my life, and my leg. Penicillin had just been discovered, and for a short period I held the world's record, having received the maximum amount ever imparted. It seemed a lot at the time, in millions of units, but the amount I was given over several months would be given nowadays in one injection.

Eventually the American surgeons were able to sew up my thigh. It had to be done in the ward because I could not be moved until encased in paster, and because it was going to take three and a half hours, it had to be done by local anaesthetic. I was asked whether I would like to watch or have a screen suspended so that I could not see. I watched the whole thing, and was full of admiration for their skill.

When I was encased in plaster for the trip home, the American surgeon plastered a broomstick between my thighs for ease of handling. He spread my legs as widely apart as possible, because this makes recovery easier later; but I could not be carried through any normal doorway without being tipped sideways. I was taken in an old Dakota across the Pacific Ocean to New Guinea, over the Owen Stanley Mountains, landing at Port Moresby to refuel; and then on, over the Coral Sea to Townsville, in Queensland, for an overnight stop. When we dropped down to land at Townsville, and I saw all the lights of the town, I was thrilled because it was my first re-entry into a world at peace. The lights had been turned on in Europe seven months previously, and in the Far East three months earlier, but I had lived in a blacked-out world since September 1939, and the lights of Townsville brought home to me very clearly that the war was really over.

The Dakota chugged its way down the east coast of Australia via Brisbane to Sydney, where I embarked in HMS *Indomitable*, for the passage home.

35
Postscript

On my way home, flat on my back in HMS *Indomitable*, the Admiralty granted me a permanent commission, which gave me a fresh incentive to recover, if one was needed. Jo was waiting for the ship at Portsmouth and I was able to greet her with this news, while at the same time apologizing for returning to her in such a useless shape. We had enjoyed a few months together in 1943, and in 1945, when I returned the second time, we had a son, born the previous year; but I was unable to get out of bed to help her with his upbringing for another year at least. When I did, from a bed in the RN Auxiliary Hospital at Sherborne in Dorset, where I had been a patient since 1945, it was 1947, and I weighed fourteen stone, eight pounds. Everyone else in hospital seemed to get thinner and thinner, poor devils, but because of all the violent exercise of my youth, I just got fatter and fatter.

When the surgeons let me get up, in an iron caliper and on elbow crutches, I managed to persuade Their Lordships of the Admiralty to put me in charge of the flying at Yeovilton, which was then a tiny little airfield of no importance. I was then able to continue at Sherborne as an outpatient. During the following year I learned to fly again, in an old Oxford, which was the only aircraft I could get into. Because my iron caliper was rigid, I had to cock my right leg up on the dashboard, and operate the rudder with my left foot; and after getting mildly lost, on a couple of simple cross-countries, it dawned on me that the caliper was affecting the compass. So, while I lay on a Yeovilton bed, the caliper was taken away and put into a magnetic field. After it had been de-gaussed, all was well and I had no further trouble.

In 1948 I was sent back to sea as Lieutenant-Commander Flying of *Implacable* again. It was very thrilling to be able to walk back on board, and start again where I had left off, two and a half years before; and by the end of the year I was able to dispense with both walking sticks altogether, which was just as well because on New Year's Eve I was promoted to Commander and two years later, given command of my own small ship in what is now called the 'Cod War'. After that marvellous appointment (and there are few delights to compare with the pleasure of standing on the bridge of your own ship) I was sent to the RN College Greenwich to do the Staff Course, when the late Evelyn Waugh suggested that I write these memoirs. He assured me that all naval officers 'retire to their country estates to write their memoirs and be beastly to the vicar'. As my second son had arrived, ten years after his brother, it seemed a good idea. Not being able to run, or play games with either of them, throughout their lives, it is a way of explaining why. Neither of them has ever known me as a whole person, and so that I could overcome this handicap, and bring them up on equal terms with other fathers, I bought an old boat, which was one of the gallant little ships which had been under my wings at Dunkirk, and which is still going strong. This has proved a boon to us all, and a few years ago I was made the honorary 'Admiral' of the Association of Dunkirk Little Ships, for life, which is a great honour.

In 1958 the Duncan Sandys axe was about to fall, and two thousand naval officers and a thousand sailors were to be found redundant. Between them they were given £9 600 000, as compensation for loss of expected earnings, known as 'The Golden Bowler'. Because few naval officers or men have ever had the time, or the inclination, to find out how to make a profit, I wrote an article entitled 'The New Way Ahead', appealing to the City to set up an advisory service to safeguard this vast sum from unwise investment in pigs and chickens and other enterprises, as happened after the Geddes axe in 1918. I wrote under the name of 'Achilles', because he had a gammy leg too, and the article aroused a great deal of sympathy in the 'Square Mile', where there has always been a close affinity with the Fleet, over the centuries. Some very eminent bankers, and gentlemen of the Stock Exchange, and others, who I was not surprised to find were some of the kindest people I have ever met, sponsored a charitable non-profit making organization to advise the whole service on financial matters, called The White Ensign Association. I chose the name, and am very proud of it. In 1958, with one of those Golden Bowlers, I left the Navy to start this Association going, and invited Admiral Sir

John A. S. Eccles, then the Commander-in-Chief of the Home Fleet, to join me as the first chairman. Because rents and rates are very high in the City – and it must always remain within the City's boundaries if it is to function properly – before retiring I managed to move it on board HMS *Belfast*, moored near Tower Bridge, where it is still doing a magnificent job of work.

During my sixteen years in the City on this active work, I met more naval officers and sailors than I did whilst I was serving, and was able to provide advice for over eight thousand officers and men, most of whom I interviewed myself. Amongst this figure were more than a hundred admirals, including Admiral Sir Denis Boyd. To me, this was most gratifying, and a wonderful method of being able to say thank you.

Providing one marries the right girl, who is prepared to put up with her husband's frequent and prolonged absences, there is no doubt in my mind that the Royal Navy is the finest way of life open to man – even in an old Stringbag.

The Men of 815 Swordfish Squadron

When control of the Fleet Air Arm passed to the Admiralty in 1938 the Air Ministry allowed those men of the RAF who were serving with naval squadrons to remain with them if they wished.

815 Squadron first formed from the survivors of Numbers 811 and 822 Swordfish Squadrons, sunk in HMS *Courageous* in September 1939. The squadron repeated history in January 1941 by re-forming from the survivors of the two Swordfish squadrons bombed in HMS *Illustrious*. Many of the men listed below were with the squadron from its beginning, but others joined later, to take the place of the men who had been killed or wounded.

If I have made any mistakes in the list, or have omitted any names or spelt them incorrectly, I apologize. I remember them all with gratitude.

Telegraphist air gunners	*Fitters* (AM (E)'s, etc.)	*Riggers* (AM (A)'s, etc)
Allen	Bartlett	Allison
Astbury	Barton, LAC, RAF	Ansell
Barrett, CPO	Bishop	Auld
Beynon	Burney	Banham
Beagley	Burns	Booth
Boddy	Cauldron	Boyd, LAC, RAF
Boosey	Cook	Brown
Butterworth	Coulson, Sgt., RAF	Burberry
Dodwell	Dobson, PO	Cook, Sgt., RAF
Faulkes	Evans	Gunter
Grainger	Greenhall	Holbrook, Sgt.,
Griffiths*	Gronow	Mather
Hazeldine	Hanley, Cpl., RAF	Nicholson, Sgt.,
Murphy	Hartland	Shilcock

*TAG Ken Dickens Griffiths followed me to Malta but was killed flying with 830 Squadron after I was taken prisoner.

Sims	Hopkins		Stoddard-Howell
Smith, PO	Jones		Warriner
Taffe	Lake		Whitington
Tapp-Smith	Price		

Armourers	*Electricians & Radio Mechanics*	*Supply Assistants & Writers*	*Seamen; Regulating & Parachute Packers*
Bonner	Ashton	Barrett	Bowles, PO
Denton, LAC, RAF	Boswell	Brooke	Fletcher
	Cameron	Donald	Hogg
Gates, Cpl., RAF	Fuggell, Cpl., RAF	Pitman	Lacy
		Turgeon	Pratt
Gibson	Mariner		
Griffin	Sheldon		
McCulley	Williamson		
Ramsden			

Royal Marines (Wardroom Attendants)
These men looked after the comfort of the aircrew and got us out of bed in the mornings. Most of them joined the squadron at Bircham Newton, and stayed with us throughout, but many were killed, or wounded, particularly during the bombing of HMS *Illustrious*. Fred Newport was my batman, shared between four other officers.

Sergeants	*Royal Marines*	
Beaven	Angell	Horrell
Booth	Brumpy	Newport
Prothero	Bryan	Selkirk
Ware	Casling	Whylet

C.B.L.